Also by Eve Arnold

The Unretouched Woman
Flashback! The Fifties
In China
In America
Marilyn Monroe: An Appreciation
Private View
All in a Day's Work
The Great British

EVE ARNOLD:
IN RETROSPECT

EVE ARNOLD: IN RETROSPECT

ALFRED A. KNOPF

New York

1995

THIS IS A BORZOI BOOK
PUBLISHED BY ALFRED A. KNOPF, INC.

Copyright © 1995 by Eve Arnold

All rights reserved under International and Pan-American Copyright Conventions.

Published in the United States by Alfred A. Knopf, Inc., New York,

and simultaneously in Canada by Random House of Canada Limited,

Toronto. Distributed by Random House, Inc., New York.

Library of Congress Cataloging-in-Publication Data

Arnold, Eve.

Eve Arnold : in retrospect. — 1st ed.

p.   cm.

ISBN 0-394-57850-3

1. Arnold, Eve.   2. Women photographers—United States—Biography.   I. Title.

TR140.A76A3   1995

770' 92—dc20   94-46574   CIP

Manufactured in the United States of America

First Edition

For my son
Frank
Lovingly called
Francis

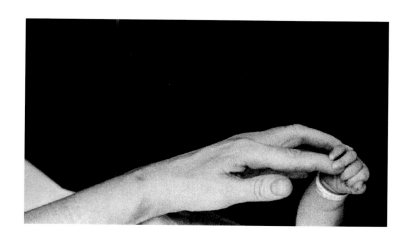

ACKNOWLEDGMENTS

It seems a miracle to me that a book gets published at all—but to make one under happy circumstances with people one enjoys is a joy indeed.

I want to thank Sonny Mehta and his wonderful staff.

I offer special thanks to my editor, Robert Gottlieb.

There are others who added to my pleasure and helped in various ways: Ed Victor, my agent; Lin Smith, my assistant; Barney Wan, who worked on the layout; Danny Pope, who made the color prints, and the entire Magnum London staff—to them all, my appreciation.

To my family and many friends who sustained me over the four decades that this book represents: my gratitude and love.

But the people who really made this book possible are the thousands who posed (either deliberately or inadvertently) for my camera. Without them I could not have done it. Blessings on them!

Hubert's Museum,
42nd Street, New York City, 1950

INTRODUCTION

Recently, when cleaning out a cupboard, I found an old suitcase in which there was an exquisite handmade Indian notebook, all purple, pink and gold. On the flyleaf was written: "China Diary: for my grandson Michael." It contained a single entry dated January 31, 1979, written on a night flight from London to Beijing. It read:

What do you hang on the walls of your mind?

When I became a photographer I began, carefully, to collect favorite images that I filed away in my imagination to bring out and examine at moments of stress or moments of quiet.

It became a game of solitaire to be played during long trips abroad—a form of meditation that kept me occupied through endless waits in bureaucratic anterooms in the USSR, fly-spattered hotels in India, risky Land Rover rides in the Hindu Kush of Afghanistan, and sleepless, breath-catching moonlit nights in Zululand—to say nothing of unnumbered hours of flying time back and forth to London.

What were the pictures?

Occasional paintings or drawings, but mainly photographs: Cartier-Bresson's children in the rubble in Spain; George Rodger's Nuba wrestlers; Elliott Erwitt's dogs; Lartigue's women; Kertesz and Brandt's distortions; Atget's Paris. Sometimes I would set them to my own music in my mind's ear, and with closed eyes and buzzing head would amuse myself by the hour.

Now, sitting with the empty suitcase and the almost empty diary, I asked myself why I hadn't continued the diary. Was it too much to do at day's end when I was fatigued with travel, interviewing and photographing? Or was it the unconscious hope that Michael (who was then two years old) would have my photographs by which to remember me, and perhaps to hang on the walls of his mind?

But which pictures? Images I had exposed to film flooded my vision—a bombardment, a veritable kaleidoscope of places, people and situations. Some had been printed in magazines or books, or had hung on gallery or museum walls; many more were still only in negative or transparency form. It was time to make an archive, to examine the failures as well as the successes, to make order out of the chaotic files that have been my life; time to unwind the film of my experiences, to expose it to view and slowly rewind it. It seemed to me it would be almost harder to do a playback of my photographic life than it had been to live it.

But here goes. To Francis, my son; to Ann, his wife. To Michael, my grandson; to Sarah Jane, my granddaughter, and to David, my newest grandson. May they live as full a life as I have.

Eve Arnold, London, 1994

EVE ARNOLD:
IN RETROSPECT

I came to photography by accident. A beau who was a keen amateur gave me my first camera and taught me to use it—a forty-dollar Rolleicord that took a twelve-exposure roll on a 2¼-inch-square format. This was the instrument with which I made my first story that was published.

My sole formal education in photography was a six-week course with Alexei Brodovitch at the New School for Social Research in New York in 1952. For the rest I am self-taught. Learning by doing turns out to be a good way to educate oneself. Since the practitioner doesn't know what could or shouldn't be done, she goes ahead and does it, and thus may find a personal approach—primitive perhaps, but fresh, at least to her.

The New School course started disastrously for me. Sixty ambitious photographers and would-be photographers, in keeping with the Socratic method used by the master ("I will not teach, you will learn from each other"), were anxious to impress the master. As art director of *Harper's Bazaar*, he had assignments to hand out. The group used their criticism of my amateur attempts at photography to gain attention for themselves. Their criticism was savage. It was infuriating and chilling, but sadly accurate. I felt bruised, but I listened. In a brief hour I learned the serious meaning of a photograph. It was my

first step to professionalism. I decided to do the first class assignment—fashion, an alien subject that was without interest to me.

I don't know why I asked Dora, my son's nursemaid, what happened in Harlem about fashion. She told me there were an average of three hundred fashion shows a year, with paid audiences. There were two modelling agencies: the Sepia and the Black & Tan, both run by the same man, Edward Brandford. When I telephoned him he recommended that I come to a deconsecrated church on the following Sunday to see the star of his show, "Fabulous" Charlotte Stribling, who had a huge following.

It was daunting to bring my pale face into that all-black audience and to get up enough courage to put my camera into their faces. I was anxious; my hands were shaking, from fear not of the people but of my ability to bring forth pictures. These were the days before the real thrust of the civil rights movement. There was then no obvious adversarial stance between the races. People smiled and started to pose for the camera. How could it be otherwise—I was so exposed. I quickly found my way backstage, where there might be a chance to take pictures without people being too aware of me because they would be busy preparing for their appearance onstage.

Fabulous had an extraordinary walk. She

Charlotte Stribling, a.k.a. Fabulous,
fashion show,
Harlem, 1952

moved like a golden animal—a leopard, perhaps, or a tiger. When she saw my white face (and black camera), she started to mince the way white models did on catwalks in those days. Lesson number one: pay attention to the intrusion of the camera.

It was exasperating photographing that moving target, because I was using flash and the gun wouldn't fire. Somehow I managed to keep the lens open and get an exposure. When the pictures were developed—hallelujah! There were images!

There is nothing to equal the excitement of seeing the image emerging from the chemicals. To go from what has been seen and envisioned in the mind to what can be held in the hand is a never-ending delight. But it's easy to be beguiled by this chemical miracle and thus lose critical judgment about the final result. The photographer has to be careful to avoid the trap of taking the happening itself too seriously.

I approached class the next day with a combination of relief that there were pictures at all and trepidation that the other students would be scathing about them. When Mr. Brodovitch put my photos at the bottom of the pile he was collecting, I was sure I was to be taken apart again.

Not so. When the class got through criticizing each other's photos, Brodovitch said he wanted to give the critique on mine himself. He praised the pictures as being fresh, original, a new approach to fashion. "You," he said to me, "do not do class assignments. Go back to Harlem and do comprehensive study."

Forty years on, I can see why I was given this advice and why the teacher considered my work fresh. Fashion photography in those days was still hidebound by fairly rigid studio techniques of lighting, posing and retouching. We were beginning to emerge from formal large cameras to smaller, more mobile ones. Most of us were beginning to use the smaller Rolleis, but still

rigidly on tripods. Although I had stumbled onto my technique by accident, my pictures looked freer than the norm of those days. They were handheld, used a reportage approach and depended on the existing light and ambience for their quality.

For a year I haunted Harlem, spending practically every weekend in a bar, a church hall or a restaurant where the black women came to show their handiwork. The clothing was made either by the models themselves or by local seamstresses, partly as a protest against the white establishment Seventh Avenue "shmatte" trade. It was one forerunner of the civil rights movement.

In addition to the shows themselves to document, there was preparation at home and backstage. There was skin whitening, makeup and hair straightening (the Afro and the wig were still to come). I was recording social history, learning to write a caption, a text block, to follow a visual story line through the beginning of the action, the peak of the action and the letdown at the end. I was starting to be able to assess the photogenic and the nonphotogenic. By the end of the year I was reluctant to wind up the project, because I feared I'd never have another idea.

As a training tool the Harlem story was a godsend, but where to find a publisher for it? In the early fifties no American picture magazine would consider such material for its lily-white pages, even though there was a market in the ten-percent-black population. So what to do with the material? My husband, who had lived in Britain and knew *Picture Post*, the great picture magazine, sent the story off to its editor, Tom Hopkinson, who published eight pages and a cover.

I was lucky to have fallen into Brodovitch's Design Laboratory. He was able to take a mixed group of photographers ranging from absolute beginners like me to professionals already widely published like Avedon and Penn and in his own idiosyncratic way prod us on to find ever more original ways to express ourselves.

The class started with sixty people. Each week found it shrinking, so that at the end of the short semester it was down to thirty. The ones who left wanted a formula, words of wisdom on how to achieve success in a hurry. They didn't like the idea of pulling ideas out of themselves for which they would have to find techniques to produce pictures; the message was lost on them. Those of us who stayed the course learned an important lesson about creative work: there are no prescriptions, no facile answers, there is only concentration and hard work.

After the Harlem fashion story was published, I ran into Mr. Brodovitch at a party. He was pleased when I thanked him and told him how much I had learned from him. He was even more shy and reticent than usual, but asked me to come see him and to bring the published pictures. Somehow I never did, and have regretted it.

Summing up the year's work, I saw that I had strengthened some old skills and acquired new ones: I was able to abandon the tripod completely and work easily with available light, and thus streamline my operation, which meant toting less equipment so that I could concentrate on basic photography. This meant that when I started to travel it would be easier in every way. Oh, yes, and I had gone beyond my forty-dollar Rollei. New and better equipment had been earned and was deserved.

But there was still more to learn from the publication of my first story. Although I had taken extreme care to report the facts accurately and to present the captioned pictures fairly, when the article appeared the layout was attractive, the pictures were used with respect, but the text was changed and the tone was snide. The magazine had had a South African black (who was obviously contemptuous of Harlem blacks) re-write my copy. She wrote: "The richer they are the whiter they want to be." She had missed the point, had reversed my meaning and had thus curdled any pleasure or sense of accomplishment to be savored from the year's work. I was going to have to learn to protect myself so that the essence of what was said in pictures and words was not subverted. It was disappointing to find that editors often changed photographers' text and captions to suit their own misconceptions. It took years until I had sufficient clout and sufficient reputation to insist upon being consulted if my text was to be altered.

Although the publication of my Harlem material had bestowed on me professional status, I had not a clue to how to go about building on it. I did make the rounds of the magazines—it seemed the logical thing to do, since this was the golden era of the picture magazine. *Life*, *Look*, *Collier's* and *The Saturday Evening Post* as well as women's and specialty periodicals were flourishing. Seeing editors, art directors and art buyers was trying, time-consuming and embarrassing. I had only the one story to show. To counteract this, I armed myself with a list of story ideas. But there were still no assignments forthcoming, so I talked the publicist at the Metropolitan Opera into letting me photograph a glittering opening night. Now I had two finished subjects to show.

I still had no direction, no guarantees, and was beginning to worry seriously about how to proceed, when I heard that Magnum Photos, a French cooperative of photographers, was opening a New York office. It was a daring thing for a rank beginner to approach these giants: Henri Cartier-Bresson, Robert Capa, George Rodger and David Seymour. I had no illusion or hope that they would consider me for membership, but I was desperate for a path to open. And I needed an assessment of my work.

There was a surprise when Maria Eisner, who ran the New York office, saw me. She smiled over the Met opening, commented favorably upon it, but when she looked at the Harlem fashion story she greeted it like an old friend. Yes, she had seen it in *Picture Post*, and in various European magazines. Oh, yes, she particularly remembered seeing the story in French and German magazines. On the strength of this she invited me to become a stringer with Magnum. The year was 1952. I was to become Magnum's first American woman member. Inge Morath and I joined at the same time, she in France, I in the United States.

It was thrilling to be asked in by Magnum, but it was puzzling, too. *Picture Post* had clearly syndicated the Harlem material without telling me. How dared it? It had no right, even though I had benefitted.

This is what had happened. A German agent had called the magazine, misrepresented herself as my agent and asked for the stuff. She then proceeded to flog it around Europe. I never saw the pictures again, nor did I ever see a farthing from her deals, but she was instrumental in placing me with what is considered the best group of photojournalists in the world.

Magnum Photos was founded on a very simple principle: the premise that the copyright of the photo belongs to the photographer, not to the assigning party. The four founders, Capa, Cartier-

Bresson, Rodger and Seymour, banded together after the war to form the cooperative, determined to pursue their efforts to retain the rights to their own work so that they could place it in many venues. They did not want to work on staff for magazines; they wanted to control their own destinies, and they divided the world among them: Rodger got Africa; Seymour Europe; Cartier-Bresson China and the Far East; and Capa was to be a roving photographer.

The battle for these rights was not a new one. The story may be apocryphal, but here it is: In the early days of the medium, Queen Victoria was displeased with the idea of "those journeymen" photographers owning rights to pictures of her; she felt safer if the rights lay with the "gentlemen" who owned the newspapers. After all, Ruskin, who spoke of photography as merely spoiled nature, had assured painters that they need not fear photographers, who merely held the ability to record. Photographers were classified with engravers (the equivalent of a fax machine in today's terms).

Magnum Photos, from its infancy, in 1948, fought a battle against the magazines. There were periods when the magazines were strong and refused to use Magnum members unless we knuckled under and gave them our negatives. Most of us were broke, but we still refused to give up rights. We joined forces with the American Society of Magazine Photographers and managed to change the law so that unless it is specified that a photographer is "working for hire," the negatives automatically belong to him or her no matter who paid for the film. In recent years, British law, too, has recognized the right of the photographer to his or her own work.

Perhaps the most important development in my early photographic career was joining the Magnum cooperative. It provided a measuring stick against which to gauge work progress, but more important, it gave us members a sense of belonging. The group was in various stages of professional maturity, ranging from beginners in their early twenties to seasoned war photographers (like the founders) in their thirties and forties. We would show our work to each other—the young avid to learn, and the elders generous with their time and their criticism.

The cooperative has been called an "exclusive club" by its detractors and a "family" by its friends. Actually, both these descriptions are true. It may at times act either snobbishly or clannishly. The "family" part manifests itself in the same problems that beset most families. You love them all—but do not necessarily like them all. So there is a tendency for small cliques to form, strange alliances to come together and peculiar games to be played.

In the beginning, even though the group was founded on democratic principles with the four founding members holding all the stock and votes, it was Robert Capa who called the turns. The young New York–based photographers, Elliott Erwitt, Burt Glinn, Erich Hartmann, Dennis Stock and I, who were stringers, had no vote, and therefore no voice. At our first annual stockholders' meeting we protested. We made noble statements about taxation without representation—meaning that we were paying twenty-five percent of our meagre earnings into the kitty— and we wanted a say. Capa listened carefully, threw up his hands in a characteristic gesture and said, "So let's each have one vote." The others agreed, and with that we all became members.

Although we voted annually, there were (and still are) those who are "more equal than others." It is hard to legislate a "family." As for my place in the family, I am an old hand at this. One (somewhere in the middle) of nine children, I long ago learned to move like a gyroscope in order to maintain absolute momentum.

I was born poor, in America, of Russian immigrant parents. I went to work early and, working, had to prove myself. The sometimes competitive atmosphere of Magnum just acted as a further goad. As a woman I was in a privileged position, even though I often resented the "there-there-little-girl," pat-on-the-head attitude of a few of my colleagues. It was no surprise that I had to strive to be at least as good as the men: it was a tough world out there.

The best bet seemed to be to use my being a woman in the best possible way—it gave me a unique edge in a man's world. The sexes think differently, work differently, so why not be myself? It turned out to be the wisest decision I could have made. I now get credit from feminists for being a pioneer. It wasn't a matter of courage but of prudence on my part; more, *faute de mieux*. At first I began consciously to think in terms of stories about women or stories best suited for a woman to photograph: the fashions in Harlem was one; then it was family, birth, women personalities, children. This approach seemed natural, but when an editor at *Collier's* saw my pictures and leered, "You'll be able to go into the dressing rooms with the actresses," I began to worry about the direction I was heading in. It was when this same editor kept referring to me as a "woman photographer" that I rebelled.

I didn't want to be a "woman photographer." That would limit me. I wanted to be a photographer who was a woman, with all the world open to my camera. What I wanted was to use my female insights and personality to interpret what I photographed. It was when I photographed Senator Joe McCarthy, a really heavy political story, that I knew I was on my way. I would have the "women's stories" but everything else as well.

Although a beginner at *taking* pictures I was experienced in the business of *making* pictures. In 1943, during the war, I had come to New York from Philadelphia, where I had worked during the day in a real estate management office and gone to school at night. For recreation I had become an amateur photographer. Even with all the activity in my life, I was restless and longing to leave home, to enter the big world. For my holiday that year I took a cruise to Bermuda via New York. New friends met aboard ship urged me to join them in the metropolis. They offered to help find me a job and suggested checking want ads in the *New York Times*. One advertisement read, "Amateur photographer: Write stating age, experience if any. Box number . . ."

As a lark, I wrote, telling of the night school and the job I held, and exaggerating my knowledge and ability as a photographer. Immediately, I was summoned to an office on Madison Av-

Self-portrait in a distorting mirror,
42nd Street,
New York, 1950

enue—but then redirected to a firm called Stanbi Photos in Hoboken, New Jersey. The whole thing sounded like a bad joke. All my nervousness and apprehension about the interview suddenly vanished. Hoboken? Stanbi Photos? It sounded like some kind of scam, like selling photographic sittings door to door. "Madame, with this coupon . . ." By the time the taxi crossed the Hudson I was in a state of high levity and feeling superior to the situation, certain that the job was bound to be something completely undesirable. I checked my appearance. I was young, well dressed—full of self-confidence.

Mr. Little, the interviewer, was an affable businessman who sat with his back to a window that framed a storybook view of lower Manhattan. He explained that Stanbi was a subsidiary of a huge corporation, Standard Brands, which sold Chase & Sanborn coffee and Fleischmann's yeast. Both products were delivered fresh weekly to shops nationwide.

Now they had added fresh film to their deliveries and people would buy the film in grocery shops and chains (instead of drugstores), expose the film, and with twenty-five cents placed in a self-addressed envelope that came with the film send it off for processing to Stanbi Photos in Hoboken. Would I like to see the plant? I played it cool. "Yes, it would be interesting."

It turned out to be very interesting. A revolutionary idea, the equivalent of a Ford Motor Company automated conveyor-belt factory for processing amateur film. The heart of the idea was a printing machine with an electric eye that measured the light and did not depend upon the judgment of an operator. The method of development was based on the way motion picture film was developed. No longer was the printer working with cut sheets of paper in a tray; thousands of feet of film were being propelled over rollers in chemical baths to be dried automati-

cally and cut up afterward. It was an impressive operation, and despite myself I kept asking question after question. The combination of my frosty manner and my appetite for information intrigued Mr. Little. He went on to explain that they expected the heavy influx of processing to be in the summer, when most people took holiday snaps, but that the plant would function year-round on a skeleton staff of about three hundred people who would act as a training cadre for another twelve hundred unskilled help to be recruited from local high schools for summer work.

Mr. Little was in the market for all kinds of employees (which is why the ad was deliberately vague), but he had a pressing need for supervisors who understood film processing and were enthusiastic about photography and would transmit their enthusiasm to the new people. He quizzed me about photography and about my work in the personnel department of a real estate management company.

By this time I had thawed considerably, and apparently my answers were the right ones. Would I consider taking two weeks' leave from my Philadelphia job? He would put me up in a good hotel and pay me seventy-five dollars a week (three times what I was earning), and at the end of the period if I proved myself and if I was happy in New York he would double the salary to 150 dollars a week so I could afford to set up on my own.

The bargaining had so absorbed me that I had not stopped to think. Did I really want to work in New Jersey? In a factory? And—it was a big "and"—would I be capable of handling the job? It was mid-war and employees were scarce—Bill Little was later to say that it was my indifference and my quick questions that got me the job.

I was to spend the next five years crossing the river. I began as a supervisor in charge of cutting and inspecting pictures, moved to plant manager, organized photographic studios in Army camps in the American South, and then spent a year in Chicago, setting up and staffing a new plant.

The five years spent at Stanbi acted as training experience for my photographic life to come. My duties ranged from learning the disciplines needed to standardize the plant's photographic quality control to learning how to speak at a local high school to recruit hundreds of students for weekend or summer work; from learning to interview a single person for a supervisory or managerial position to learning how to write lucid photographic instructions for amateurs to be sent them with their less-than-perfect photographs.

Each day I had to handle new problems. I was involved with technology and I was involved with people. I had to learn to gain the confidence of those I dealt with. In so doing, I began to trust my own judgment and matured quickly because of the responsibilities I had assumed. In normal times, it would have been almost unthinkable for someone so young, so inexperienced and so female to have been placed in such a position of trust, but the war presented extraordinary opportunities to the young.

As the employment market tightened, with even youngsters sucked into war jobs, it became more difficult to keep the factory staffed. We tried everything: a shift of housewives who had only a few hours to spare for part-time work; a twilight shift for the aged who did not qualify for war work; we even placed advertisements in Chinatown newspapers for a night shift. Here we fell lucky.

Our needs were greatest in summer, and we wound up with Chinese men who had worked long hours in steamy laundries and were delighted to work in our air-conditioned plant. When winter approached they all returned to the warm laundries. Meanwhile, we had weathered yet another season.

At one point I asked the Chinese men if they could help me recruit women as well. They said that if we got a good Chinese cook and served Chinese food they would help. Within a week, ten women had started in the department where photographs were collated with their negatives, inspected and mailed to the customers. The scheme seemed to be working well. The women were at separate tables from the men, but there was always banter and laughter. We all remarked on the speed with which these apparent strangers seemed to make instantaneous friendships. The day supervisor who was training the women kept saying, "What a wonderful culture." Things certainly didn't happen that quickly with our American employees.

The Chinese women stayed just long enough to receive their first biweekly paychecks. When they failed to return to work, I asked for an explanation from the men. They giggled and refused to answer. Finally the Number One, who was their supervisor and bolder than the rest (and also better able to express himself in English), sought me out and explained that the women, who were the local Chinatown prostitutes, had been doing their own recruiting at Stanbi, and having established a bridgehead had gone back to Chinatown to exploit it. Incidentally, my informant turned out to be the man who collected the bets for the numbers racket. He left soon after the women did but returned weekly to wait outside the plant (in a chauffeur-driven limousine) for the men to come out after work so he could collect their bets. He had added Stanbi to his usual rounds—his customers were mainly employees in Chinese restaurants throughout Manhattan. When asked about the limousine and the chauffeur, he shrugged. Oh, that was to impress the suckers.

But perhaps my strangest chore was the vetting of what the inspectors called "dirty pictures." We received hundreds of pornographic films for processing. Since this was a mail-order business, the senders felt they could remain anonymous. It was better than taking the pictures into the local drugstore. However, according to New Jersey law it was illegal for us to handle them. If I'm remembering accurately, they could not be processed, handled, or returned to sender: it was a federal offense to send them through the mails. Our lawyers decreed that all we could do was notify the sender about the law. We bought a new file, and the two keys were kept by Bill Little and me. I also handled the complaints. Irate customers would write furious letters. Invariably, the letter would come from a man stating that the pictures were legally his, and moreover the woman in the pictures was his wife. No matter his conjugal rights, we were prevented by law from returning his property.

The pictures mounted in the file. Every few months a top executive from the parent company, Standard Brands, would come over in his limousine and ask for the keys to the file. For an hour guffaws would issue from the office where he checked over the latest crop of "dirty pictures."

What were the pictures like? The usual badly exposed, occasionally in-focus nudes. Each partner would have photographed the other. The more sophisticated would have used a delayed-action timer to photograph themselves in action. Of all the thousands that I saw, only a single set of pictures is memorable—a group of nude black men and women enjoying themselves in broad daylight in Central Park. These were in focus, and, yes, properly exposed.

In my five years at the photo-finishing plant, I had absorbed a great deal about the chemical and physical properties of photography. At the New School came the realization that I knew little or nothing about the aesthetic and emotional content of a photograph. Now I began to haunt the files at Magnum, to look at pictures by the various photographers, and to go over their contact sheets to try to understand how they worked. Why this specific angle and not that? Was this great shot made in a public place taken without the knowledge and agreement of the subject, or was it a planned picture, done with co-operation and consent? Had the photographer shown us something unique and unexpected that we might not have noticed on our own? What had the photographer had in mind before the button was pressed? These files became my university.

There were no easy answers. There were just endless questions to be solved separately for each photograph. I was facing subjective values that cannot be taught. One can only dredge up ideas from within oneself and apply them to the real world.

Sometimes the magic works; more often not—but the photographer must continue to try to understand the subject, to get the proportions right, to try to establish not only a personal style, but an empathy with and a sympathy for the sub-ject. If the picture is about unspeakable evil like war or poverty, then hatred helps. Above all, I decided, the photographer must have a point of view, a passionate personal approach. All this, I thought wryly, before you even consider technique—and in the 125th part of a second!

It has been said that Henri Cartier-Bresson, the poet with the camera, was the photographic emphasis at Magnum and that Robert Capa, the reporter with the camera, was the journalistic emphasis. Together they made up photojournalism. Although the two men may have been polar opposites, the combination of their very different approaches to photography created a heady atmosphere in which the rest of us members could develop. In the beginning this was particularly true because photojournalism had not yet solidified and become institutionalized. Daily we created our own rules and improvised.

A codified structure for the group seemed irrelevant, or rather it was Capa's genius that was the structure. He would spawn ideas for us all, from arranging group assignments to sending Cartier-Bresson off to Russia. We were young and idealistic and we were a brotherhood, but a contentious and competitive one. When Werner Bischof and Bob Capa were both killed in 1954, we were suddenly leaderless—no, we felt fatherless.

In the crisis that ensued in New York we looked among the founding members for contenders to take over Bob's mantle. Could it be Cartier-Bresson? That was not his forte; he wanted to assuage his grief in taking pictures. Could it be David Seymour? He was needed in the Paris office. How about George Rodger? He was ill.

With one of our best photographers and our leader gone, there were questions as to whether the Magnum cooperative would survive. But the deaths of our beloved friends had an unexpected effect upon the rest of us. Instead of weakening us it strengthened our resolve to continue in the spirit of these two men who had died in pursuit of their profession. Lucky for us, Cornell Capa, Bob's brother, quit his profitable job as a photographer at *Life* to come and get us going again. The Magnum photographers were in disarray, confused about the future, and in our unhappiness some of us behaved like spoiled anarchic children. I cringe every time I think of how inconsiderate, uncooperative and ungrateful we were to Cornell, who with his wife, Edie, worked his guts out for years to keep Magnum afloat.

The Cartier-Bresson approach to photography—the classical, brilliantly organized photograph—and the Robert Capa historic haphazard photograph still act as competing forces at Magnum, often causing the members to erupt into strong arguments at current annual stockholders' meetings, as to whither the agency. When you add to these basic differences age (we range now from twenty-one to eighty-six), gender (there are only four women), nationalities (a polyglot lot—French, German, Iranian, American, Brazilian, Austrian, Japanese, British, etc.) and the fact that now Magnum is institutionalized, you have some idea of what the years have wrought. Also, we must add to this the current changes in the marketplace.

When I started in photography, in the early 1950s, our pictures were mainly based on how the photographer himself (or herself) saw the story. Now, more and more, photographers have become illustrators for editors' preconceived ideas. Finally, the dwindling number of magazines and newspapers has forced many photographers to go into advertising, art and industrial work to survive.

But despite the adverse conditions in our field, Magnum's four offices (Paris, New York, London and Tokyo) remain active, and although the standards of excellence set by the founders are hard to maintain, they still obtain. I look back at the four decades of my membership at Magnum and remember numerous images, their authors and what I learned as a beginner from each:

From Henri Cartier-Bresson I learned the need to try to tell an entire story in a single definitive image.

From Gene Smith I learned the intricacies of the picture story and to be humble when putting the whole together; if a lesser picture tells a better story and enhances the overall, make sure to use it.

From Robert Capa I learned to dare, to gamble, to hurl myself around the world in search of adventure. Whenever I pick up a camera I can almost hear his injunction ringing in my ears: "If your pictures aren't good enough, you aren't close enough."

From Inge Morath I learned to introduce a leavening and a lightness into my work.

From Ernst Haas I learned a great deal about color. Even though in the beginning my color influenced him, he pushed color farther and faster than I did.

From Erich Hartmann I learned technical restraint and discipline.

With Burt Glinn I was able to discuss a

projected story and to arrive at a sensible plan of attack before setting out to photograph.

From Elliott Erwitt I learned that it is possible to find laughter and humor in photographs.

There were others, like Dennis Stock, who were friends to bounce ideas off. What was important was the friendship of my colleagues. It was particularly so when I moved to England and both George Rodger and Ian Berry were available to me at the end of the telephone line.

Let me return to my early days at Magnum. I became mired in theorizing and increasingly frightened of going out to photograph. I was growing more and more daunted by the fear that I would not be able to measure up to the photographers I was studying when I met Janet Flanner, the *New Yorker* ("Letter from Paris") writer. She put things in perspective for me. Since I was with Magnum Photos, did I know her friend Robert Capa? Yes. She talked glowingly about him: his courage, his intelligence, his ability to nose out where each new global trouble spot was emerging. She talked and I listened.

Noticing my silence, she started to probe. I blurted out that his pictures I had been studying were not well designed. She looked at me pityingly. "My dear," she said, "history doesn't design well, either."

I listened and I heard—and I went to work. There was so much to learn: reportage, printing (traditional and experimental) and learning to work on my own ideas and generate my own stories, to say nothing of learning how to write better captions and text blocks. Then there was research and there was color photography, just beginning to be seriously used editorially. It all became a great jumble in my mind. The only way to deal with it was to take things day by day and enjoy whatever that day brought.

Those were yeasty times. The cramped and badly equipped Magnum office was filled with photographers and filled with enthusiasm. We talked photography, we talked ideas, and we showed each other our pictures. There would be bellows of laughter and Capa would be holding forth. Or there would be sudden silence and Cartier-Bresson would be looking at our pictures. He would hold a print upside down and talk about its photographic merit, or he would squint at it while making a right angle with both arms bent at the elbow. His judgment was always to the point: direct, thoughtful and fair. I would be tremulous when I approached him, but I shall never forget his kindness and the time he took with me. I remember very little specific criticism he offered. He had that ability great teachers and great editors have of making you excited. He created an awareness and a consciousness that went beyond the picture in hand to form a space into which you could be more demanding of yourself. He carried you beyond analysis into a world that could make you think the unthinkable, that made you free. He acted as a catalyst that enabled you to go beyond your own expectations.

I remember one New York spring evening when Henri, Gjon Mili, Ernst Haas, Inge Morath and I stopped for coffee on our way from a gathering of some sort. Ernst, who loved to talk about photography in great elliptical terms, was expounding on form, color, design and photography as art. We all listened, then Henri leaned across to me and said, "Eve, when we are good, we are maybe little better than the watchmaker."

It was good to hear Henri puncture the preciousness that was creeping into our métier. The term "photojournalism" was beginning to take on a pejorative cast. There was a story going the rounds that when Cartier-Bresson was having difficulty being accepted as a serious photographer he asked Capa for advice. Bob said, "Stop calling yourself a photojournalist and call yourself a surrealist."

For years I have sought a meaning for the term "photojournalism." What is it? The dictionary defines it vaguely as "journalism in which photography dominates written copy—as in certain magazines." The best definition I know came from an article Gene Baro, the art critic, wrote about my work for the catalogue he prepared for my China show at the Brooklyn Museum. He said, "The photojournalist doesn't illustrate a story but explores a subject by way of the camera and provides a supporting text. The assignment may come from an editor or a publisher or it may be generated by the passionate interest and social insight of the photographer-writer. But the best photojournalism transcends its subject and gives us images that have a timeless quality, so acute visually that no other explanation is needed finally. The art is in what remains when the occasion has faded."

I am glad that I turned to the real world for my pictures. I cannot imagine working otherwise. In the beginning, I did try photographing in a studio. I did learn to light and to compose in front of blank, no-seam paper. But I found the exercise sterile. Being a storyteller with a camera is much more rewarding. How I came to photography at all has always puzzled me. In my family, as in many Jewish families, literacy was the chosen direction. The Orthodox belief was that one did not make a graven image. The only photograph I remember seeing at home when I was growing up was a photo of my grandfather taken in a studio in a small town near Odessa. Over the years my mother talked about our having a family portrait taken to send to her father, but it never happened.

Who knew from art? I didn't even visit a museum until I was fifteen, but from early childhood I loved to arrange things, to make order out of chaos. I remember a story of my early childhood that might be a clue to the kind of skills I've developed and use now.

When I was five years old my mother's cousin Rose came from Canada with her new husband, Yanye. It was a big occasion in our household. I recall my mother's excitement. She baked knishes, cleaned up her brood (there were then six of us) and admonished us to behave ourselves. The guests were to come for tea and knishes and then go on to our rich uncle Labe for dinner. When she arrived, Rose put a beautifully wrapped parcel on a chair along with her wraps. I could hardly contain my curiosity, and when the adults went for their tea I snatched the package and raced up to the attic with it. There I unwrapped the treasure. It was a box of chocolates. I had never seen a box of chocolates before, nor anything as lovely.

I got out my little facsimiles of Turkish carpets (my father smoked Hasaan cigarettes and these premiums were my playthings). Carefully and lovingly I wrapped each chocolate in a little rug, then I proceeded to arrange them in various patterns. I still remember the thrill of finding that I could wring different designs from the same elements.

When our cousins were ready to leave, an alarm went up because the box of chocolates was missing. It had not been intended for us, but for Uncle Labe, so there was a bit of embarrassment all around. When the family caught up with me I was still making abstract patterns of the chocolates. I had not eaten a single one. Very carefully we placed each intact chocolate in its paper wrapper. No one would have known the box had ever been opened.

During my first years as a member of Magnum I stayed close to home, using Brookhaven Township, Long Island, where my husband, my son and I summered, as a crucible in which to forge ideas. Thus when we left New York City to live on Long Island I was already launched on my ten-year study of the Davis family, whose ancestors had been granted their land by Queen Anne, in 1710. The family was a cache for all sorts of stories, a rug under which to sweep everything from a church supper at which the Davises ate their ears of corn and barbecued chicken in among the tombstones of their ancestors to a story on migratory potato pickers who came north seasonally, like the birds, to work for Mr. Davis, who was a farmer.

This chronicle was almost too good to be true. American Gothic faces, the same family on the same land for almost two and a half centuries: farmers, a teacher who taught in the one-room schoolhouse, a local grocer who tended the post office and sold penny candy, an undertaker, a justice of the peace, a librarian who kept the local library open two hours a week, Daughters of the American Revolution. It was a bonanza for a beginning photographer, and all within a radius of twenty miles from home. Even as I photographed the area and its people, the Brookhaven Township I knew started to disappear, to be replaced by housing on quarter-acre plots. Many landmarks and many people have gone, as has the underlying character of the place. All that remains is the memories of those of us who are still around and our mementos and photographs. I am glad that my son will have my pictures of a vanished world to show his children.

Brookhaven Township was the source of another ongoing saga for my camera: "The First Five Minutes of a Baby's Life." I had lost a baby and gone into a deep depression, and in my anguish had turned to photographing births as a catharsis. It seemed madness to go to the source of the pain, but it did assuage my grief. For an entire winter I went back and forth to the Mather Hospital in Port Jefferson, looking for the exact five minutes when the infant leaves the warmth and security of the womb and is thrust into the alien world where

> the cord is cut
> the child is slapped
> > tagged
> > footprinted
> > weighed
> > washed
> > anointed
> > measured
> > swaddled.

The above describes the way birth was han-

The Davis family church supper,
Mount Sinai,
New York, 1952

dled in the United States (under ideal clinical conditions) in the 1950s. All of this was to change, as I found out in the sixties when I did a story in Britain on motherhood. The new approach was to leave the child alone as much as possible immediately after he or she had navigated the birth canal. It was closer to what I photographed later in primitive countries like Haiti and Tibet, where the child was placed in the mother's arms to rest even before the cord was cut. The rest of the initiation into life would come in due course.

Life magazine loved the birth story and ran the layout over eight pages, calling the closing shot (which ran over two pages) "classic." It was one of two hands, the child clinging to the mother's hand. This picture has been used to advertise everything from insurance to corn flakes. Its sale has generated mad money to pay for independent projects I could not otherwise have risked tackling. The costs of being independent run high.

When I joined Magnum Photos my expectations were very high: my difficulties would disappear—Magnum would provide work, I would do it. All would be well. But that is not what happened. Magnum's loose organization, its lack of capital, its dependence on the vagaries of the editorial market, its insistence upon the photographers owning their negatives, and its limited number of editors in proportion to the number of photographers it represented made it difficult to launch new people while striving to service the established ones.

The above were the problems from our side. From the publishing side (magazines, newspapers, etc.), editors wanted to meet the photographers, wanted to see their work, wanted to know whom they were asking to carry out their assignments. So the burden was thrown back on the photographer. It was time-consuming but productive, because it forced the photographer to come up with ideas and independent projects.

I chose to photograph Joe McCarthy, who in the fifties was holding America to ransom for his witch-hunt for Communists. When I came up with the idea, I spoke to Robert Capa about it. He was silent for a moment, then asked me if I minded waiting a bit before starting on the story; he said he had an important reason for asking me to wait—unfortunately, the reason would have to wait as well. He spoke to me a week later: he was leaving for Paris in a few days and would cable me from there. It all seemed mysterious and worrying, but the day he arrived in Paris he cabled thumbs-up so I could proceed. The reason, which I only heard years later, was that he was having trouble with American immigration authorities, who were threatening to lift his passport. As far as I can check, friends rallied to his aid, the situation changed, and he could step back from the shadow cast by McCarthy and okay my story. He had not wanted either Magnum or me involved in his troubles.

McCarthy and his gang were repellent to me. I had done my homework and brought my concerns and my questions with me to the assignment. I had to keep remembering some of the things I had heard from people whose life he had blighted, because he exuded an oily charm that made it hard to think of the terrible things he had done. One of my interviewees told the following story. He was an instructor at New York University who refused to play McCarthy's game and name names. He had talked back at a hearing in New York. The man was dismissed from his post with prejudice, and in the climate of that time he had little chance of a job without references. He went to Baltimore with his wife and young child. After many months he landed a job. Because he had no references and because he was an honest man, he told his employer the truth. He had to learn to drive a car. He managed that in three

Childbirth,
Port Jefferson, New York, 1952

20

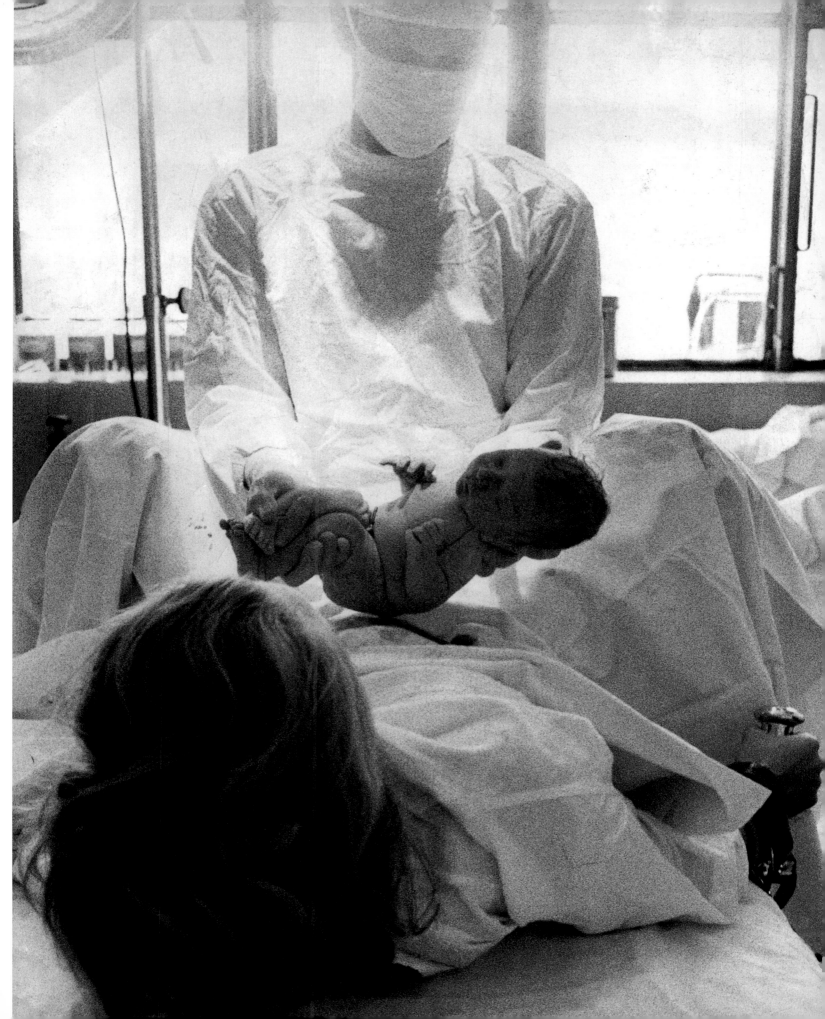

Sailor and his family,
Newport News, Virginia, 1954

days and then took off for his duties. The job was selling toilet seats in West Virginia. He told me that the nadir of his life came when he saw a hit-and-run driver run over a child. He felt he could not be involved—his family's life was at risk. He could not go to the child's aid; others did that. He noted the car's license number and reported it from the nearest phone box, then he sped away.

I tell this as an example of how involved in the story I became before I even picked up the camera. I felt that research like this, although it might not appear in the final reportage, was essential to my understanding of the situation. I likened my preparations to those of a boxer training for a fight.

In contrast to the above and to the other sad tales I had heard, the Senate hearing room where the McCarthy investigation was being held was a crazy circus complete with heavy press, television crews, batteries of lights and on a dais McCarthy flanked by his cohorts, Cohn and Schine, and various senators. Under the table where they sat were crouched two photographers, Speed Graphics at the ready, to pounce on the witnesses they faced. At noon when we broke for lunch, Senator McCarthy held a press conference. He came over to me (I was the only woman there) and put his hand on my shoulder as he asked me whether I had any questions. I instantly put my hand up to remove his, but my brain telegraphed that this wasn't a good idea, so we remained for a beat, my hand covering his.

As gracefully as I could, I managed to extricate myself by saying I had to get to work. Later when I went down to the Senate dining room to get a bowl of the famous bean soup, the thirty or so newsmen who sat at the same table ignored me. Not one of them would talk to me, because they had witnessed the scene with the senator. Such was the climate of distrust that I didn't dare tell them what had happened for fear of betrayal. Looking back now it is hard to believe the climate of terror that existed in the fifties in America.

I found it very exciting to be doing political reportage, to be where history was being made, to be able to express what I felt about the injustice being practiced. The ugliness of it all was evident in the faces of McCarthy and his henchmen, and I tried to capture it on film.

I came away from Washington convinced that this kind of documentary photography was an area for me to pursue. It was rewarding because everything from the initial idea through the research, photography, editing and captions and text was mine. The whole effort was crowned by good sales in good magazines abroad and a pat on the head from Capa. It followed an assignment by a British magazine to cover the 1952 Republican Convention in Chicago. This was another kind of circus, with little old ladies in sneakers trying to start a third party to promote Joe McCarthy at its head.

I was a total novice at this kind of work, and, what was worse, I had come to the convention three days late—after the main candidates had retired from the scene to await the outcome of the contest. The only thing I could do was to photograph the mood of the event, the hysteria, but I knew that without the principal players, no matter how good the pictures, my editors would consider the shoot a failure and me a washout. Of course, I had a picture of Eisenhower's (and Nixon's) acceptance speech, waving their arms about—the shot photographers call the "armpit"—but that hackneyed image is hardly something to stop the presses. So what to do? I figured that there had been tough, acrimonious dissension within the Republican Party between the Taft and the Ike supporters and that they would want to show a united front. I guessed (and luck was with me) that at the end, Eisenhower, the

Roy Cohn and Joseph McCarthy,
House Committee on Un-American Activities,
Washington, D.C., 1954

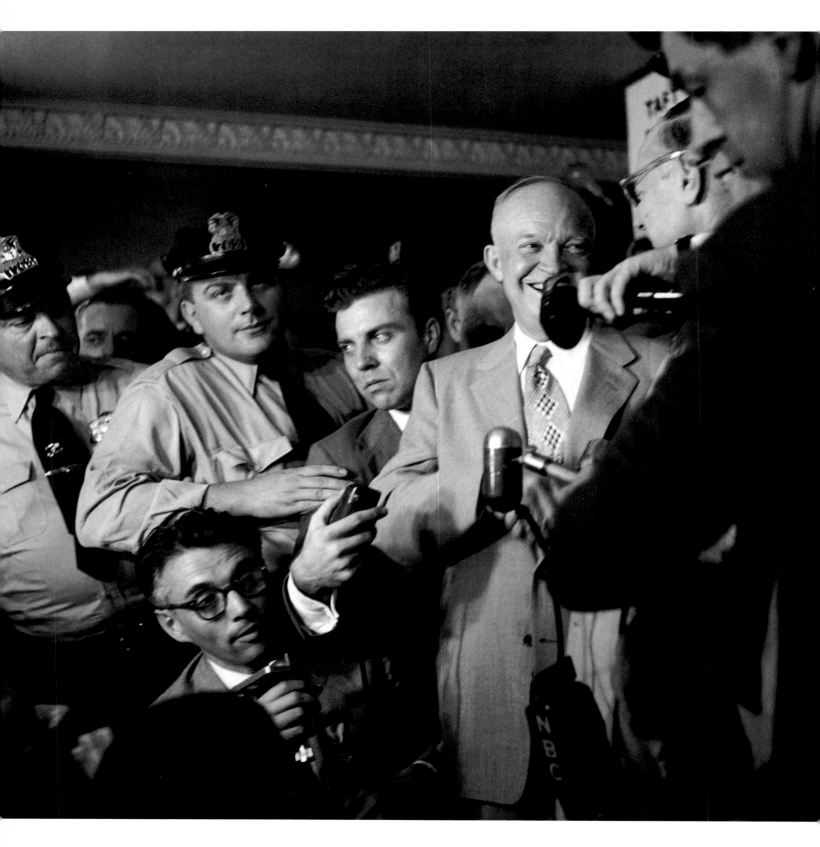

Dwight D. Eisenhower and Robert Taft
after Republican nomination,
Chicago, 1952

winner, would be magnanimous and come to Taft's headquarters at the Blackstone Hotel to try to heal the Republican Party's wounds.

When I arrived there, CBS was setting up lights and there were practically no stills photographers about. The CBS crew winked at me and let me inside the circle of locked arms when Eisenhower arrived, hardly able to hide his smile of triumph. Taft forced a grimace and I got my picture. It was a relief, because I was shooting for *London Illustrated*, and my friend Eddie Feingirsh was shooting for *Picture Post*—I didn't want to be outshone by him. In order to get his picture he did a daring thing. He managed to find a waiter's coat and a tray with glasses and champagne, gave the future president a celebratory glass and then whipped out his Leica. Before he could make a single exposure the Secret Service men grabbed him. I saw them marching him out of the lobby of the hotel to interrogate him. I blessed my bumbling intuition. I had beaten the competition.

The 1952 Republican Convention had initiated television as a news medium, and all over New York during the period leading up to the election you could see clusters of people on the streets in front of TV shops and in the bars watching TV. There were still very few home sets. It seemed a good idea to document the phenomenon, though there were many who thought TV a fad and would smile at the thought that it might oust mighty *Life* magazine.

I also went on with Brookhaven pictures and expanded my take to the migrants on a Long Island farm my four-year-old-son, Francis, called the Awful Place. Then late one rainy night I received a call to cover a recording session of Marlene Dietrich in which she would sing the songs she had sung to the Allied troops during the war: "Lili Marlene," "Miss Otis Regrets," "Where Have All the Flowers Gone," and others. I was a replacement for Ernst Haas, who was not avail-

able. But I didn't mind; Marlene was my first "personality," and I was thrilled.

I had heard that when she recorded she dressed in trousers and a beret, but on the evening we worked she arrived in a short cocktail dress on which there was a large gaudy diamond clip. The other getup would have been more appropriate, but there were the wonderful legs instead. She was trailed by two men. One was Jean Gabin and the other a short, pockmarked man whom she introduced as a friend from Hollywood. Adroit questioning revealed that he was her astrologer and that he had decreed that this miserable wet night was the propitious time to make the recordings.

The time was certainly propitious for me. She worked diligently, "like a ditchdigger," said my notes, from midnight when she arrived until six in the morning. I followed her from rehearsal to recording to playback and back again as she worked, and nothing was questioned or off-limits. I heard later from our mutual friend Leo Lerman that she called him when we finished and complained that I had been there all night taking pictures. He asked why she hadn't stopped me. She said it had never occurred to her, I had done it with "such authority."

Magnum had been informed by Columbia Records that I could have either twenty-five dollars with the negatives belonging to them or I could receive no payment and own the negatives. Of course, I chose the latter. There was also a stipulation that Marlene would have to vet the pictures and have final right of approval. And she wanted to see them immediately. I went straight from the session to my darkroom (an improvised cupboard that had formerly housed a large refrigerator in my bedroom and which I had to enter sideways because it was so small). I printed carefully to make her look as young and attractive as possible.

While I worked, there were phone calls from Columbia Records to arrange a time next day for me to see Miss Dietrich with the pictures. There was also a call for me to meet Mme. Edmonde Charles-Roux, then editor of French *Vogue*, to show her my portfolio. I arranged to go to *Vogue* first, and from there to Marlene.

Mme. C. loved my portfolio, she said, but what was a second envelope I was carrying? Could she see it? Another time, I said. But what was it? Embarrassed, gauche, I told the truth: Marlene, I said, but she must see the pictures first. Nonsense, said Charles-Roux: just let me see them—I'll never tell Marlene I saw them. Too inexperienced to deal with the situation, I showed her the pictures. Again she reassured me that she would say nothing.

I went directly from *Vogue* to Marlene's house, where there was a message to say that she was away for the day and for me to leave the pictures and my phone number. That night the *Vogue* editor went to a party given by Condé Nast for Marlene and told her she had seen terrific pictures of her done by me. Marlene's fury was predictable. She called the record company and raged. I had broken a sacred trust. She was to have seen the pictures first. How dare I? She said she had been so angry that she had torn up the pictures without looking at them. The PR person from Columbia Records called me. What to do? I had another set of prints made by a commercial printer and sent them to Miss Dietrich.

When she went through the pictures she wrote instructions on each (in eyebrow pencil) for retouching: narrow down the chin, cut down the waist, remove the dimple from the knee, the ankle should be slimmer, etc. I went into the darkroom again, printed them well, wrote captions and a short text and took the pictures to *Esquire* magazine, which used them across two pages. I did not retouch them—just printed them

well, and removed two prints she might have found offensive.

The story was to be reproduced in many magazines around the world and to be a forerunner of the changes taking place in portraiture—a documentation, a form Brodovitch called a "portrait in action," unglamorized and unretouched. Capa when he saw these pictures said my work fell, metaphorically of course, between Marlene Dietrich's legs and the bitter lives of migratory potato pickers. (He was right. My work still continues with the celebrated and the poverty-stricken.)

Marlene loved those pictures, and for years I was her "white-haired girl" (I went grey early) and was brought in on many occasions, from her opening the circus to an appearance at the Museum of Modern Art to more recording sessions.

It was flattering to be invited to photograph Dietrich, who knew a great deal about photography. She knew exactly how she should be photographed to bring out the exquisite line of her cheekbones, the luminosity of her eyes, the arch of her neck, the beauty of her legs. When she was in Hollywood she would discuss with the cameraman where her key light should be, the angle of the fill light, etc., etc. A story that went the rounds was that she was particularly pleased with the cameraman after *Rancho Notorious* was filmed and offered, as a reward, to go to bed with him. When he demurred she laughed and sent him a Cadillac instead.

Recording sessions were stimulating to photograph, because everything was in motion: the subject, the musicians, the technicians and therefore the photographer. You needed fast reflexes to keep up with moving targets and sensitivity and skill to get the pictures while keeping out of the performers' eyeline so as not to break their concentration. You also needed to be careful not

Marlene Dietrich,
recording session,
New York, 1952

to photograph during soft musical passages so the click wasn't heard on the recording. Even now when I think about it I feel the tension in my muscles that I felt then while waiting for fortissimo passages in the music.

Photographing recording sessions was particularly difficult because at that time I was still using the square-format Rollei, an awkward camera to compose in. Pictures seem to design best in rectangles (the eye sees that way). Filling the square space (at least at first) takes longer to arrange and one always worries that with a fast-moving subject, pictures are being missed; that you're just a beat behind. But the Rollei was the camera of choice in the fifties. Historically, it bridged the period from the even larger studio format camera to the smaller and more flexible 35mm camera.

In quick succession I photographed the following artists recording for Columbia Records: Tony Bennett, Guy Mitchell, Lotte Lenya (singing "Mack the Knife" and other Weill-Brecht numbers), Benny Goodman, Lili Pons, Bruno Walter, Eileen Farrell, Mary Martin, David Oistrach, the saxophonist Lillian Briggs, and a very young boy and a singing nun recording "Rudolph the Red-Nosed Reindeer."

I fell out of favor with Marlene in the early sixties. She did a show at the Olympia in Paris and, hearing from a friend that I was there, got in touch with me. She had demanded that *Match*, which was doing a feature on her, guarantee her a cover. It was during the time of the Algerian crisis, and plastic bombs were exploding all over Paris. When the magazine pointed out that under the circumstances it might need the space for a more compelling situation, she asked me to photograph as well, so she could threaten *Match* with the competition of other French magazines. When I saw the pictures I made, I knew she would hate them. It was almost a decade since the first session, and to paraphrase an old Hollywood joke, the photographer was ten years older. I decided to retire them, and sent her a note saying that I had lost my touch, had done a bad job, and was so sorry; I had tried to reach her to tell her myself, but had been unable to. Then I left for London for assignment. Stupidly, I left the pictures at Magnum in Paris with strict instructions for them to be locked away and not be used, but she was clever—she came to the office herself and with a combination of charm and intimidation managed to see the pictures.

She was imperious and pitying: "Sad," she said, "but poor Eve has really lost her touch."

Republican Convention,
Chicago, 1952

The following year, when Queen Elizabeth of England went on her first world tour, I was assigned by a British magazine to cover the event in Jamaica. It was my first foreign assignment. I was green and scared and game. I arrived in Kingston two days before the event to document the anticipation and the preparations on the island. In order to get a feel of the place and some background material, I checked in at the *Gleaner*, the local newspaper, where I met Kathleen McColgen, a reporter who had been the first woman to write leaders for the London *Times*. She knew the island and its problems, and was generous and open with her information.

She told me that the police were uneasy about security. They were carefully watching the Rastafari, a group of black militants who did not look on the British queen as their sovereign, but believed that Haile Selassie was their king, and that ships would one day arrive to take them home to Ethiopia. When men joined the movement they vowed never to cut their beards or their hair, which hung in matted dreadlocks to their shoulders, as long as they remained in exile.

The Rastas, as Kathleen called them, lived mainly in Trenchtown, a makeshift area that had been set up by the Red Cross after the 1938 hurricane hit the island. Now, fifteen years later, they were still in tents, and the trenches were stinking latrines. She said the drug and alcohol consumption among the Rastas was high, and that the police feared that there might be trouble when the queen came.

This was an interesting sidelight to the royal tour, but also a good story on its own. I was intrigued. Kathleen put me in touch with a man she described as the black Charlie Chaplin, a Jamaican comedian the Rastas adored. He agreed that for a fee (I remember fifty dollars) he would drive me to Trenchtown at ten o'clock that night to introduce me, so that I could come to work the following day at my leisure.

Except for a single kerosene lamp that was burning on a lectern, the tent-covered wasteland of Trenchtown was in pitch darkness. Charlie and I stumbled over a rutted path toward the light, where four bearded hairy men stood. One was reading from the Old Testament. When Charlie explained why we had come, they looked at me with bloodshot eyes and muttered about money. Charlie handled that. They then agreed to pictures, but no names, otherwise the police would be able to trace them. I felt it incumbent upon me to point out that their faces would identify them even if no names were used.

The head man said that he would have to consult the Bible, whereupon he picked up a long

Queen Elizabeth,
first royal tour,
Jamaica, 1954

33

knife that lay on the lectern and slipped it haphazardly in among the pages. He then read aloud the line the knife tip had touched: "For we are the Jews, the Chosen People." The men all nodded at each other. Even then, things might have been okay except that I piped up, saying, "I too am a Jew." With this the leader picked up the knife and started for me. Charlie grabbed my arm and we ran stumbling and falling back down the pitted track, the drunken men lurching after us with the knife. We made it to the car and took off before they could reach us. My guide told me that the men were full of white lightning, the home brew they didn't want the police to find, and so hadn't been very fast on their feet. We had been lucky. They looked on Haile Selassie as the king of Judea and deeply resented a white woman's claim to Judaism.

For the queen's formal appearance a dozen Rastas showed up—guarded by the police. They were clean and sober and stood quietly in the corner of the square under a banner that said, "Haile Selassie, King of Judea." When the queen's cavalcade passed they were the only ones in the throng who didn't cheer.

The experience was an exotic and stimulating one that gave me a taste for more. In 1954 I returned to the Caribbean: to Cuba on a story about a child that was part of a Magnum series called Children Around the World, and to Haiti for a story about a doctor that was part of a series called Women Around the World. Bob Capa had sold these two series to *Holiday* magazine for fifteen thousand dollars after an all-night poker session in Paris with its editor, Ted Patrick. It is part of the Capa legend that first the editor lost all his money, then Capa sweetly inveigled him into the sale, which was to keep us all working and keep the agency afloat for a year.

Juana, the child who lived on Bahía Honda, an island in the Caribbean that housed eleven families, was eight years old. When my single-engined plane landed, a swarm of children raced toward us, Juana leading the pack. She immediately climbed a palm tree and threw down coconuts to be opened for me to drink. She was a vibrant loving child who was a delight to photograph in this idyllic setting—idyllic, until one noticed the poverty. The men fished for a living; fish, was the staple diet, along with coffee, rice and lard that came from the mainland. There was a school set up very cleverly by Batista's repressive government. When he came to power he instantly drafted graduate university students into the army. They were then deployed all over the country to teach a practically illiterate population of adults as well as children. The teacher brought toothbrushes and toothpaste and taught the children how to take care of their teeth.

In the three weeks I lived on the island, Juana and her family became my friends. I wept when I left. The parents had asked me to adopt Juana. She had no future there except to emulate her mother and live in poverty. If she escaped to the city the chances of her not turning to prostitution were slim. Alas, there was no way I could fit her into my peripatetic life.

I did get one more story in Cuba in 1954. I went with Helen Lawrenson, who had written *Latins Are Lousy Lovers*, to Havana. She called the story "The Sexiest City in the World." It was hard to do, because Helen kept talking about the softness of the air, the *ambiente*, the excitement, while the curfew was strictly enforced after ten at night and Batista's tanks roamed the city. She remembered the opulent whorehouses of the decade before, and told a story of a South American dictator who had rented a house into which he would drive his limousine. He and his mistress would then spend weeks in seclusion and sexual bliss, only taking time out to send for food.

Fisherman and family,
Bahía Honda,
Cuba, 1954

Bar girl in a brothel,
Havana, 1954

Alas, the elegant red velvet brothels were gone, the dictator's house empty and dull like some empty concrete box.

What to do? Days of worry, particularly difficult because I spoke no Spanish. Helen wasn't daunted. We went to the Tropicana, an expensive nightclub (before curfew), and photographed; then we gained access to a rather poor man's brothel which was frequented by American sailors when the fleet was in. The place was called Christmas Tree Alley, because it was in the red-light district. We photographed the sailors dancing with the ladies of the night. But I ran into trouble with the lawyers at *Esquire*, for which the story was done. They vetoed the pictures of the sailors, saying that their "bulges of lust" showed through their tight white thirteen-button trousers. I solved the problem by having the bulges airbrushed out, and all was well.

Through Yvonne Sylvain, a woman doctor, I learned about Haiti in an intimate way that would not have been possible otherwise. She was one of the fifteen percent French (not Creole) descendants who were the elite. She led me to both the rich and the poor (there was practically no middle class). She arranged for me to go to the insane asylum where an American drug company was carrying out its first trials of Miltown, an early tranquilizer. First it was rats, then Haitians, and if the drug proved safe for humans, Americans would have it.

Yvonne also introduced me to voodoo Haitian-style. It is a combination of Catholicism and African tribal ritual, so the litany to Erzele the goddess is chanted in a cadence (Erzele Erzele) that sounds like Hail Mary, Hail Mary. It is said that Haitians go to church and are Catholics on Sunday, but are voodoo all the rest of the week. Voodoo was illegal, so officials of the temple simply strung pictures of the then president, Magloire, on strings all over the place, presumably appeasing the authorities.

It was in Haiti, too, that I met Margaret Mead, the eminent anthropologist. She had her own hang-ups. She was not working in the temple—it was too dark. She had simply taken an entire purification ceremony out of doors into the light, where she reset and photographed the scene. She told me that when she had worked in the South Seas she had found it tiresome that births usually took place at night, and so she had waited until sunlight so that she could recreate the birth. I tried to tell her that I had managed to shoot the actual voodoo scene *in situ* even with my slow Rolleiflex, but she felt that was silly when it was possible to set things up outdoors to make them more dramatic.

Nineteen fifty-four was the year Magnum suffered its two crippling losses. Werner Bischof, Swiss, handsome, sensitive, gifted, was killed on assignment in Peru. The same week Robert Capa, Hungarian-naturalized-American, good-looking, volatile, prescient, was killed on assignment in Indochina. Werner was thirty-eight years old, Capa was forty.

When news of Capa's death reached Paris, those of Capa's friends who were in the city met in the bistro downstairs from the Magnum office to hold their own wake, to spend the night drinking magnums of champagne and reminiscing about their friend. In the group were John Huston, Irwin Shaw and John Steinbeck.

In New York, John Morris, our bureau chief, arranged a fitting memorial service for both men at a Quaker meeting house in Purchase, New York. As is customary, there was no pastor; people sat quietly and then when moved to speak rose to their feet and did so. It was interesting that each of the people that spoke that Sunday afternoon in

Miltown experiment,
insane asylum,
Haiti, 1954

May seemed mindful of his own mortality and spoke out in terms of his own life.

The first person to speak was Steichen. He had been an admiral in the American Navy during World War II. He raised his right hand to his forehead and said, "Salute to Robert Capa—he was a great soldier." He extolled Capa's virtues as photographer and military man and sat down.

Julia Capa, mother of Bob and his younger brother, Cornell, spoke heartbreakingly of her "sonny boy."

Cornell spoke of his relationship to his brother and the bond they had in photography.

Others followed and talked of interests shared with Capa: one had gone skiing with him in the Alps; another had been gambling at Longchamp, where they had placed bets on the wrong horses; a third had been involved in his wild poker games.

A writer, John Winocour, who had worked for *Picture Post* in Israel with Bob, began a tale of daring by saying, "In 1948 I was on the road to Jerusalem with Capa."

Among the last to speak was Eliot Elisofon, a fellow photographer and a man of no small ego. His memorial to his friend Capa began, "I was not jealous of Robert Capa, I was as good a photographer as he was . . ."

There were, of course, also tributes to Werner throughout the service, but he was not as well known or as charismatic as his fellow corpse, so what was said about him was muted. Elisofon would not let him have the last accolade either. When we returned to the Magnum office later that day he went through Bischof's book on Japan comparing his own Japanese work with Werner's. The last thing I remember Eliot saying was "My bride was prettier than his, my pictures are better . . ."

Emboldened by favorable acceptance from editors and readers, I began to produce work independently, knowing not only that working on my own, unassigned, would offer freedom in the photographing itself but that if the material merited it, Magnum would sell the pictures for more money than normal. Also the chances were that the pictures would appear in more venues than if they had been tailored to the editorial needs of a single magazine. They would also go into the archives in our offices and those of our agents, and so they became an ongoing source of income, especially if they were images of historic events or classic images of personalities. Without the agency the photographer would have been happy with a single fifty-dollar sale (the going price in the fifties). Now most of us at Magnum who have a body of work in our libraries can live off the income from our archives.

The list of "personalities" I photographed in the fifties and early sixties (after Marlene) is interesting for its diversity. Actors and performers Paul Newman, Jack Benny, Josephine Baker, Joan Crawford with her daughter Christina, Gina Lollobrigida, Mary Martin, Haya Harrareet, Margaret Sullavan, Shirley MacLaine, Clark Gable, Montgomery Clift, Danny Kaye, Lilli Palmer, Marilyn Monroe (alone and with Laurence Olivier), Susan Strasberg, James Cagney, the Lunts, Silvana Mangano and Lotte Lenya; world heavyweight boxing champion Rocky Marciano; radio and television commentators Alistair Cooke, Arthur Godfrey and Mike Wallace; directors Jed Harris and John Huston; musicians David Oistrach, Igor Stravinsky and Bruno Walter; politicos (including wives and a daughter) Richard Nixon, Patricia Nixon, Mamie Eisenhower, Mme. Khrushchev and the daughter of the shah of Iran; religious leaders Dean Pike and Oral Roberts; dancer Vera Zorina; singers Rosemary Clooney and Leontyne Price; writers Arthur Miller, William Carlos Williams, and Christopher Isherwood and W. H. Auden (together).

Some details of the picture-taking stay in the mind: Danny Kaye conducting the Boston Pops Orchestra with a flyswatter while they played "The Flight of the Bumble Bee"; Rocky Marciano talking about the difficulties of training for a world championship bout, especially abstaining from sex to build up the killer instinct; Mamie Eisenhower's dictum that to look her best no woman should leave her bed before noon. James Cagney was particularly touching in his concern for the environment (we called it conservation then). He spoke of his poverty-ridden childhood on the streets of New York, and he told a singular story. As a child he was sent by a charity organization (with other poor children) to a summer camp on a meadow overlooking the sea. He vowed then that if he ever became rich he would buy the meadow on which they were encamped and build a house. When he became famous—and rich—he returned to Massachusetts to fulfill the dream. Alas, the people who owned the land refused to sell, saying that it had been in their family for generations and they wished to keep their holdings intact. Disappointed, Mr. Cagney bought land on the sea not far away and built a modest house.

Then came the hurricane of 1938 and he and his wife, Willy, found shelter on the roof of their house, which was pulled up from its cellar and sent spinning into the sea. It came to rest on the spot that he had always coveted. The people who owned it came to him and sold it to him. It was, they said, an act of God.

Before I met up with Clark Gable I wondered how the private person would match with the public person. It was an important question, because on it rested the degree of intimacy he would permit between us, and that in turn would affect the kind of pictures I could take, whether there could be collaboration between subject and photographer, whether the sitter (a loose term, as he would also stand, move, ride a horse, and so on) would be generous with the person behind the camera. A great deal depended on the tact and diplomacy of the photographer. I remembered my brother Jack's definition of a diplomat: someone who maneuvers an adversary into a corner where there is a door.

At the beginning of my work on John Huston's *The Misfits*, Gable was pleasant but formal. Since I knew we would have a long time together (two months, it turned out), I was careful to wait for him to get used to me on the location in Nevada. Then one day from the darkness of watching the "rushes" I heard a voice I thought

belonged to the set dresser asking what I had thought of the three minutes of film just seen.

Without thinking, I said they had knocked me on my ass. I heard a great guffaw and looked around to see that it came from Clark Gable. He wanted particulars about my reaction. Red-faced and sputtering, I told him that he was marvellous in an extremely difficult drunk scene in which he barrels out of a saloon looking for his children, hops up on to the hood of a car and then falls off the other side. This was a scene that would normally have been played by a stuntman.

Apparently I said the right thing, because next day he told me that when he heard I was shooting for *Life* magazine, he had decided to be aloof. He had had dealings with *Life* before. They had, he said, followed him around a golf course for a month—or at least it seemed like a month—and then had not used a single picture. But with that devilish Rhett Butler look that was his trademark, he said that anybody who could be as good a sport as I had been the other day when he had laughed at me deserved a break—and he would be happy to cooperate.

Memories of Gable slide into memories of John Huston. Although I was to work on a number of his films and to become a good friend, seeing him often on holidays and weekends at his baronial house in Ireland, it is images from the days of *The Misfits* that are most vivid.

He had been a great friend of Robert Capa's, and he welcomed me warmly as a member of Magnum Photos. People who knew John as a great practical (even sadistic) joker who loved to "take the mickey" out of you had warned me to be on the lookout for pranks he might play. He was, however, unfailingly kind and considerate with me, usually finding a spot closest to his camera for mine.

I worked as stills photographer on other films of Huston's: *A Walk with Love and Death* (in Aus-

James Cagney and his wife, Willy,
hoofing in their barn,
Massachusetts, 1955

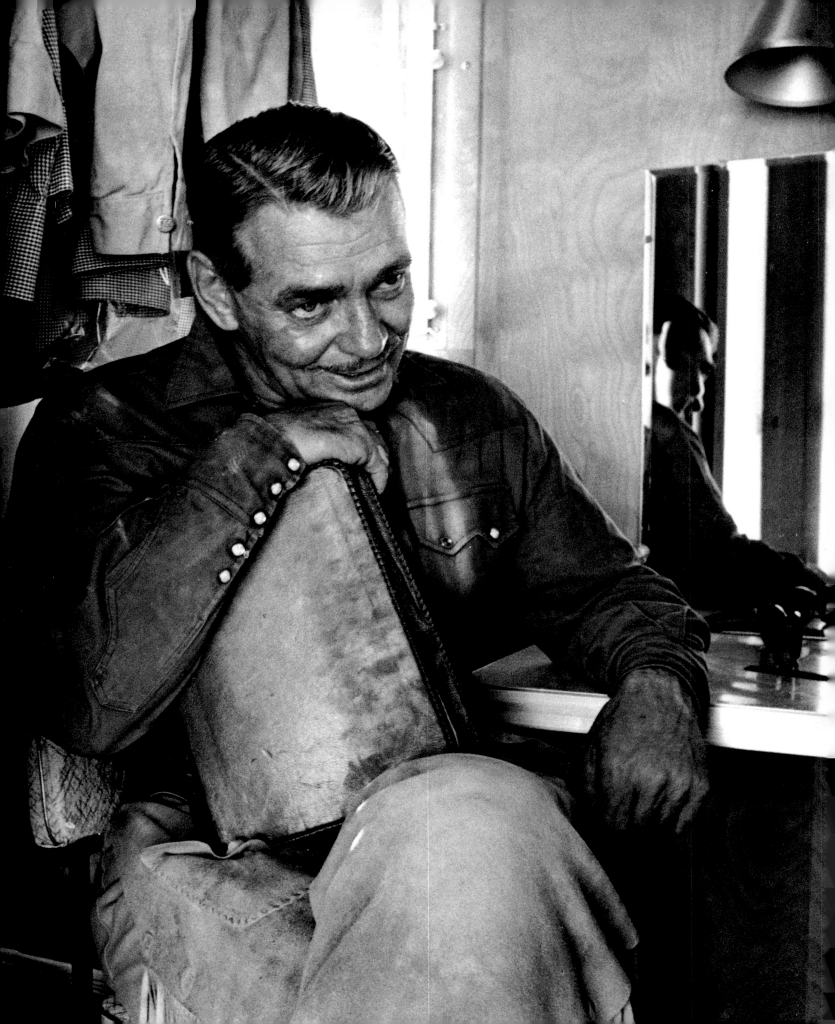

tria); *The Bible* (in Italy); *The Man Who Would Be King* (in Morocco); and *Under the Volcano* (in Mexico). Since I was frequently a guest at St. Clarens, his home in Ireland, I was able to observe him away from the location where he was filming. He would frequently be working at home on a film script with Gladys Hill, his assistant, or with other writers. Often over lunch or dinner, if we were *en famille*, he would discuss a scene, act out a character, or, when relaxed over coffee, make sketches for his storyboard.

His preparations were prodigious. He would be brilliantly prepared for each new film. As a director who had aspirations to be a painter, and who painted in his spare time, he visualized scenes in meticulous detail. He would come to each movie with images already set in his mind and with his enthusiasm high. As he filmed each new situation he would appear to flag. It often seemed to me that he had let the perfume stopper out of the bottle; that for him the real creation lay in the visualization and that the act of getting the film into the can was an afterthought. Often on location there would seem to be an anticlimax, then he would gather his forces and the adrenaline would flow again. But always it was the next, untapped project that fascinated him.

Perhaps it wasn't film that gave him his greatest satisfaction, but the hunt. Watching him in his elegantly tailored velvet dinner jacket seated at the head of his magnificent marble dinner table listening with acute attention to a local horsewoman extol the virtues of the bloodlines of her horses, I couldn't help feeling that he would rather be Master of the Galway Hunt than make a fine film. Then we would retire to the drawing room and he would take up his sketch pad and begin to dream a new film. There was no question that he needed both worlds—and of course he *was* Master of the Galway Hunt.

I learned a great deal from John Huston. When I started to do photo reportage on the making of motion pictures I was naive enough to think that film was multiplied stills with sound and motion. Not so. The still photo is essentially the distillation of the *mise-en-scène*, and even though it is the basic component of the movie, mastering it doesn't make it easier for the practitioner who works with the single image (the photographer, painter, illustrator, etc.) to learn filmmaking. They must put aside what has been learned from the still image and start fresh.

I became an unacknowledged apprentice to John Huston. By listening, sitting in on story conferences, and being given carte blanche to go wherever John was, I began to understand about structuring a scene, directing an actor, dealing with a lighting cameraman and all the minutiae necessary for a director to know. My passport was my camera. John enjoyed being photographed, and he was a splendid subject. He would go about the business connected with his work seemingly unaware of the camera, but he was both actor and director, and I would see a sudden extra flourish, a slight movement of a hand or an eyebrow, to enhance the picture.

His style of directing was no style at all. He did not direct. He did not rehearse. He would elicit from his actors their best in very few words. Some actors would deeply resent not being given specific instructions. If they asked, he would give, but that was not his natural way. He felt that leaving the actor free to bring forth his own interpretation gave him a greater chance to create his own special character. True, it set up tensions and often worries among cast and crew, but this only provided an ambience in which to probe and to develop ideas. This method—or "no method"—of working acted as a guide to me in my work with my subjects, especially when I photographed actors.

Clark Gable
on location for *The Misfits*,
Nevada, 1960

An assignment that was as theatrical as any Huston film was of Nikita Khrushchev. While we were still in the middle of the cold war, Khrushchev and his family came to America. Magnum had organized heavy coverage for practically all of us. I asked to be assigned to Mrs. Khrushchev, finding her babushka appearance appealing. Cleverly, she was to exploit her peasant appearance to compete with the Hollywood hoopla her American hosts were offering.

There was a crush of press when Mme. K. started her tour. The authorities had decided that it was impossible to accommodate all the photographers, and so the "pool" method was to be used, one photographer to take the pictures and share them with all the others. I argued that that was fine for domestic use but would not accommodate the European press, which I, as a member of Magnum, represented. The system would be too slow (years before fax), so could I be "pool" for Europe? This was granted, grudgingly, and I was to be permitted to follow Mrs. Khrushchev into lunch with Governor Rockefeller's wife.

The governor's lady and her guests convened at the Waldorf Hotel, and the other "pool" person and I waited outside in the lobby until after the first course, when the picture session was to take place. As we stood outside the banqueting hall, a small nondescript man came up behind me and started to whisper. I was startled, but he shushed me by putting his fingers against his lips, at the same time indicating the police that stood guard all around us. What he whispered to me was, "Hey, lady, how would you like to earn a thousand dollars?" When I asked what he was talking about, he thrust a greasy paper bag at me and said he represented the American Doughnut Trust, and if I could get a picture of Mme. Khrushchev eating a doughnut the way the Queen of England had eaten a hot dog, then I would be paid "a thousand smackeroos."

I told him to get lost and went over to the nearest policeman to find out who the man was.

"Oh," the cop said, "I don't know. I thought he was with you."

So much for the security protecting our guests. When I seemed troubled, the cop assured me that there isn't much that can be done if there is a dedicated assassin on the loose. "All you have to do," he said, "is to go to a theatrical costumier and hire a police uniform for ten bucks"—this was before inflation—"and do the deed and you could disappear without a trace."

Silvana Mangano,
Museum of Modern Art,
New York City, 1956

All through the fifties in the United States, I continued with portraiture. It was usually part of a reportage done for magazine publication or as an assignment for a film production like *The Misfits*, which also included magazine assignments. One of the most intriguing of these was a pure publicity puffball done for *The Woman's Home Companion*. It was intended to publicize *Autumn Leaves*, a movie starring Joan Crawford.

A Hollywood publicist had dreamed up a scenario. Miss Crawford was to come to New York with sixteen-year-old Christina, her adopted daughter. She was faced with a dilemma: should Christina, who wanted to be an actress like Mommie, plan to go to college and take up drama there while going on with her education, or should she come to New York to try to take the direct path to an acting career?

Since Miss Crawford knew no one in New York who could help, I mapped out a plan of action. We would go to theatre and supper afterward at Sardi's every night for a week. This would give Joan maximum coverage to be seen, and it would also (theoretically) give Christina a chance to see real theatre and give her a more concrete idea of her chosen métier. During the days there would be talking to people in the theatre who might be helpful: drama school heads,

producers, directors and a young actress, Susan Strasberg, currently starring in *The Diary of Anne Frank*.

Let me describe our first day's outings. We met at Tina Leser, the dress designer's, where Miss Crawford and her daughter were to buy clothes. Joan swept in, her square-shouldered suit and very-high-heeled clear plastic shoes making her appear tall (she was in reality only five feet four). On her wrists were the tiniest of dogs—one pissing poodle as a cuff on each. If she put her hands together there was a muff. As she handed the dogs (Mommie's darlings) to her secretary, she kissed each on the mouth, then kissed me on the mouth (we had never met before). She then proceeded to the dressing room, where an entire wardrobe awaited her. She ignored the fact that Christina had not arrived and started to strip. When she was completely nude she imperiously told me to start photographing.

It was obvious that she had been drinking, and it was also obvious that there was something that impelled her to behave the way she did, something I only dimly began to understand years later when I had learned more about her.

At any rate, there she was nude—but sadly, something happens to flesh after fifty. I knew she would not be happy with the pictures she kept insisting that I take. I tried playing for time.

Joan Crawford
on soundstage,
Hollywood, 1959

49

Shouldn't we wait for Christina? No, we should not, emphatically not. So I picked up the camera and started to photograph. By the time I had finished a roll of thirty-six exposures, Christina arrived. I breathed more easily, Joan put on her undergarments, Christina took off her outer clothes, they both started to put on the lovely Leser clothes, and I began to take pictures.

Late in the afternoon I staggered out of the dressing room.

I had been a fool to let her terrorize me into taking the nudes, and—bad news—I had exposed them on color film; I had been too nervous to notice that I had color film in the camera in anticipation of the colorful frocks I expected her to pirouette in. I realized there was no one I could trust to process the film; the risk was too great that it would be copied and exploited. Then what? I would have to process it myself, and I had never processed a roll of color film. I raced to the nearest camera shop and bought a manual on basic color development and the necessary chemicals, and asked for a short course from the clerk who served me.

I hurried home, mixed up the chemicals, and dressed for the evening's revels. In our party at *The Diary of Anne Frank* were the Crawford ladies; Joan's husband, Al Steele, chairman of the board of Pepsi-Cola; two young actors whose names escape me; and a man built like a Quonset hut who was Steele's chauffeur and drinking buddy. It was his job to find out where the best bar nearest the theatre was located, and to set up the drinks so that at intermission, Mr. Steele and his guests could get straight to their tipples.

Of course, Joan made a last-minute entrance for the first act, but by the beginning of the second act she was fortified by her favorite 140-proof vodka (a good choice—vodka has no odor). Just before the curtain was raised she made her slow dramatic entrance down the aisle, then paused, turned, and stood at her seat blowing kisses at the audience. The curtain had to be held for ten minutes while she took her bows. I should have photographed this spectacle, but the play was so serious and disturbing that it would have been sacrilege to have raised the camera at that moment. At dinner at Sardi's later, Joan said she had done it just for me and she hoped I appreciated it. I gulped and said nothing.

The entrance into Sardi's was a triumphal procession. People craned their necks, applauded, asked for autographs. Joan seated us all, ordered our meals without asking us what we wanted, and then, without apparent cause, started to berate Christina, accusing her of behaving like a harlot. I made a few token shots, excused myself and rushed home to process the roll of color film. Intuition told me that when my subject sobered in the morning she might demand the roll of film. Hallelujah, the chemicals brought forth images—not great technically or photographically, but still passable; a weapon with which to placate my adversary.

Next morning, early, I called the Columbia Pictures publicist whose job it was to deal with Joan and the story we were involved in. I told her that Miss Crawford might call her to say that during the dress session I might have taken some questionable pictures. Well, they were now processed by me, no one else had seen them— and they were ready for her. All she needed to do was ask and they were hers.

Berenice, the publicist, was mystified but said okay when I told her it would be breaking trust to tell her more. Fifteen minutes later she was back on the phone. Yes, Miss Crawford had phoned— how had I known she would call? Laughter from my end.

The saga continued for the rest of the week, and Joan did not ask for the questionable transparencies that were ready in my camera bag. The

Joan Crawford
undergoing a beauty treatment,
New York, 1959

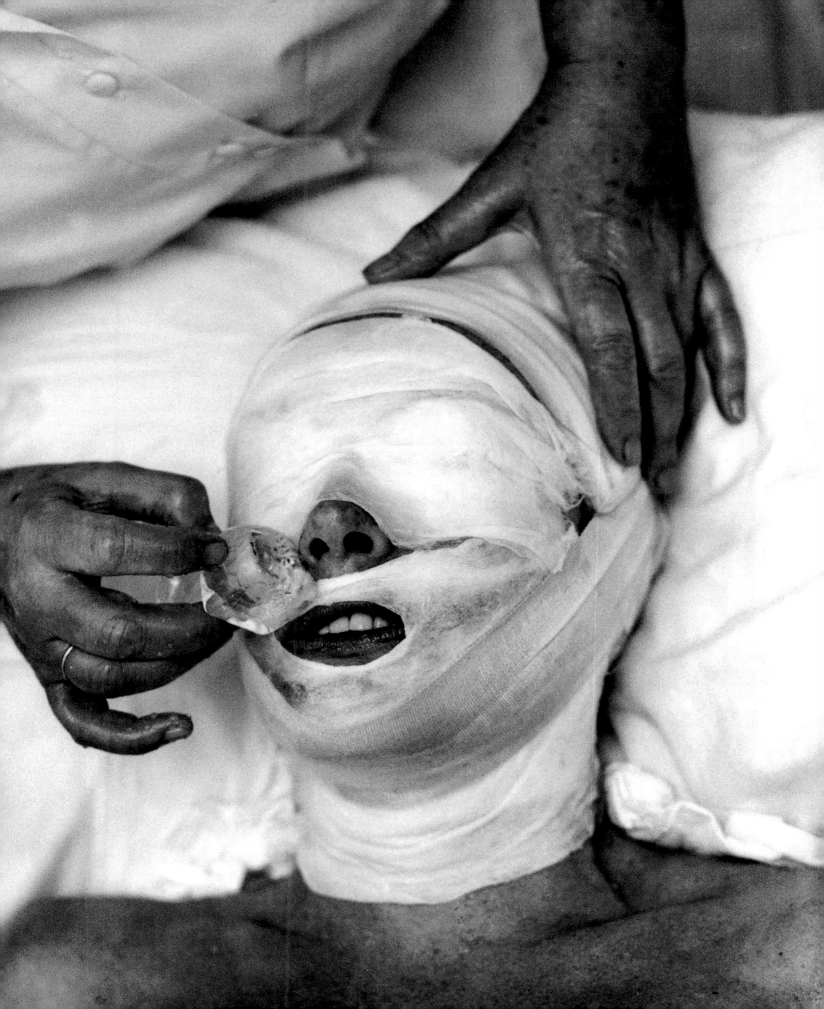

day after the photography was finished, she phoned me herself. Command performance: lunch at "21." This time I made the late entrance. She was waiting for me, hand outstretched—I put the little yellow box of transparencies into it. She held up the transparencies one by one to the light. She sighed, leaned across the table, kissed me, raised her vodka glass and said, "Love and eternal trust—always."

I had reason to remind her of this toast five years later when at my suggestion *Life* magazine assigned me a photo-essay on her. She was working on a film called *The Best of Everything*, she was recently widowed, she had four adopted children, she was still echt-Hollywood, and she was on the board of Pepsi-Cola, a mix that should yield interesting pictures.

I called her at Pepsi-Cola in New York, and within half an hour she was back on the phone to me from California. Yes, she would love to be in *Life*; yes, she would love to be photographed by me; but there was one small favor—she would like to go into the darkroom with me the way Marilyn Monroe had with Richard Avedon. Translated, this meant that she wanted editorial control, and this I felt neither the magazine nor I should permit. I said I would ask the magazine and that we would get back to her.

At eight o'clock next morning, Ed Thompson, a harassed managing editor of *Life*, phoned. During the night his employer, Henry Luce, the publisher of *Life*, had had a wild call from Miss Crawford complaining that that Arnold woman was trying to withhold her (Crawford's) editorial right to say which pictures were to be used. The editor thought we should agree to her terms so Mr. Luce could get his sleep. I suggested we drop the story, then played a hunch that we wait until twelve o'clock New York time on the chance that in the sober light of day she might back down. At

eight o'clock her time, she called me. I reminded her that she had trusted me once before; perhaps she should again. "Yes," came her dulcet tones, "I agree," and still in that sweet voice, "but if I don't like what you do," and here Mrs. Steele's steely voice came through, "you'll *never* work in Hollywood again."

It was not the best way to start an assignment, but when I arrived in Hollywood she was welcoming. We discussed the story line—she wanted to show how dedicated she was to hang on to the top of the cliff of success for thirty years. We started with nothing off-limits and wound up after eight weeks the same way. In fact, so inventive was Joan (she would simply dream up situations and go ahead waiting for the camera to follow after) that we could have filled an encyclopedia instead of the twelve pages at our disposal.

The research about her was revealing. Joan had adopted her four children during the Hollywood days when it was easy to do so. She was between husbands, and the little blond heads beside her own in the current *Screen Gems* or other movie magazines made perfect copy for her. She is said to have stopped the show when she attended the wedding of a former lover with all four of them being ushered into the church with her.

My notes about her early history were interesting too. She grew up as a prostitute in her mother's establishment; she started her film career doing pornographic films. She spent the next ten years of her professional life as an actress trying to buy back the ever-proliferating blue movies, but they eluded her. Where there was a positive someone would make a negative and from that negative a positive—all in a never-ending chain. In Germany someone said they are still on sale, but I have never seen one. In California, a director said he was present when she and a brand-new husband had a dinner party. For entertainment the groom had ordered some blue films, and one of them turned out to star his bride. True or not I do not know. But she was the stuff legends are built around.

She was the last of the queen bees. She would arrive at the Twentieth Century–Fox studio lot in her limousine. Her chauffeur would follow her in carrying a large thermos box marked "Pepsi-Cola" (in which, packed in ice, was her 140-proof vodka) and a smaller elegant black alligator case in which were her jewels. She insisted upon wearing real gems in the film, the idea being that their authenticity gave her a greater sense of authority (about authority: she kept repeating that she had "balls"). Her precious gems were in matched sets like costume jewelry: necklace, two clips, a pair of earrings, two bracelets and a ring of black pearls, emeralds, topazes, rubies, aquamarines, diamonds, or whatever precious gems. As clasps on a pair of diamond bracelets there were priceless baguette diamonds—one from the engagement ring given her by Douglas Fairbanks, Jr., and the other given her by Franchot Tone.

It was remarkable to see her on the set made up and ready for a scene, surrounded by her retinue of hairdresser, makeup artist, wardrobe mistress, secretary, chauffeur and stand-in. They would line up beside the Pepsi-Cola dispenser Joan kept outside her dressing room. She would stand nervously, clutching her fingers and repeating her lines to herself. For big emotional moments the director would arrange for her to literally run into a scene. She would take off twenty feet from the lighted set, run, hit her mark perfectly and start to emote for the camera.

Every other day or so her twelve-year-old twins, Kathy and Cindy, would be brought to the set all dressed up—ruffled, beribboned and awkward. They would sit, legs crossed at the ankles, in the shadows, drinking Pepsi-Cola and waiting for Mommie to summon them. When she did, all that could be heard from them was a litany of "Yes Mommie, yes Mommie."

Weekends we would spend at her house in Bel-Air photographing. Those would be her days for having her nails done, her hair colored, her legs waxed, her eyebrows dyed; all of which she wanted me to record on film, to show her devotion to her public.

In the mornings she would come down the stairs slowly, pause midway at the niche in the stairwell where the spotlighted Oscar she had won for *Mildred Pierce* was housed, genuflect and continue to the bottom. Only then could the day's work begin.

The more I saw of her, the more complex she seemed and the more perplexed I became. Hollywood is a parochial town where everyone knows everyone else's business. When word got around that I was doing a *Life* story on her, people got in touch with me to tell me Joan Crawford stories—everybody from clapper boys to executives. Mainly they were stories that had to do with the children and her cruelty to them.

After six weeks the picture was finished and we returned to New York, where Joan wanted to be shown at work for Pepsi-Cola. (She had been made a member of the board after her husband's death.) She was hostess at a party in her triplex on Fifth Avenue for two members of the West Nigerian trade delegation who had contracted for ten Pepsi-Cola plants.

Normally guests in her house were asked to leave their shoes at the door and walk around on her white carpet in their stocking feet. Her cleanliness fetish also dictated that all her white upholstered furniture be covered in clear plastic, which looked like giant condoms. For the party she relented: the covers were removed from the furniture, the guests could keep their shoes on, but the waiters—who came from "21," the

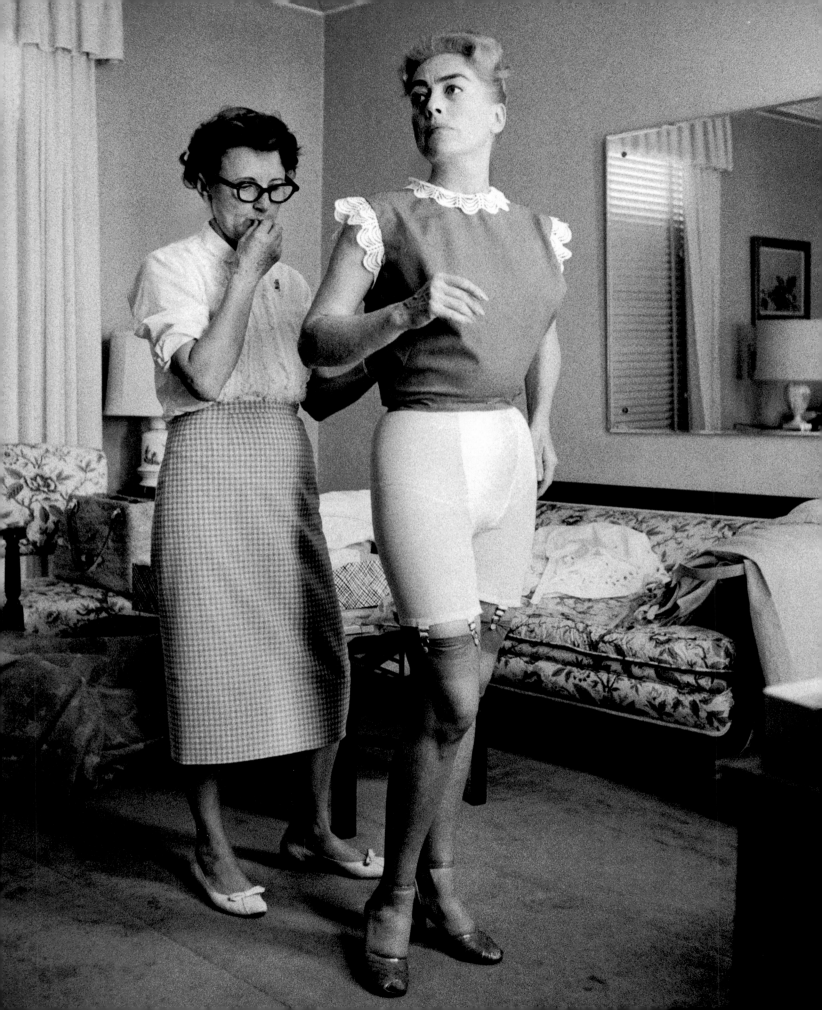

restaurant which catered the party—had to cover their shoes with the kind of socks provided by airlines for first class travel.

Midway through the evening, when the party was beginning to sag, Joan suddenly spilled something down her dress. People gathered round; napkins were produced to clean up the mess. Joan made her way up the dramatic staircase in the middle of the triplex, followed by me. She changed into the garment she had prepared for this emergency. When she made her entrance the party seemed to have a new lift.

Joan had invited me to spend the night, because the party ended quite late. When I woke at nine the next morning I was locked in my bedroom. She heard me calling and banging, and came and unlocked the door, protesting that she had no idea how it had happened. I could never decide whether she thought I was going to steal something!

That day while we were at breakfast, a lovely small Picasso drawing of the Cubist period was delivered as a thank-you gift from one of the guests who had been at the party the evening before. The picture puzzled and bothered Joan. She told me that when she had gone to Paris with Al Steele she had brought back French paintings—she pointed to them on the wall. She had found an artist who for twenty-five dollars would copy "that guy Utrillo," and she, Joan, had improved on Utrillo. She had her man straighten up the streets. She looked at me for a moment seriously and said she didn't understand "modern art"; could I explain it to her?

I thought for a beat trying to figure out a way that would be right for her. Then I said that if you think of modern art like sex in all its forms—heterosexual, bisexual, homosexual, multipartnered, bestial, whatever, with absolutely no holds barred and with everything available and permissible—that would be "modern art." I felt rotten after I'd said it: it was a cheap shot. But she was delighted with the analogy. She laughed and said that at last she understood what "modern art" was about.

Joan was fond of telling about her days—her heydays—when she was at Warners. She talked about Bette Davis at Warners but would end up by saying that she, Joan, had been the "baby of the lot," implying that Miss Davis was much older. Actually, Joan saw Miss Davis as her formidable rival. When the *Life* story appeared, she cabled me and again said, "Love and eternal trust always." It was a tough intimate story, but she had wanted it that way. When next I heard from her it was perhaps a year later and she wanted me to come and work on her next film, *What Ever Happened to Baby Jane?* She said she would be starring with Miss Davis and that I should be able to do some wonderful things. They hadn't been together since Joan had been "the baby" on the Warners lot. I had to decline. I was living in England, my son was in school there, and I didn't want to leave him. About three months later, Joan called in the middle of the night. She was ecstatic. The film was finished. She said, "You would have been so proud of me. I was a lady, not like that cunt Bette Davis."

Joan Crawford,
dress fitting,
Hollywood, 1959

Marilyn Monroe, another Hollywood legend whom I photographed over a period of ten years, runs like a thread through my work of the fifties in America. We met when we were young women, each just beginning her career. She was a starlet, I a neophyte photographer. Neither of us knew very much about her chosen métier, but this formed a bond between us.

It was at a party at "21" given for John Huston that we met. When we were introduced by another photographer, Sam Shaw, who had shown her my published Marlene Dietrich story, she said, "If you could do that well with Marlene, can you imagine what you can do with me?"

My decade of documentation of Miss Monroe has been published as a book, *Marilyn Monroe: An Appreciation*, so there is no reason to repeat it here. There are, however, two small anecdotes that tie two legends, Crawford and Monroe, together.

The mad day in 1956 when I photographed Crawford in the nude, she talked venomously about Monroe, whom she had just seen at the Actors' Studio. "She didn't wear a girdle—her ass was hanging out. She is a disgrace to the industry."

Some weeks later when I ran into Marilyn, she told me that she had seen Miss Crawford at the Actors' Studio. She was breathless with awe, stagestruck at meeting the movie star whom she had aspired to emulate when she was a child.

Speaking of posing in the nude, later that year I saw Marilyn in action. Like Crawford she loved it. She was more original and also more provocative about it. She had been suspended from Twentieth Century–Fox, the studio to which she was contracted, and was in New York at loose ends: going to the Actors' Studio, seeing friends, keeping her publicity going. One day I was invited to come talk to her about an idea she had for a picture story. The meeting place was the Waldorf, where she was living.

She met me at the door in a diaphanous black negligee. She had a hairbrush in her hand. Would I mind sitting through an interview for a European magazine—then we could talk? Almost immediately the reporter showed up. Marilyn greeted her, and while the woman had her head down, looking in her purse for notebook and pencil, Marilyn asked if she minded if she (Marilyn) brushed her hair during the interview. No, of course not. When the woman raised her head, Marilyn was brushing her pubic hair.

What was particularly interesting to me about Marilyn was that each time I photographed her she was different—not only a variation from session to session, but a variation from frame to

Marilyn Monroe,
airport ladies' room,
Chicago, 1955

Marilyn Monroe
in the bulrushes,
Mount Sinai, Long Island, 1954

frame. She would look different in mood and attitude. This one could expect, because she was an actress, but it was the shadings of mood and attitude that she called forth that were impressive.

There were six sessions when we worked together. They ranged from the press conference that lasted two hours to the period of two months when she had the lead role in *The Misfits*. Whether it was the pressure of the short click-click of the public session or the prolonged, more personal daily session during the making of the film, the surprising thing was how she managed to keep herself fresh throughout.

So over the ten-year stretch during which I photographed her, the infinite changes she could wring from situation to situation never failed to surprise me. We went from personal snaps in the ladies' room of the Chicago airport, through intimate reportage, through formal color studio shots for covers.

These changes are only possible if the photographer has forged a relationship which permits an atmosphere in which the subject feels relaxed and safe, an intimacy that allows the person being photographed to be uninhibited and to reveal hitherto unknown aspects of herself.

My most poignant memory of Marilyn is of how distressed, troubled and still radiant she looked when I arrived in Nevada to work on *The Misfits*. She asked immediately how she looked, and she wanted and needed reassurance.

It was four years since we had worked together, and she looked into my eyes for a long moment to make sure she could still trust me. Then she drew in her breath, sighed and said, "I'm thirty-four years old. I've been dancing for six months [on *Let's Make Love*]. I've had no rest, I'm exhausted. Where do I go from here?" She was not asking me—she was asking herself.

This was less than a year before she died. It occurred to me then that when she had lived with the fantasy of Marilyn that she had created, that fantasy had sustained her, but now the reality had caught up with her and she found it too much to bear.

Photographing movie stars was child's play compared to the problems to be hurdled when *Life* magazine assigned a political story on Malcolm X, the emerging leader of the Black Muslims.

Before asking the magazine to commit itself, there was a major research job to be done. The Muslims were a virtually impregnable wall to broach. Through sources I no longer remember I contacted a man called Louis Lomax who was a journalist with access to Malcolm X. We agreed to lunch to discuss the possibility of my hiring him to set things up for me.

We were to meet at Del Pezzo's, an Italian restaurant, now defunct, on 47th Street. When I had waited for him for two hours and the restaurant was about to close for the afternoon, he breezed in. I tried to contain my displeasure and ordered him a drink, and before I could say anything about the Black Muslims he said, "You don't want to do a story, you just want to sleep with a black man, don't you?"

I was enraged, let rip a few nasty sentences, and started to walk out. He caught up with me, apologized, said he was just testing, and led me back to our drinks. We agreed that for a sum he would be the fixer for the story. We then went down the street to the Magnum office to get him a check to seal the bargain.

Lomax was invaluable during the years I worked on the story. He meticulously carried out everything he had promised, beginning with the introduction to Malcolm X. What he had not told me was that I was just one of his many clients. At every public meeting he raced about servicing both major television networks as well as several newspapers. He was a busy man indeed, leaving

Marilyn Monroe with Arthur Miller,
on location for *The Misfits*,
Nevada, 1960

me to wonder how he found time for the sexual exploits he bragged about.

The first contact with Malcolm X was at the Uline Arena in Washington, at a national convention of all chapters of the Black Muslims. People had come by the busload from all over America. The males (even boys) were in black suits, white shirts and black ties, their boots highly polished. The females (even the youngest) wore white dresses, and their heads were modestly covered in white scarves. There was an honor guard for the Prophet, Elijah Muhammad, the messenger of Allah, as well as an elite young military guard called the Fruit of Islam who carried no guns but had been taught to kill with their hands.

We were frisked for weapons—I by the women. The meeting hall was festooned with banners that bore the legends "We Must Protect Our Women" and "There Is No God But Allah." The arena was packed—estimates ran between five and six thousand. Who were these immaculate people? What were their teachings? their beliefs? They were taught that the black race is the superior race, that all black men are brothers, that allegiance must be to the flag of Islam, that the white man is the devil and must be overthrown, that unless America changed its wicked ways it would burn for 360 years. They were enjoined to bathe daily and were forbidden to smoke, drink alcohol, take narcotics or eat pork. They demanded separation or death, calling upon the U.S. government to give them the states of the Eastern Seaboard so that they could establish their own autonomy.

The seating plan segregated the men and women—the women upstairs, the men downstairs. In the front row facing the podium sat George Lincoln Rockwell, the head of the American Nazi Party, with his henchmen. They were in military khakis and sported swastika armbands. The reason for this unholy alliance was that the Nazis and the Muslims had a common goal—to divide America between them. The Muslims would get the entire Eastern Seaboard, the Nazis the rest.

When I raised the camera to photograph Rockwell and his men, he hissed at me, "I'll make a bar of soap out of you." I hissed back, "As long as it isn't a lampshade," and kept on photographing.

Over the next year (1960) I followed Malcolm from Washington to New York and Chicago and then back to New York. He was cooperative and considerate. As we worked together, the passionate orator who could whip a crowd to euphoria, who could convince a University of Chicago student audience with sheer sophistry that the white man was the villain who had introduced the slave trade in Africa and that the Arab was blameless, began to unbend and to think of situations for me to photograph.

First he asked me to dinner at a restaurant in Harlem owned by the Black Muslims. The place was spotless (the Muslims were always saying the whites didn't bathe and smelled bad). Malcolm was charming, made small talk to put me at ease, and said some gracious words about my work. The food was delicious. I was served a dish that in my ignorance I referred to as a "sweet potato pie." The waiter froze. When I asked what I had done, Malcolm told me that their religion forbade them to eat the food they had eaten in slavery.

"Then what," I asked, "is in the pie?"

"It's made with beans—*white* beans."

The "white" was underscored with such venom that I wondered if it was meant to make me feel like a cannibal. But his eyes glinted behind his spectacles, and he laughed. From that time on he would tease me and make jokes.

That night Malcolm took me to a rally on 125th Street. As I walked about the crowd taking photographs, there were cries of "White bitch!"

and "Kill the white bitch!" and I was spat upon. It was a mild spring night and I wore a light wool dress and a light wool sweater. Luckily for me my clothes were wool: wool doesn't burn, it smolders. Later when I took off my sweater to remove the film from its zippered pockets, I saw that the entire back was polka-dotted with cigarette burns. As I had moved about the crowd, they had stuck burning cigarettes into the sweater. I must have been moving too fast for them to get to the flesh.

When I went to Chicago it was to see the way the Muslims dealt with whitey through their economic boycott. They set up clothing factories, bakeries, grocery shops, restaurants and other small businesses that were owned and operated by their members to service their own people. The Chicago community was thriving, so Malcolm thought it should be photographed as part of my article.

For the two weeks I worked in Chicago, at eight o'clock each morning I received a telephone call. Someone with a Southern accent said, "Get the hell out of town before it's too late," and hung up. Half an hour later Malcolm would call, polite but brisk, and give me an address in the black ghetto where I was to meet him. He called each morning with instructions, but so did the person with the same message to get the hell out of town before it was too late. I don't know why I wasn't frightened, but I wasn't, and although it did occur to me to tell the *Life* bureau in Chicago, I didn't—because I was afraid *Life* would take me off the story.

I felt that Malcolm wouldn't let anything happen to me. He continued to be friendly, and surprised me by bringing ten Muslim women in their white habits to be photographed. He was a really clever showman and apparently knowledgeable about how he could use pictures and the press to tell his story. He set up the shots while I clicked the camera. It was hilarious. I tried several times to get him in the act of framing a photo with his hands, but he was too quick for me. With the photos of himself, he was professional and imaginative. He obviously had an idea of how he wanted the public to see him and he maneuvered me into showing him that way. I am always delighted by the manipulation that goes on between subject and photographer when the subject knows about the camera and how it can best be used to his advantage. Malcolm was brilliant at this silent collaboration. He knew his needs, his wants, his best points and how to get me to give him what he required.

I was amused recently at an International Center of Photography group show of pictures of Malcolm. The lead picture was one of mine: a huge smiling profile of him looking smart; hat, gold watch and Masonic ring worn jauntily. A group of young black photographers came over to talk to me. "Thank you," they said, "for making him look like a dude."

"It was a collaboration," I said.

In addition to making sure that I got the pictures necessary for a large photo-essay, Malcolm arranged interviews for my text.

I talked to one indoctrinated Muslim who was a cook in a Detroit hotel before he became a captain in the elite guard, the Fruit of Islam, the group taught to kill with their hands. He said, "I want my gold shoes now. I want my white robes now. I want my milk and honey right now. I have sung too many songs in the Baptist Church and had too much water poured over me. I want now what the white man has."

Sitting opposite this man and looking at those fanatic eyes and seeing the purpose that this movement had given him, I understood. He looked like any other cook, but cleaner: neatly pressed grey flannel suit, neat black tie, polished shoes. But there was a difference: he had a dignity he had never had before. True, he had been

overleaf: Malcolm X
collecting money for the Black Muslims,
Washington, D.C., 1960

Though *Life* returned the Black Muslim essay unpublished, it was to have a long editorial life. *Esquire* printed it large and impressively, it was syndicated worldwide, and it acted as a launch pad for me in 1961 when I began work with the London *Sunday Times*, which had just started its *Colour Magazine*.

I was to be under contract to the Times for ten years for a given number of assignments, my time spent not to exceed six months per year in England and abroad. Mainly I worked on my own ideas, handling everything from initial research through finished prints. There were also captions and text to do—often used as commentary if I worked without a writer.

The *Sunday Times* under Harold Evans as overall editor, with Mark Boxer as editor of the *Colour Magazine* and Michael Rand as its art director, created a high in picture journalism in the sixties which maintained itself until the end of the seventies.

So strong was the style set that when Mark left to edit a new magazine called *London Life* and Godfrey Smith came in as editor, he was able to strengthen and build upon it. James Fox, writing recently about Francis Wyndham (who, for lack of a better description, acted as idea man and catalyst to the staff), said, "At that time everyone— writers, and photographers—seemed to want to write for the Magazine, then under the editorship of Godfrey Smith. It was both a serious and a very glamorous publication, soon to be the apogee of photo-journalism, its style was a vital part of the machinery of the Sixties—all hard to imagine now. The newspaper itself was perhaps the best in the world, well financed, brimming with talent and zeal," and "the photographers, the galaxy of glamour: Snowdon, Bailey, McCullin, Duffy, Donovan, Eve Arnold . . ."

Color photography was a come-on for advertisers in the prosperous sixties in Britain. It could easily have become a gimmick, but the editors were careful not to use (or abuse) color for its own sake. Instead, we photographers were encouraged to develop our own styles, to explore, to experiment, to come up with departures from the basic color look offered by the film manufacturers. This proved to be a clever approach, because it gave greater visual diversity to a magazine in which the editorial matter was used to keep the advertisements apart.

I did not usually go for the blatant color element in a scene (unless there was a reason to), but tended to use color as accent or as part of the design. Very often, muted color would be more effective than blazing tones—depending upon the subject, of course. I began to expose color for form, to try to get the subtle tints the eye sees.

Often I worked on the very edges of the film, taking chances, pushing my luck, daring the emulsion to bring forth optically what I wasn't sure would reproduce on the flat page. Then Michael Rand would send me Stanley Daw, his production man, who could (sometimes) bring forth miracles.

One such episode happened in 1963 for an assignment on music in Britain, which included everything from opera to jazz, from classical music to the Moog, from the busker to the concert performer—but what to put on the cover? What was needed was a generic symbol that said MUSIC, that complemented what was on the inside pages of the magazine, but was not too literal or specific.

I came up with a girl violinist tuning her instrument while sounding her A on the piano keyboard. I wanted a silhouette of the girl—more a shadow—but with the instrument distinct. The picture was almost smoky monochrome black/brown except for the hand and the ivory keyboard. There was no detail in the shadows and a borderline question as to whether it would reproduce. But Stanley managed, and we got a unique cover.

When the *Colour Magazine* started, it used black-and-white photography as well to accommodate advertisers who had yet to be wooed to color or who had less to spend. If we were lucky, Michael Rand would wangle a color page on which to print our black-and-white pictures. Printing them four-color instead of just black gave the pictures greater punch and quality. Michael and his associates expended a great deal of thought and ingenuity to try to get the best possible results from the porous newsprint used.

Because I loved variety and because, perversely, I liked to set myself the most difficult obstacle course possible, I would photograph black-and-white and color in the same situations one right after the other—a very difficult thing to do, demanding total concentration. The photographer has to be endlessly visualizing the image in either form, being careful not to think in color while working in black-and-white—or the other way round. It can make for a schizoid experience. I find in my 1960s archive picture after picture for which I did matching monochrome and color. I persisted in this until the beginning of the seventies, when the black-and-white market seemed to disappear, only to surface on the walls of picture galleries. For the next decade it was almost essential to photograph in color to survive as an editorial photographer.

Although it was difficult to try to juggle color and black-and-white, it was fascinating to compare them. Monochrome is an abstraction; color comes closer to reality. I had graphic proof of this when John Hillelson, the Magnum London agent, asked me to follow my black-and-white picture essay "The First Five Minutes of a Baby's Life" with a color essay on the same subject. On the original I had done only black-and-white and had worked tirelessly in that medium for four months to try to achieve the definitive five minutes. I returned to the Mather Hospital on Long Island to try to duplicate my essay in color. On the first exposure I slipped to the floor in a faint at the first sign of blood. I had been able to sustain four prolonged months of photography because I was working in black-and-white, which was an abstraction to me, but when I approached the same subject in color it became real and thus not bearable.

The early 1960s were frantic years for me, torn between my need to stay close to my son, Francis (who came to Britain when he was thirteen to enroll at Bedales, the boarding school where his father had matriculated), and my need to keep working. My marriage had ended soon after we came to England, and it was essential for us to be

Music student
sounding her A,
London, 1963

71

in constant touch with our son. I was in England as often as possible, and my ex-husband, who had returned to America, spent every available holiday as well as summer vacations with Francis. We also kept a lively correspondence going with him.

The family as well as the national uprooting required difficult adjustments. We arrived in England in a very wet autumn which was followed by the coldest winter in a hundred years; the long tits and the bearded tits were dying in great numbers, so that food was being dropped for the birds by helicopter. We were not used to the gloom, during which house lights were turned on upon waking and not extinguished until bedtime. There was little or no heat, and what there was usually came from a single electric bar that was turned on by putting coins into a meter. We were accustomed to overheated rooms and changing seasons that brightened the year: brilliant foliage in the fall, snow and clear skies in the winter. The endless grey and chill days of England seemed like a punishment and added to our sadness at the sudden changes in our lives.

During this time I researched a story on families who immigrated from Africa to England. The parents told me that their children's first questions in their new environment were:

Who turned off the sun?
Who faded the colors?
Who darkened the days?
Who stopped the smiles?

I understood their misery and was concerned for my own child. I couldn't turn on the sun for Francis, brighten the colors, lighten the days, or bring back the smiles, but I could at least be on the other end of a telephone for him every day. We agreed that I would try to make sure that he had a number where he could reach me at five o'clock every afternoon if he so chose, and that if I was travelling or otherwise engaged I would call him. I don't know whether this helped him, but it eased my mind to know that if he was troubled he could talk to me no matter the distances that separated us. It wasn't always easy if I was on the road; often I was in places that had no telephone or, if they did, calls had to be booked in advance. And there was the additional problem of different time zones. I remember a particularly difficult connection when I tried to reach him from Russia the day before his O-level examinations (the equivalent of American junior high school finals). I was in Sukhumi on the Black Sea. It was a Sunday, and it seemed that the whole Russian populace was trying to reach the outside world. I spent the entire day waiting in line, but it was worth it to hear his voice.

In England there was a series to do on public schools for girls and a series on people who advertised in the personals columns of the *Times* (which the Brits call the agony column).

Although it was wearing to go back and forth between Britain and America, it was both informative and amusing to be able to compare the two. Part of the personals column story showed three girls in search of a fourth to share a flat. All the girls, aged twenty, were in advertising; their boyfriends—public school and university graduates—were in either advertising or public relations. It was strange to see these young, long-haired British kids from well-to-do families training at ten quid a week to be account executives. They resented the Madison Avenue jargon, but felt that Britain was bankrupt and that their only chance was to go with advertising or its sister field, public relations. They had tested high in their interviews, IQ tests, psychology tests, examinations, medicals, personality tests, etc., and it was amusing to hear them talk about their experiences in their Oxford and Cambridge ac-

One of four girls who share an apartment,
London, 1963

72

Fencing mistress,
Wycombe Abbey,
High Wycombe, England, 1963

cents. Slowly I began to adjust to the endless mist and rain, the tepid tea, hot-water bottles and British food. And I fell in love with the British, their eccentricity and their individuality.

In 1961 I photographed the following in the United States: Adlai Stevenson at the UN, a continuation of the Black Muslims story, Danny Kaye at Tanglewood, a cancer story, and a recording session with Stravinsky.

Despite all the activity in my professional life I was having a tough time financially. The amount of money it took Magnum to stay afloat was exorbitant. We had upped the percentage for handling a new story from twenty-five to forty percent and to fifty percent for archive sales. It was a large drain on my meagre resources. I owed Magnum a thousand dollars (about four hundred pounds by the 1960 rate of exchange). This sum seems piddling by today's standards, but if you realize that I was paying my assistant three pounds three shillings a day, car included (I paid for fuel and lunch), then you can realize how worrying the burden of debt was for me.

I had to find another source of income to try to reach solvency.

Two windfalls bailed me out. I started getting work to do "specials" stills for films—and Wayne Miller, who was then president of Magnum, generously advanced the money to cover my debt. It took me five years to repay it. I have never forgotten his kindness.

Although I had done stills on only two films, *The Misfits* and *The Best of Everything*, they were big films with big names, and my picture stories on both had garnered an enormous amount of magazine and newspaper space. The first might not have done so except for the fact that Clark Gable died almost immediately after *The Misfits* was finished, and these not only were the last pictures taken of him, but showed him at home, something he seldom allowed. The other bene-

fitted from my irreverent intimate *Life* story on Joan Crawford. The track record for the column inches commanded in the press for these two essays both in America and abroad (thanks to Magnum's distribution system) made me a viable candidate for hire for assignments on other films. Britain was booming in the sixties as a film capital. It was a natural for locations for American film productions: ready-made film crews, processing facilities, skillful supporting actors, good financial terms, and even though the natives spoke "funny English" it was not too hard to understand.

For a quarter of a century, from 1959 to 1984, I documented the making of feature films, sometimes assigned by a motion picture company, sometimes by a magazine and sometimes by both. Because the photographer becomes part of the film unit for an extended time and is expected to be accepted as such by cast and crew, it is easier to come to understand them and thus be able to portray them both more intimately and more realistically than is possible in the usual limited time accorded for a photo session. The atmosphere is more relaxed, and since the photographer is on hand for weeks and sometimes months she does not have to run in shooting. Also the locations are usually more interesting and exotic than a photographic studio. Over the years, I made stills on motion pictures in Morocco, England, Ireland, Italy, Sicily, Spain, Majorca, Austria, Tunisia, Mexico, Finland, Portugal and America.

The concern, beyond worrying about the merits of the photograph itself, is how it will ultimately be used. In the case of movie stills, which are used to promote and sell the movie involved, care must be taken by the photographer not to wind up a "flack" but to try to be as straight and as factual as possible within the reality that we live in a commercial world. In the beginning I felt uneasy about my pictures publicizing and promoting the films I was working on, but as I became more adroit at dealing with the situation I began to accept the fact that this was the real world. I started to enjoy the film work both on the sound stage and on location, even though I had to acknowledge that I was in demand for major films not only because I was giving value for money but because I was under contract to the *Sunday Times Colour Magazine* and could usually command space. Also, I had Magnum's distribution worldwide, and, as a further plus, because I lived in Europe, travelling expenses for me were minimal.

I was in the unique position of being able to pick the films on which to make photo reports, for instance Richard Burton in both *Becket* and *Anne of the Thousand Days*; John Huston, acting in and directing *The Bible*; and Paul Scofield and Orson Welles in *A Man for All Seasons*.

At one point I was even written into a star's contract: Terry Stamp's in *Modesty Blaise*. All that is changed now. During my time, only major stars like Marilyn Monroe or Clark Gable would have the right of veto on the stills made of them, simply putting an X with a grease pencil on a contact sheet to indicate a "kill," leaving it to the integrity of the photographer not to violate that trust. Now it is said that Madonna and other stars demand the right to destroy negatives and transparencies they do not want used and insist upon a large portion of the earnings from pictures of them in perpetuity.

The first film I worked on in Europe was of Princess Grace showing the palace in Monaco the way Jackie Kennedy had shown the White House. It was a TV special, but shot by a professional Hollywood motion picture crew. They were disdainful of television and kept muttering that this was a "cheapie"; they said that more money was spent on wardrobe in an equivalent California film than was being spent on this en-

tire opus. It didn't help that in the month we worked in the palace, we were never offered a cup of coffee.

Even though we were living in the deluxe Hôtel de Paris and going to the casino nightly, we were homesick and anxious to leave. The municipality had the sad abandoned feel of all watering places off-season (it was November). Not even the gambling forays helped. We had expected the Monte Carlo Casino to be glamorous and full of mystery. Instead, it was filled with "little old ladies on fixed incomes" who came nightly for a bit of excitement. Rumor had it that off-season the casino paid these people to fill up the place to make it look lively, and that during high season the casino paid these same "regulars" to stay away.

It is not surprising that, given these downbeat memories, the most vivid image that surfaces is of Grace Kelly, impeccably dressed by Givenchy, posing on the grand staircase of the palace with Prince Rainier. He is dressed in a dark blue flannel blazer. In a possessive wifely gesture she begins to pick away bits of lint from his lapel. This domestic scene is too much for him, and just as the cameras begin to roll, he mouths, "Leave me alone," and the clapper loader has to mark the scene all over again.

The atmosphere during the making of a motion picture would vary from film to film depending upon the person in charge of the finances, the magnitude of the stars, their personalities, and, for the photographer, the degree of acceptance accorded her by director and cast. This, of course, depended upon tact and whatever relationship could be established on location. It seemed that the handling of the camera was the least of it. Patience and diplomacy were of the essence.

Becket, the film version of Jean Anouilh's play, began with the usual honeymoon that most films enjoy, went on to difficult days and ended with a party. There was more than the usual tension during filming, because the producer, Hal Wallis, was there watching both the budget and his director, Peter Glenville. Usually the producer is not in evidence and the director is in total charge, but in this case a great deal of consultation with the producer went on.

The film starred Richard Burton as Thomas Becket, Archbishop of Canterbury, and Peter O'Toole as King Henry II of England, who has him murdered. It begins with Henry talking to Becket's effigy and then flashes back and forth, with Henry remembering the gay times the two men shared before they became mortal enemies, when they wenched and hawked, played and drank together.

The two actors took their roles seriously and kept in character, at least as far as the drink was concerned. They took to returning tipsy from lunch, where they, along with supporting Shakespearean actors, would be reciting from various plays they had graced. Each tried to outperform the other. Their merry mood kept Hal Wallis' color high and his anger barely suppressed. All this against the splendid "movie set" cathedral that cost more to build than did the original Canterbury.

By the time the murder scene was to be filmed, the levity had disappeared and the mood was heavy. Burton spent that lunch hour playing with Elizabeth Taylor's sons Michael and Christopher Wilding, showing them his costume. They played with his mailed gloves and his sword. Then Taylor and her daughter Liza Todd arrived to watch the brutal murder of the "meddlesome priest" by the barons. Out of camera range in the shadows with Liza snug in her arms, Miss Taylor watched, while facing her in the brilliant klieg lights lay the murdered Becket. To the side, hugging a column and looking solemn and bemused, were the Wilding boys. It had become a family affair for my camera.

Orson Welles,
deathbed rehearsal
for *A Man for All Seasons*,
England, 1966

78

Richard Burton and Elizabeth Taylor
during the filming of *Becket*,
Shepperton, England, 1963

The sixties were a testing ground for me, it seems, to see how many different kinds of assignments I could juggle and still keep up decent work standards, play around with both color and black-and-white, travel and enjoy different countries, earn a living, and, most important, remain in contact with my son. The energy level was high, the curiosity insatiable, and each new experience seemed to set off a chain reaction for still further experience. In retrospect, it sounds daunting, but at the time it was the natural way to go.

When I would return home from photographing, my life would settle into a three-tiered routine:

1. Editing and writing the current story.
2. Preparing the next assigned story.
3. Reading for and researching a third story.

Meanwhile there would be film to buy, cameras to clean, money in foreign currencies to secure, injections against various diseases to have, while my beloved assistants (Helen Craig, Lin Smith and Beeban Kidron) made last-minute phone calls, paid bills and sent off letters. Friends would drop in for last-minute hugs. The apartment would be festooned with clothing on hangers in plastic bags. On the morning before departure I would pack.

Then as I raced for the plane, the cameras strapped to my back, already homesick, the depression would hit. To allay it would come ironic memories of my friends telling me what a glamorous life I lived!

Although practically everything I did was assigned, most of it was based on my own ideas. The nature of the work itself leaves the decision to the photographer. The chameleonlike changes of light, expression, attitude, happen with the rapidity of clouds moving across the sky, making the endless choices impossible for an outsider to dictate. Even when the basic idea is fixed by the assigning editor, the execution has to remain at the discretion of the photographer. Only at what Cartier-Bresson calls the "decisive moment" is the picture determined. It is always a game of chance, fugitive and ephemeral. The terms used by photographers best express the medium's mutability: catch, grab, capture, seize.

Working on films gave me additional earnings that spelled at least temporary independence. They were needed to augment the *Sunday Times* rates, which were low, even considering the purchasing power of the sixties compared to now. I earned on a sixties *Sunday Times* four-month contract exactly the amount I earned recently for a single day's work for a Saatchi & Saatchi ad. Ironic, but I would not have missed a single mo-

Andy Warhol
lifting weights,
Silver Factory,
New York, 1964

Alec Douglas-Home, Prime
Minister of England, and his
wife, Lady Douglas-Home,
The Hersil, Scotland, 1964

ment of the *Colour Magazine* adventure, because it was exactly that free and open, giving staff and contributors a chance to bring our best efforts to it.

Michael Rand and I would meet and discuss my future work. He was extraordinary in his ability to convey almost wordlessly a sense of trust and confidence. Nineteen sixty-three could serve as an example of the way we worked together. The British material: Alec Douglas-Home, the prime minister; the Royal Societies; the Church of England; the *New Statesman*—all of them cover stories. Then there was one-time reproduction use of the American material I did that year: a cover story on fringe religions in California; a political story on Barry Goldwater, the Republican candidate for president (cover story); and another cover story on the Negro aristocracy.

The *Sunday Times* also had access to British use of my assignments done for other venues: the young Alan Bates (American *Vogue*); Robert Kennedy (independent project); Barbra Streisand (*Seventeen*); Kingman Brewster (cover for *Newsweek*); Andy Warhol (independent project).

Of all the assignments that year, the most amusing was Andy Warhol. I had met him in the mid-fifties when he was a shoe illustrator. Even then he had a penchant for self-promotion and suggested pictures I might take of him for various magazines. A decade later, when he set up his all-purpose salon-cum-film-studio at the Silver Factory, he invited me to come photograph it.

It was incredible: a low-ceilinged, single dark room over a hundred feet long whose ceiling, side walls, pipes and structural columns had been covered with Reynolds aluminum foil. The floor, cabinets, pay phone and toilet bowl were all painted silver, and Andy wore a silver wig. The whole thing photographed well in black-and-white with Andy sitting on an unconnected toilet in the center of the huge empty silver loft.

I also photographed him directing his first sound film. His early films were made on a hand-held Bolex camera. For *Harlot* (Harlow) he was using a full-fledged 35mm movie sound camera on tripod which trailed acres of cable. When I arrived, Andy was standing behind the camera on an upended orange crate ready to commence shooting. He looked puzzled.

"Eve, what do I do?" he asked.

"For openers, flip the switch," I said.

He did, and as the camera started to move the film sprockets, he began to direct the white cat and the white evening-frocked transvestite with the freshly shaven face who was playing Jean Harlow. As he filmed, two young poets kept either reading lines they had written or making random comments as soundtrack for the movie. At the end one of them asked, "Who's the old dame with the bare feet who's taking Andy's picture?"

"Oh, that's the broad from the London paper. Came all the way from England. Doesn't seem to know much. Doesn't even have a flash . . ."

The connection with the *Sunday Times* had the advantage of snob appeal to Anglophile Americans. It certainly worked with Barry Goldwater, the senior senator from Arizona, soon to become Republican presidential nominee. By sheer good fortune, I arrived at his Washington office the morning he had been made a member of the Royal Photographic Society.

He was a mad keen amateur photographer who worked in his home state of Arizona on an 11 x 14 plate-back camera anchored to the earth on a sturdy tripod. His subject was landscape. He had been trained by a pro, given a specific exposure for a specific time of day and a specific season to be exposed on specific film—none of which he ever varied, and which someone else processed.

He was amused to see me darting around his office with a miniature camera. We talked photography. I used the one shot I was concentrating on as the point of discussion and conveyed the idea that there was only one angle in that room from which to work—ergo, only one picture. I said it would be good to do more pictures. He then invited me to fly back with him to his home in Phoenix, so that I could continue my documentation. I explained that I had been asked to do a cover story. He seemed pleased and turned me over to one of his assistants to handle logistics. We were to fly in his own plane, piloted by his son.

When we entered the aircraft, Mr. Goldwater put on a pair of earphones, sat at a radio console and proceeded to contact radio hams. He would verify that he had reached a specific number, speak his own number and tick off the number on a sheet of paper. He tallied the calls, four vertical lines crossed with a fifth for each five calls.

There was never a personal word spoken, just the numbers out there in the ether. When he reached one hundred, his quota for the day, he stopped. He was an avid ham and prided himself on this daily diversion.

This was a significant time for him. His candidacy for the nomination was heating up. The convention was only a couple of weeks away—and his daughter was to be married the following weekend. The timing couldn't have been better. I was invited home, photographed him raising the American flag outside his ranch house, met his wife and daughters and was in the house taking pictures of the bridal party and helping to affix a flower to a recalcitrant buttonhole of the father of the bride, while outside the press, both "flat" and electronic, waited impatiently to grab whatever news shots they could.

I had followed him about locally to church breakfasts, American Legion lunches and Rotary Club dinners, so that by the time the last grain of rice was thrown at the couple taking off in their honeymoon chariot—a small plane—all that was needed to complete my picture essay was Goldwater's nomination. I had spent two weeks of intensive work, had so far a fairly intimate story, but without the payoff of his becoming the nominee it would all have been a footnote to just another story of just another man's attempt at elevation. I went to San Francisco to the convention to check it out. Here too my way was eased because I knew the possible candidate and his family.

Yes, he did make it and I got my story. It ran in color: a madwoman supporter with a large broom on one shoulder and a pair of crazy glasses, the right eye shaped as a large G and the left eye shaped as an O, making go. The bridge of the spectacles read GOLDWATER. Behind the O and aslant her nose and mouth was the stem of an American flag popping out of the left side of her head. I had delusions of Goldwater's making it to the White House and my having easy access to photograph in the Oval Office.

The mood of the country seemed right for a right-wing President, but Goldwater was badly advised by the think tank that planned his election campaign strategy. In an effort to give him some intellectual plumage, they put words into his convention acceptance speech which gave the Democratic Party a whip to beat him with. The words were "Extremism in the defense of liberty is no vice." The media picked it up, and editorials ranging from fear of right-wing repression to fear that Goldwater would want to "nuke" the Russians helped defeat him.

It would have been interesting to follow the candidate into the White House, to see this man who had silently reached into the airwaves and to whom his fellow radio operators were numbers on a sheet of paper become the most powerful man on the planet. How would he have handled himself and the world's problems? It would have been provocative to photograph power and its

Father Gregory Wilkins,
Kelham, Nottinghamshire,
England, 1963

camp followers, which are naturals to the camera.

The work in the early sixties was divided between the United States and Britain, with an occasional assignment in France. In 1965 I branched out and went to Italy to work on two films: John Huston's *The Bible* and Joe Losey's *Modesty Blaise*. I also photographed in the Soviet Union—the first of the stories on the Russians who were over a hundred years old.

The Bible was said to have been financed by an unholy trinity: Hollywood, Vatican money and the Mafia. True or false, it makes a good story. John Huston invited me to Rome, where he was filming the section on Noah's Ark. He suggested I come for a week to see the three hundred animals and one thousand birds who were learning to live together in the ark. He figured that he would have finished the interior shots with the animals by then and that they would be sufficiently accustomed to each other so he could lead them peaceably into the ark two by two. He himself was playing Noah. He had wanted to cast Charlie Chaplin or Alec Guinness, but Chaplin refused and Guinness was elsewhere committed. When Huston tried to think of the person of the proper stature and authority he saw his father, the late Walter Huston, in the role. He must then logically have seen himself. A most fastidious man, he started appearing in the ark unshaven. He started to act out scenes with the animals, and his beard got longer and longer.

There were hazards of birds overhead and elephant dung underfoot. Experienced journalists turned up with plastic hats, plastic macs and Wellingtons. When all the animals were in place and the lights blazing, the stench was overpowering. A man walked about with a huge atomizer from which he sprayed a deodorant that anesthetized one's nostrils, which was almost worse than the smell. The noise was overpowering, too: the roar of caged tigers, barnyard braying, bark-ing, jungle calls, wild screeching and singing birds. The humans added their babble of tongues: the German trainers' baby talk to their charges; the Italian actress who played Noah's wife learning her lines from a coach; Huston giving instructions in English to his first assistant, who repeated them in Italian to a Danish interpreter, who translated them into German for the actors playing Noah's sons.

When Huston, in sackcloth costume, greeted me, he was patting the dugs of an elephant, who loved the attention. "I had a nightmare," he said. "I dreamed I was directing *The Bible* and I woke up screaming." He had reason to scream a few days later when he came down with an excruciating attack of gout, and filming had to be stopped. This happened at a propitious time, because De Laurentiis, the producer, had run out of money. Meanwhile the animals had to be fed, and the food bill was enormous.

Even the "featured" animals who were circus-trained and used to performing found it difficult to get used to the ark and each other. The first few days after their arrival at the vast compound in the Rome studio they were ill at ease.

The arc lights made the cocks neurotic. Every time the full brilliance came on they thought it was dawn and crowed wildly. The flamingoes were tense and nervous and in danger of breaking their spindly legs if they were startled by a sudden movement. The giraffes were neurotic and worried—until Huston and the trainers hit upon the idea of feeding them sugar lumps mixed with corn as a tranquilizer.

As the days stretched into weeks there were so many interruptions, holdups and changes in the production schedule that I decided to do my own two-by-two—just photographing the animals and birds in pairs, because it seemed unlikely that I could spare the time to await the triumphal march into the ark. When I went to say

Republican Convention
fund-raising,
San Francisco, 1964

goodbye to Huston he was sitting on a bale of hay, dressed in his sackcloth Noah outfit. While Professori, the raven, picked at corn in his hand, he was being interviewed by the religious editor of a French publication:

Why is he making *The Bible*?

Is it a religious experience?

In what way will it differ from other vehicles for bosoms and battles?

Whose idea was it that Adam and Eve should be naked?

"God's," said John Huston.

Two weeks later a jubilant Huston called me. He had led the animals, and miraculously all three hundred of them had followed him in neat pairs into the ark. He got it on film on the first take. For insurance he tried it again. No luck. The animals refused to budge.

Each type of photography has its own compensations. Working on film stills is particularly rewarding because it is a group effort. The camaraderie is especially welcome after working on a series of reportage stories, which can be a lonely effort. After *The Bible* with its zany problems, it was good to go on to a serious documentary essay on women. The women's liberation movement was just beginning and I had suggested the idea of a picture essay on women without men. We picked various situations: a divorcée (with children), an abandoned wife (also with children), nuns, the women's army, lesbians and spinsters. It was before the public outlook changed to acceptance of men and women living together openly without benefit of clergy and women having children out of wedlock. The women I photographed were still timid about going public with their life stories, so it was a very delicate and solitary job that went on for months.

Occasionally I could wring a chuckle out of a situation, but generally it was a fairly lugubrious setup. There was only a single leavening time. I had photographed the nun story, called "The Brides of Christ at Ladywell Convent Chapel," at a final profession ceremony, the serious ritual that marks the final withdrawal from the world. The mother superior suddenly got cold feet and decided to refuse permission to have the story published. This presented a problem, since these were the best pictures in the overall story. What to do?

Thinking quickly, I told the nun the truth: it would wreck the entire project and get me in trouble with my editor. Then I asked if my editor and I could call on her to discuss it. She grudgingly set a date. I figured that Peter Crooksten, the managing editor of the *Colour Magazine*, who was handsome and had an attractive personality, could charm the nuns. He had them cooing with pleasure over the teacups. They gave unconditional consent and we smiled all the way back to London.

I was amused in going through my archive to find how often women who had taken the veil or veiled women appear. In the Women Without Men series there are two unexpected weddings—both of them featuring veils. The four brides of Christ wore white bridal dresses complete with lace veils and orange blossoms. There was also a wedding cake. The women took their vows lying prone on the floor.

In contrast, there was the other incongruous wedding: two lesbians who celebrated after their veiled ceremony by watching a male guest lying on the floor—this time supine—being whipped by a member of the wedding party. She stood sadistically on his belly in her stiletto heels.

It seems ironic that these services were the seed that germinated into the series (beginning in 1969) in which I photographed in the Middle East and Africa. This time veiled Muslim women—some of them in harems.

John Huston as Noah
(with hippopotamus) in *The Bible*,
Rome, 1965

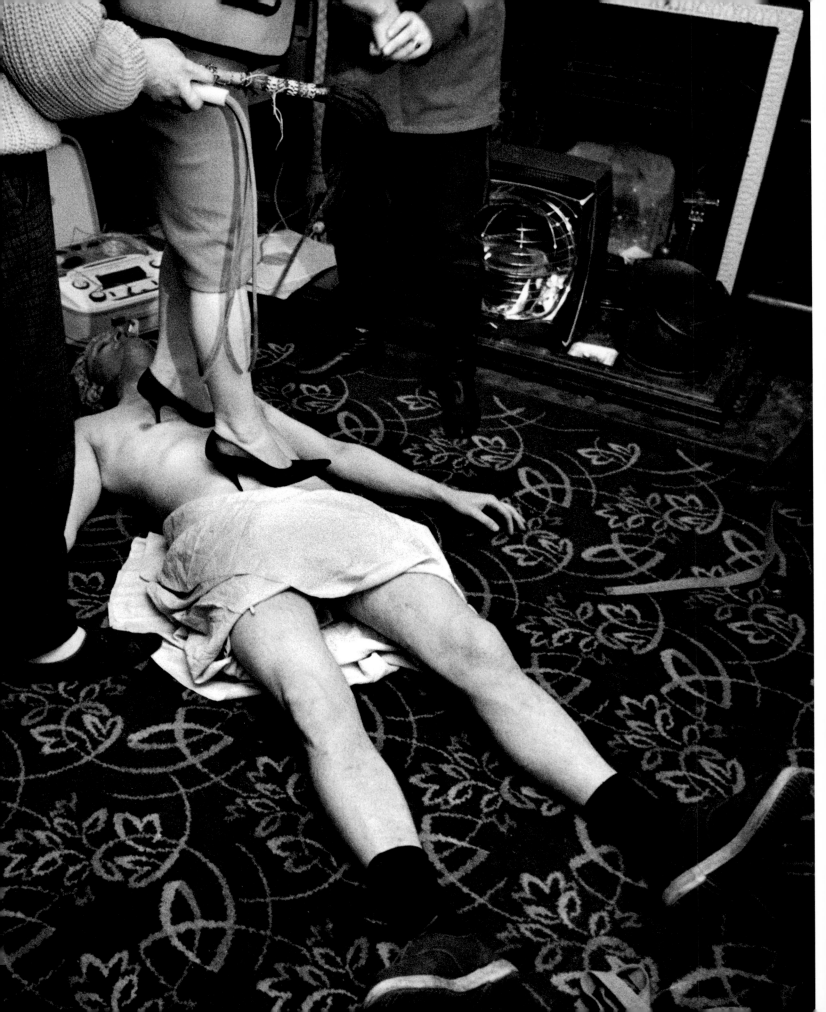

I then went to Sicily to join the cast, crew and director of *Modesty Blaise*. It was a relief to be with this spoof of a comic strip after the downbeat Women Without Men, even though the film had its own problems. The star, Monica Vitti, was an idol of art-movie houses. She had started out as a theatre actress in Italy, gone on to dub Italian films in her seductive voice, and then to making celebrated films with Michelangelo Antonioni. Now she was going for the big prize—stardom in a popular film.

Joe Losey, the director, was a serious man who had been savaged in America by McCarthyism. He had made earnest films before (*The Servant* and *Accident*). Now he, too, was making a bid for a wider audience. This was a comedy.

We seemed to have more fun off camera than on. One night at dinner at the Domenica, the superb monastery-turned-hotel where we were lodged, Monica Vitti did a priceless spoof of Marilyn Monroe. At our table Dirk Bogarde, his manager Tony Forewood and other members of the cast were convulsed but also strangely moved.

Wonderful, I thought. Joe Losey will have an easy time of it, and so will I with the stills. Not so. Miss Vitti, who was playing a lampoon, a sort of female James Bond character, had an obsession about her nose which made filming her almost impossible. She felt she had a housemaid's nose that made her look common in profile. Her endless jockeying for camera position complicated the shooting. I was told, "No profiles, please," even though I thought her profile Nefertiti-like and quite lovely. I managed, but it made improvisation difficult when all I had to work with was just one angle, full face. For Joe Losey it was tougher. He would map out a shot and she would try to outwit him by moving in a different direction to avoid her profile. It was particularly worrying one day when the director of her successes, Antonioni, came to the studio and watched her from behind Losey's camera. She kept looking to Antonioni and he kept directing her with his eyes. The atmosphere was suddenly very heavy. Mr. Losey kept his temper, but from then on the film was difficult to work on.

Lesbian wedding celebration,
London, 1965

In the autumn of 1965 I went to the USSR for the first time. Peter Crooksten had dreamed up two stories which he called "The Oldest" and "The Coldest." "The Oldest" was about the oldest men in the world. According to a current Russian census, there were two thousand people in the Republic of Georgia over one hundred years old. "The Coldest" was about an area in Siberia where temperatures drop to sixty-five degrees below zero. This assignment I refused. The idea was enough to give me chilblains in a heated room.

These were cold war days, so the trip was very difficult to arrange for an American. The Russians refused me a visa, then relented when they saw a picture story in the *Sunday Times* that they savored. The Novosti man in London said, "Oh, you work for *Sunday Times*. Not good paper, but last week I see so decadent story about debutante. Her father spend ten thousand pound for her party. I buy many copies. Send to Moscow, they see how low is the West. *Nekulturny*."

When I told him it was my story, he looked me over and gave me a journalist's visa. Then I flew to Moscow and my troubles really started. I met with the writer Gloria Stewart. For a week we haggled, harangued and waited for things to open up. Then through good luck, good handling,

sheer accident or the Russians' eagerness to get rid of us, we were in Georgia.

I was wildly excited to be in the land of my ancestors, the land where my mother and father grew up, but still mindful that here my mother's brother and ten members of his family had been slaughtered in a pogrom in the 1920s. The only survivor was Ben, who was two years old and whom someone had shoved under a bed.

I was confused. There was jubilation and there was trauma, which changed to anger at my parents, who spoke Russian but hadn't taught the children their native tongue. They feared we might be handicapped in the new world if we spoke the language of the old country; they wanted us to be Americans, not foreigners. So I had to depend on Gloria to interpret. She was a jolly young woman from Birmingham who had wangled her way into Russia, spoke the language idiomatically and was street-smart.

We had been given visas—for Sukhumi on the Black Sea, where we were to contact the Soviet Institute of Gerontology. They were reluctant to tell us where the old men were, but they gave us long lectures and showed us grotty medical films of old men with caved-in clavicles and dangling genitals. When we thanked them but said we wanted to see live ancients, they passed us on to yet another specialist. Apparently no one wanted

The oldest men in the world,
the Caucasus, USSR, 1965

to take the responsibility of pointing us in the right direction.

After a week of this I suggested that we go to the local newspaper for help—we might find colleagues to take pity on us. We were lucky. The editor introduced us to a team of two men—a journalist and a photographer—who were in the region working on the same story for a Moscow bureau. The journalist fell in love with Gloria's generous bottom and the photographer became enamored of my long lenses. They bought us a vodka and vowed to come at ten the next morning to take us to the old men. Indeed, they arrived on time in their car and drove us to a nearby village, where they mobilized a posse of twelve Communist Party members in three cars. We were then driven thirty miles to the farm of Astan Schlarba, a 112-year-old. When we arrived he was leading a goat to the slaughter for that night's feast.

He sent his fifty-year-old son, Varlaan, off to catch a wild horse for me to photograph. When the son had difficulty the father took over and led the horse he had lassoed past my camera.

The eight men who had gathered to welcome us were all centenarians, and they were all vitally alive. They worked hard in the vineyards and tobacco fields and were (by Russian standards) prosperous. They told us that when any of them left the near-perfect climate of the mountain villages of the Caucasus and moved to the cities they died at a much earlier age, just like everyone else. When we had asked the doctors at the institute about longevity, they had grinned and said it was high sexual potency that kept the ancients going. The old men spoke of the sex factor. They cited the case of a 123-year-old friend who had married a black woman, a descendant of Pushkin's slave, who was only twenty-three. The old man died on his honeymoon, but, and the men shook their heads admiringly—what a way to go.

We were invited to bread and salt. Translated, this meant a banquet of grilled goat, chicken, cheese, fruit, vegetables, salad. All of this was served with huge soup plates piled with *mamaliga*—a cornmeal mush one rolls into balls and eats with the fingers. The whole is topped with hot pepper sauce and washed down with vodka. For a time I imagined I was at the Yalta Conference. There were toasts in vodka to the hosts' long life, to Gloria, to me, to peace, to the end of war, to the banning of the nuclear bomb, and toasts to each of the other guests. For each toast one knocked back a vodka. Then it was my turn to toast. I drank to our 112-year-old host. His reply was: "When a woman drinks to me, I feel that I am once again in the world of men."

When I reached saturation with the vodka, our gracious host remarked that there were parts of Georgia in which one is murdered for refusing to drink. But he let us off the vodka and appointed a toastmaster, whose duty it was to drink a tumbler of wine for each of the dozen-plus guests. We others were only obliged to drink six glasses of wine. The banquet lasted five hours and wound up with our drinking a toast to the women who served us; they never sat down with their men.

This ceremony was repeated on three different occasions in three different villages. We would be met by local party bigwigs, talk briefly, photograph, then on to the banqueting. We would be greeted by the hostess, who touched her cheek to each guest's cheek. Then she said, "I offer you clean food with a clean heart," and poured fresh water over our hands. Then we proceeded to the table to be outdrunk by the ancient men.

There are other memories that surface: a betrothal party at which the old men danced, and a photograph of a balalaika orchestra of a hundred men performing onstage, all of whom claimed to be over one hundred years old. When the *Sunday Times* story was published, a friend, Sherley Roland, sent it to Alexander Schneider, the leader of the Budapest String Quartet and a disciple of Casals. He asked for a print, which he sent to Casals on his ninetieth birthday with the inscription "Maestro, you are just a baby."

As long as I kept drinking I did well, but one day, cold sober, I stepped backward off a porch to get a more interesting angle and fell down a flight of steps, wrecked two teeth and broke my jaw. I worked in great pain for three days, afraid to go to a local doctor. I had a nightmare of returning to the West with a mouthful of stainless steel. I was then five days in transit. Sat two days in an airport on the Black Sea—Moscow was snowbound, and the Russian planes had no deicing equipment. Saw a pig amble down the runway as a plane was about to land, but didn't photograph it because I didn't want the authorities angry and feared they might take away my exposed film. Waited for a French plane that was winterized, but it didn't arrive. Our permits did not allow us to go by train, but I was so ill that Gloria covered me up with scarves to make me look like an old babushka and enjoined me not to open my mouth so I could pass for a native, and we took an overnight train to Kiev. The train was wonderful—people wandered around in the heated cars in summer striped pajamas, played stringed instruments and sang folk music. We shared a compartment with two young men who were kind to the mute babushka—they gallantly gave Gloria and me the choice of bunks and waited in the corridor while we changed into our nightclothes. One was a young soldier whose mother had baked him a white loaf of bread, a luxury in the USSR. Gloria and I looked at each other and went to the buffet, where she bought caviar and butter for the bread and champagne and chocolate to be drunk and eaten together Russ-

ian-style. I, of course, couldn't eat, but I drank a bit.

From Kiev we went by plane to Moscow, only to find the connecting flights icebound and grounded. So two more days in the Moscow airport. Finally I arrived in Paris. All flights to London booked. Spent the night in Paris. At last a connection to London, a dental surgeon and the blessed oblivion of two purple hearts.

During the weeks we spent searching for the Russian centenarians, I amused myself by fantasizing a major photo-essay on the USSR. Gloria and I talked endlessly about an ideal assignment in which we were given freedom to move about and investigate anything we chose. We made lists that grew longer each day. I would ask questions: What about the jails? Divorce? Psychiatry? Religion? Spending months in a single village? Remnants of the aristocracy like the Tolstoy family? And on and on. If Gloria knew the subject, she would answer, but answer or no, on the list it went.

When we finished "The Oldest" and were emboldened by Gloria's daring (and success with the forbidden train ride), we began to take the list seriously. We planned to see if we could get the *Sunday Times* to underwrite the project and the Russians to give us the necessary visas and cooperation. Back in London when my jaw began to heal, I began a research blitz of the story possibilities on my list, and when I felt secure in the facts to back up the project, I asked Godfrey Smith, the editor of the *Sunday Times Colour Magazine*, to lunch. He had heard about the difficulties we had encountered doing the old men story, so his first remark to me was: "I'll bet you never want to see Russia again."

On the contrary—and I presented him with my list.

What percentage do you expect to come back with?

overleaf: Psychiatric hospital, Moscow, 1966

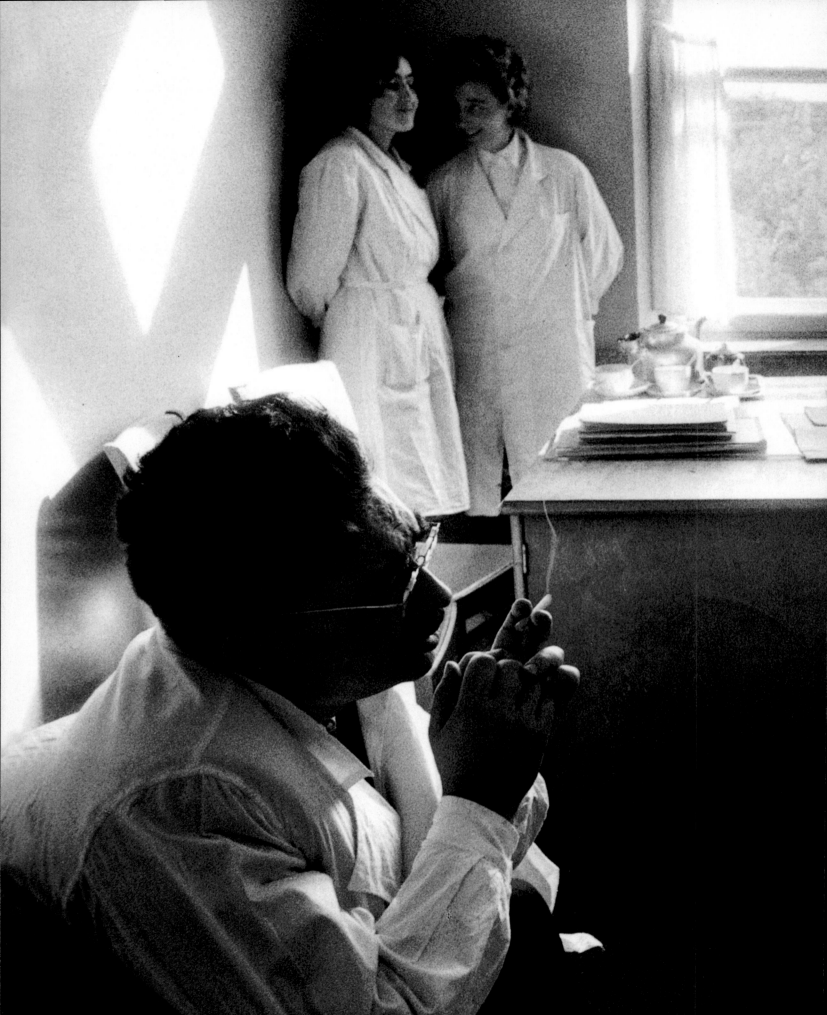

Fifty percent.

Go ahead. I'll be happy with thirty percent.

Unfortunately, Gloria couldn't make it. While Peter Crooksten searched for an appropriate Russian-speaking journalist, I took off for Spain to photograph the Spanish aristocracy. Then on to a cover story on Vanessa Redgrave, and stills of Charles Chaplin directing Sophia Loren and Marlon Brando in *A Countess from Hong Kong*; Fred Zinnemann directing Paul Scofield and Orson Welles in *A Man for All Seasons*; Sidney Lumet directing Simone Signoret and James Mason in *The Deadly Affair*.

Signoret was a delight to work with. She was professional, inventive, informed and friendly. She loved to come to London (and when I got to know her better, to go to the antique barrow markets). After our shopping expeditions, we would go up to her suite at the Savoy, kick off our shoes and talk. I remember one story she told. Her husband, Yves Montand, was on a film with Jeanne Moreau, Simone's competition for first lady of French film and stage. Ms. Moreau showed interest in Yves, but, said Simone, Yves fucked the ingenue in the film instead—here she shrugged her shoulders—and now Jeanne wouldn't talk to Simone.

Eventually, Peter Crooksten settled on George Feifer, a Russian-speaking American journalist who had been a Harvard exchange student in the USSR, to do the Soviet story with me. It took almost a year to organize the trip, but at last on August 26, 1966, George and I enplaned for the USSR. When I had begun my quest in 1965, I had no idea of the politically seismic changes that were taking place in the USSR. Khrushchev was out and Kosygin and Brezhnev not yet settled into control. There was a vacuum and a glimmer of goodwill which made it possible for a journalist to slide in. I was to encounter the same situation when I went to China in 1979. Nobody quite knew what the regime would do, so the apparatchiks played it safe and let in the more persistent and more desirable types. But the "guests" were under constant surveillance by the KGB even though our work came under the innocent heading of stories about the daily lives of their people.

I could still feel the prickles in the back of my neck from the last Russian trip, the feeling that I was being followed. I would tell myself that it was madness, that my head was filled with too many spy movies, that it was sheer paranoia. Then I would look around and there would be a watcher. My muscles would tighten in the attempt to throw off the fear, but there it was.

One incident in Sukhumi had really bothered me. It was too much like a cliché to be credible. Still, it happened. I was checked into the bridal suite of an art nouveau hotel on the Black Sea.

The rooms were vast. In one room there was a small thin-mattressed cot, a rickety chest of drawers and a bare bulb hanging from the ceiling. The other room held a sad, badly sprung two-seat sofa and another bare bulb. In all this splendor I lost a shoe. I found it under the cot, where there was an exposed bugging device. I sat on the cot and talked to myself. I said the windows were filthy, the floors unswept, the bathroom unspeakable, and on and on with my file of complaints. Ten minutes later, two maids showed up with mops, brooms and cleaning cloths. Not only did the hotel have listening devices but it must have had interpreters to monitor them.

I tried to put my fears behind me and gave a party in London to celebrate our departure, and George and I took off. George was young, in his thirties, and enthusiastic. He knew his way around the bureaucratic snarls that could easily defeat a less intrepid reporter. He was painstakingly meticulous when he interviewed (in Russian), filling pages of a very large notebook. Our interpreter tried to fill me in on what was being said so I could visualize the necessary pictures.

It was frustrating to come into a new area or situation, see what was possible photographically and then have to wait endlessly for the polite atmosphere to be established, the brief to be discussed, the tea to be drunk and the interview to be endured.

George tried valiantly to keep things running smoothly, but it wasn't easy for either of us. The partnership between writer and photographer is difficult at best, especially if it is complicated by working in a foreign language. Both members of the team need the time and the sole attention of the subjects, who can concentrate either on being questioned or on being photographed, not both. It is especially hard for the photographer, who has to depend often on first impressions, on the element of surprise and on the light—all of which are ephemeral. Often by the time the essential preamble is over, the light is gone and the subject is either tired or bored or both. This makes it hard for the photographer to produce a sense of freshness or spontaneity, especially if she doesn't have direct contact with the subject, but is depending on an interpreter for communication.

We started in Moscow, where George spent days organizing our trips for the next three months. We were to travel with one interpreter, whom we hired through the news agency Novosti. Wherever we went we were to be joined by a local person (usually a member of the KGB) who was familiar with the area and who could smooth our way.

We worked in Moscow and at various country sites around the capital. We went to the Black Sea to document the Russians at play; to Bolshevo to

report on juvenile delinquency and its rehabilitation in a labor colony, which was a prison; to the Kuban, in the Russian heartland, to spend a month living in a village.

The village was part of a vast, rich collective farm called Our Motherland. Its black soil was so fertile that a local proverb had it that today you shove a stick into the ground, tomorrow a tree will come up. At last there was time to observe, to inquire, to establish friendships, and, yes, to photograph. We lived with the peasants—their word—had our meals with them, took our Saturday-night bath when they took theirs, went to bed when they did, and rose with the dawn. They talked to George about their lives and wanted to know about ours. There were jokes and laughter. A friendly rivalry arose about our countries. To hear the head of the collective, Chairman Cherkasov, tell it, American farms were not a patch on Russian ones. He had read that American farms were only seventy acres big. Now compare this with Our Motherland, which had 28,000 acres. When we began to unravel his garbled account of the seventy-acre farms, we realized that the figure was an average of the vast acreage of farms like the King Ranch with family allotments of a few acres. Our host was chastened when George explained, but the friendly one-upmanship ended in laughter when George came up with the last word. He said, "The best Russian vodka is Polish, the best Russian caviar is Iranian, and the best Communists are Yugoslavs."

My idea of using the collective as a microcosm to represent the USSR proved to be a good one. There were a clinic, a hospital, a dairy, schools, a town hall called the Palace of Rest and Culture, and people doing many and varied jobs within the framework of Our Motherland. It all came together into a representative document of the

overleaf: Divorce, Moscow, 1966

daily lives of the Russian people. There were even cowboys (whom the Russians called cahvboys). If you brought in a film crew you could make a western on the spot.

On the day before we left, Chairman Cherkasov made us *pelmeni*, a Siberian ravioli served in broth and garnished with a mustard sauce. It was fun to see him roll out the dough, add the meat and make up the paste into triangular shapes. In the evening he added the *pelmeni* to the broth and we sat down to dine with him and his family for the last time. We brought four bottles of vodka to add to the four the Cherkasovs provided, making it a bottle each for the eight of us. Since according to Russian custom it would be unthinkable not to finish every drop, all eight of us, seven men and I, were pretty tight when we left the dinner to go on to a party in our honor. I remember how we lurched down a broad moonlit road arm-in-arm. I would like to think it was pure camaraderie; alas, we were afraid to let go for fear of falling. When we arrived at the party, there was a balalaika player who played music for the *cossatchka*, the Cossack dance of my childhood. I was disappointed that none of my new friends knew the dance, so I formed a circle and taught the others the Russian dance my parents had taught me.

Next day there were more festivities to speed the parting guests, this time at the community hall. There were the usual monthly rituals: instead of a baptism there was the ceremony of the Party parents (in a Christian country they would be godparents) taking on the responsibility for the politics of the infant, there were birthday celebrations and a marriage, and there were speeches of farewell for us.

Then we all sat the ritual five minutes of silence for the parting guests, and there were kisses and wishes of Godspeed, and the whole congregation walked us to the train. They had brought so many flowers that I calculated that they came to ten times my girth in autumn blossoms. Thank you, *tovarishchi*.

We returned to Moscow to do a story on the way the church functioned under communism and stories on Soviet psychiatry, advertising, jazz, a circus school, fashion, a movie star, clinical death, a divorce court, and Tolstoy's eldest grandson. The authorities told us that nothing as detailed or as comprehensive had ever been tried in the USSR.

We ended up with twenty-nine separate stories, seventy percent of the list I had offered Godfrey Smith—not the fifty percent I projected, or the thirty percent he would have been happy to receive.

George and I had tried to arrive at a cohesive understanding of what we had seen and experienced on our Russian travels. We had gone to the USSR to investigate how the people lived fifty years after their Revolution, and we were given unprecedented access—but still under control of the authorities and always under the surveillance of the KGB. So we had to try to figure out the distance between what we were shown and what we could gather existed elsewhere in the country. We knew that what we saw was prepared specially for the outside world, but as far as the amenities for daily living went, they still trailed way below American standards. Comparison with the West was depressing.

During the month we spent living closely with the people in the villages of the collective and the other three months in the cities and moving about the country, we did walk about and explore on our own, and we could and did talk to people, many of whom were open in their criticism of things as they were. The main complaints were lack of space and lack of privacy, the high cost of food and the shortage of goods that made shopping a nightmare, and the primitive transportation and restrictions on travel. Above all, the lack of free choice, the alcoholism and the suffering economy were particular *bêtes noires*.

Against these problems they cited how terrible living conditions had been under the tsars, and they spoke of the good things: free medical care, day-care centers for their children, free education, the low cost of utilities, the assurance that cradle to the grave you were looked after (if you conformed). When we raised the obvious questions about the high price in conformity that had to be paid for these privileges we would usually meet with a cynical shrug of the shoulders, an attack on capitalism or questions about our own way of life. Often they might repeat a joke that was going the rounds. "What is the difference between America and Russia? In Russia it is man's inhumanity to man—and in America? It is the other way around."

None of this was new. What we saw simply confirmed what we already knew in the West. What bothered us as we travelled around the country was the unhappiness on the faces of the people and the grey grim look of their surroundings. This was true everywhere except in the better places the authorities had prepared as demonstrations of the triumphs of communism.

We wanted to understand what had happened after 1945, after the Russians had coped with the ravages of war and the loss of thirty million people; how they faced up to the cold war with their former allies in the West. We wanted to know the aftermath of Khrushchev's denunciation of Stalin for his setting up of the show trials in the thirties that resulted in the death of countless people; what was happening with the de-Stalinization program since the removal of his body from the mausoleum in the Kremlin wall; what was the result of Peking's denunciation of Moscow as "defaming the dictatorship of the proletariat, the socialist system and the international Communist movement."

What had happened was that Russia, which historically had always been Janus-faced (with one face turned east and one face turned west) and which would periodically turn completely in whichever direction suited her at the moment, had broken with China and turned to the West. It was this phenomenon we were witnessing now— the period Kremlin-watchers now call "the silver years."

When we had asked people who did trust us sufficiently to discuss how they felt about the defrosting of official attitudes to the West, the consensus was that although things were easier since Stalin's death, they were still under strict constraint not to speak out freely and still walked in fear of their lives, and they cautioned us not to be misled by what we were being shown.

overleaf: Hydrotherapy for political prisoners, psychiatric hospital, Moscow, 1966

When I returned to London after the Russian trip, I went to Dingleton Hospital on the Borders in Scotland to photograph a story called "A Therapeutic Community" and started research on a photo-essay I had long wanted to do on the Vatican. I was in good form, back at my three-tier way of working.

The Vatican was an old idea of mine. It started when I read an article in *Fortune* (in the dentist's waiting room). The American Management Association rated company efficiency. Its research showed that on a scale of 1 to 10, if it assessed AT&T, one of the world's most efficient companies, at 7, then the Vatican would rate 9. Somehow this stuck in my mind. It was sufficiently intriguing to make me want to investigate one of the world's last absolute monarchies.

My research read:

> One sixth of a square mile in area, with a population of not much more than a thousand, itself barely thirty-five years old as an independent state within a state, Vatican City is the administrative center of a spiritual and material empire with a citizenry in the hundreds of millions and a history of two thousand years. No one, whatever his faith or national allegiance, lives unaffected by decisions taken in this tiny community, where past and future meet, even collide.

To bolster my point about the collision of past and future, I unearthed the fact that the Vatican owned a Dutch pharmaceutical company that manufactured the birth-control pill. The story also included early computers. We used a nun at the computer console on our cover.

I went to Rome at Easter to investigate the story. It was, like so many interesting stories, hard to get permission to do—in this case, to go beyond the Swiss Guard and the public arena. There were very tight controls for journalists and even tighter ones for photographers. Permits had to be requested and obtained on a daily basis. There was an exclusive sub rosa arrangement with a specific Italian photographer, who kept other photographers out.

I tried to get around the red tape. My first permit was to do pictures and an interview about the Vatican's own newspaper, *Osservatore Romano*. Thus, I met Don Levi, the editor who had been secretary to Pope Paul VI. He was interested enough to go out of his way to help me, so that by the time John Mortimer arrived to write the article we were personae gratae and except for a few sticky spots were able to move about freely.

Since Vatican City is self-contained, running everything from a food store to its own fire department, from a furniture workshop to a department where nuns pressed cardinals' vestments, it

Nuns,
the Vatican, 1965

seemed a good idea to investigate practically everything behind the scenes. There were also the more obvious situations, like an investiture of twenty-six cardinals in the Sistine Chapel; the Ethiopian College, where black students played drums for a ritual mass; and the American college the students nicknamed Collegio Coca-Cola. It had a huge swimming pool, in the center of which was a bronze crown of thorns.

The more we did the more there was to do. I had arranged a meeting with the secretary of state for John Mortimer and me. When I arrived, the Swiss Guard blocked my entry. They told me that John had arrived with his wife, the writer Penelope Mortimer, and her daughter, and that they had been refused access because the women were wearing sleeveless dresses. Strange that there was no problem about wearing miniskirts, but the rule about sleeveless attire was inviolable. It took me another two weeks to wangle permission to see the secretary of state. Meanwhile, Penelope Mortimer decided to go back to London and went to the airport. She was early, and after checking in she sat down and fell asleep. When she awoke the plane was gone. In her lap was a Polaroid of her sound asleep.

An official at the Vatican had advised me when we started work, "This place is like an artichoke. Pull it off petal by petal, until you come to the heart." In trying to get to the heart, I decided to detour a bit and do a series on the Catholic sacraments. I started with baptism in St. Peter's. Every Sunday, three priests would do a production-line simultaneous baptism. You would hear a group of howling infants and then, as the parents and relatives of each of as many as ten babies watched, the priests in a single sentence would intone their names: Giuseppe, Marco, Michelangelo, Roberto . . .

I went on to confirmation, communion, confession, marriage and ordination. All the rituals were standard except extreme unction. The ordination service, where eight young Filipino men dressed in green (seven of them wearing glasses) lay facedown before the altar of their college chapel (Collegio Coca-Cola), was deeply moving to me. The atmosphere was highly charged. A row of nuns stood weeping, handkerchiefs clutched. The litany was beautifully sung:

> Inasmuch as you celebrate the mystery death of the Lord you should endeavor to mortify in your members all sin and concupiscence.

It continued:

> From the snares of the devil
> From anger and hatred
> From the spirit of fornication through tempest, earthquakes, plagues, famine, war and everlasting death
> Lord have mercy on us.

If the taking of holy orders was painful to photograph, the service for the dying was sheer farce. My interpreter, Jan Frejese, found out that there was a priest who was dying in a nearby hospital. She got permission from the family. The priest who was officiating told them a white lie— he said the picture was for the Pope. In order not to damn his soul to hell, I promised to send the Pope a print. Then my interpreter and I, wearing medical white coats, were permitted into the sickroom. I shot off a roll of film. The sound the camera makes when the film sprockets are engaged sounded wrong, but I went on. To make sure, I took up another camera and got the same response. I realized that for the first time in my photographic life, I had failed to load my cameras.

I mouthed "Let's go" to Jan. When we got out into the hall I explained, and she exploded into nervous laughter, the kind of laughing jag that is almost impossible to stop. When she did finish, the priest demanded an explanation. He was horrified, and refused to let me back into the sickroom. He kept saying, "You came to the war, but you didn't load the cannons." I was heartsick about both my unforgivable stupidity and Jan's involuntary laughter. Next day I went to try to make peace with the priest. He was still hurt and angry, but said he would try to help us, and next day he sent a message for us to load the cannons and come to the hospital. When we arrived, he was mysterious. He said he had not only brought the holy oil but had paid for the candles himself. He then led us into a private room where a healthy, ruddy-skinned young priest lay, his leg suspended above his head. He had been in a skiing accident and was in traction. The older priest lit the candles and started to apply the oil to various orifices, all the time moving his lips for the picture. The whole situation was so ludicrous that the four of us dissolved into laughter. I took a few token shots and thanked the priests. Alas, there was no picture to send to the Pope. Ever after I have wondered how our friend the priest dealt with his conscience. Did he tell his confessor?

Among my notes about the Vatican I found the copy of a letter sent to John Hillelson, the then London Magnum agent:

Dear John,

Please note that in the enclosed expense account I referred to entertainment, tips and bribery—all of which made it easier to work within the framework of the church. I was advised by one of the Paulist Fathers that the simplest way in was through corruption, and that a thousand-lire note to an usher makes life easier in any church in Rome. For the invoice I'm sure you will find a more pleasing term for "Bribery."

The Vatican had drained me. The planning, socializing and setting-up necessary for a major photographic essay can be a tiresome exercise in which the pictures seem an anticlimax. There is some small satisfaction in the game of wits that takes place, but the overwhelming need to get to the camera has to be subordinated to all the preparations.

The foreplay is frustrating, but necessary; it is the armature on which the whole is built image by image. It is a slow process, but without acceptance and trust there can be no story. I always admonished myself to pack patience and understanding along with my other equipment into the camera bags. The popular notion that the photographer is someone who flits about the world clicking gaily away could not be more wrong. Getting a story takes concentration and hard work.

In London I sought something light, not too taxing, with the ground rules agreed beforehand. Something like the amusing film *Doctor Dolittle*, which I had done the year before, in which Rex Harrison romped with the animals and all there was to do was follow the action. What turned up was a film called *Salt and Pepper*. It was a feeble attempt to create a team of adventurers like Redford and Newman in *Butch Cassidy and the Sundance Kid*. Only this time it was Sammy Davis, Jr., and Peter Lawford. All I can remember was Sammy's energy, matchless dancing and endless questions about photography. He owned many thousands of dollars' worth of equipment, of which he was inordinately proud, and he talked a jargon gathered from the various photographic manuals he had read. He was a nut on the subject.

It seems that films always came like bookends—in pairs. The next one was *The Magus*, in Majorca. I was still tired and wanted to spend some time with Francis, so we went two weeks before the film started and came to rest in a pensione run by Juan, one of Robert Graves' sons.

overleaf: Nun ironing cardinal's vestments, the Vatican, 1965

113

The place was untidy, the meals so-so, but it was easy and relaxed and we loved it. Our host's mother invited us to lunch. Robert Graves was away, but Mrs. Graves gave us a delicious lunch, and there was a surprise for me. On the wall of her bedroom was a tear sheet from the *Sunday Times* of my Russian story. It was of a middle-aged man with a sheet of bees on a frame.

Mrs. Graves said, "I learned my Spanish reading *Don Quixote*. Now I'm learning Russian reading *War and Peace*. When I looked at that picture I thought, if fifty years after the Revolution people can be raising bees, then I want to go to Russia. I don't know who took the picture." I didn't tell her it was mine.

The two films had served their purpose. Now I wanted something more challenging to do. I tried to get an assignment to go to Vietnam, but had no luck. The next best thing was to do a story on Marines training for Vietnam. I went to North Carolina, where the Marines had set up replicas of Vietnamese villages. The text I wrote read:

Vietnam, North Carolina. With Marines bearing the brunt of the toughest fighting in Vietnam, extraordinary efforts are being made to perfect their combat training. This Vietnamese village in North Carolina, one of three built in North America, is the latest aid.

It is as authentic as the Marines can make it. Here Puerto Ricans dressed in coolie pajamas play the part of Vietnamese peasants and Negroes wearing saffron robes kneel in make-believe temples pretending to be Buddhist monks. Besides the typical houses and temple, the village has refinements like a Vietnamese barber's shop (haircuts, fifteen cents) and even a cemetery. The men are planning to bring in a bull, since water buffalo are not too easy to come by, and they use smudge pots to produce the authentic village smell. Perhaps the only shaky detail is the calligraphy—the writing over the entrance to the village was copied from a Japanese newspaper, and in the cemetery the lettering on the headstones (made from Coca-Cola crates painted yellow) came off a perfume bottle labelled Jade East. But, apart from this, the realism is almost total: the men wear sandals copied from the ones the Viet Cong improvise from the tires of American planes shot down in the North. Called "Ho Chi Minh gloves," the soles are made from the treads, the straps from inner tubes. Overall authenticity of the villages is so good that, after searching all over Southeast Asia, John Wayne used one of them as the setting for his film about Vietnam, *The Green Berets*.

The men are taught by combat veterans returned from Vietnam. The village is riddled with Viet Cong booby traps—electrically charged bridges and sharpened bamboo whips that swing down from trees when triggered off by the victim. The grim motto of the operation is: "Let no man's ghost say our training let him down." They learn "quick-kill": a man-sized target is thrown up, a snap identification made and the enemy shot immediately. They are taught how to behave if captured: never to accept favors, because obligations create a relationship.

Alongside the camp's efforts to make the Marine an even more effective fighting man, his public relations officers are trying to soften his domestic image. "We used to try to portray the Marine as a steely-eyed killer with hair growing through his clothes," said one. "Now the image we strive for is the hometown boy fighting for his country; the boy who hypothetically won three Bronze Stars, is only nineteen years old and did it without thought of reward." In fact, with the pace of the war so intensified, the Marine's chances of winning the Bronze Star certainly seem much higher than his chances now of ever setting foot in an ordinary, undamaged Vietnamese village.

Beekeeper,
Krasnadar, USSR, 1966

116

Returned Vietnam warriors,
Fort Bragg, North Carolina, 1968

The story seemed a series of surface exercises until I photographed wounded troops who had just returned from combat in Vietnam. It became deadly serious when I made one distinctive photo: a Marine in a wheelchair (reading a comic strip). His right arm is in a sling; he is flanked by two Marines on crutches. The one in the wheelchair has literally had his career shattered. He had been a professional baseball player and his pitching arm was so badly broken that the prognosis was that he would never pitch again. The men on crutches had suffered equally disabling injuries that would render them *hors de combat* for years.

It was about this picture that Michael Rand said, "Give me one great picture and I'll give you an eight-page layout." So strong was the "double truck" he made of the three Marines that the other six pages seemed redundant. For once I had achieved the objective so devoutly to be wished: the whole story told in a single picture.

In 1968 when John Huston decided to make a film with his daughter Anjelica called *A Walk with Love and Death*, he called to ask me to photograph her. Twentieth Century–Fox didn't know her, was uncertain of the way she would photograph and wanted to see pictures of her.

I was third down the list. Cecil Beaton and Bailey had photographed her before me. In their pictures, although she looked glamorous, she looked too old; the part called for a fourteen-year-old. The studio bosses would sit still for adding a few years, but it would not do to present them with the soignée lady the photographers depicted.

When John called, my first question was had they used color or black-and-white. It was black-and-white, which, with the dramatic lighting used, added years. Anjelica was then sixteen and caught between her mother's wish for her to get her A levels (high school diploma) and her father's wish for her to learn to become a film actress. To make matters worse, Anjelica had cut off her hair, which had hung way past her shoulders. This, too, made her look older.

Somehow a photographic session got organized. Gladys Hill, John's assistant, managed a wig and a fall from Alexandre, the movie stars' hairdresser in Paris. I got Ricky, Anjelica's mother, involved, so she provided an Empire-line dress that was youthful and romantic. Anjelica and I then flew to Ireland to St. Clarens to photograph. I thought that with color, soft Irish ambience, a broken-down castle on the grounds of John's country manor, we had a chance.

The film is about a medieval troubadour, a Sorbonne dropout, and his highborn lady love. The year is 1358, and the story is set against the background of war and rebellion. The idea was to evoke comparison with the youth rebellion going on presently in France. In fact, while the film was being cast, the barricades were up in Paris and the students throwing paving stones. The film, scheduled to be made in France, was then moved to a venue outside Vienna.

It was raining when we arrived at St. Clarens, which meant we would have to work indoors. Over lunch, John asked us what kind of pictures we planned. I told him that it's a bad idea to talk about pictures beforehand—it tends to rob both photographer and subject of spontaneity. For me, a thoroughly planned photograph seems to rule out ideas engendered during the photographing, because the original idea hijacks the sitting, leaving no space for improvisation. The photographer has to be able to take advantage of accidents that occur. For that an almost blank mind—like a blank canvas—is essential. The idea is to set the place and the time of day, surround oneself with whatever props are necessary and then proceed. The subject and photographer, sometimes even

Anjelica Huston at sixteen,
Ireland, 1968

120

without words between them, then are free to create the essential bond that makes the image.

I also felt that all the talk might make Anjelica nervous, so told Huston he had a nervous photographer on his hands—no talk, please. He understood immediately, and we spoke of other things. Next day the sun shone. We worked out of doors. Anjelica came through: young, lovely and vulnerable. We flew back to London, I to process the film, Anjelica to get back to her studies. When the pictures were shown to the studio people, they were enthusiastic. I was then asked to go to Austria to work on the film. It was ill-starred. Assaf Dayan's accent was against him, Anjelica was inexperienced, and not all Huston's great skill could save the picture. It was released briefly, just for a few days in New York, then quietly faded away.

Huston wanted to give me a gift, since I refused to be paid for the St. Clarens pictures. One day when he was in London he came to see me in my new flat. He started pacing the bare floor of the drawing room, putting one size-twelve boot ahead of the other. When asked what he was doing, he said he just wanted to see how big the room was.

Months later a beautiful handmade carpet arrived from Ecuador. Even the way the gift arrived was calculated to give maximum pleasure. It came, in a great princely gesture, by air, and two strong men carried it up my stairs on a wet London day. The men unrolled it and it shone forth in its sunny yellow, beiges and browns.

I had need of cheering. That week a letter had come from my brother George, who was dying of cancer. He was forty-three years old. He wrote to Francis and me: "I've always had a tremendous amount of love and respect for you. I just want to make sure that you hear about it too. I regret the many years during which the loving respect could not be shown." Two weeks later he died. It was hard to be in a strange land, away from those I loved. I didn't return for the funeral. I wanted to hold his memory close in my heart.

When I felt stronger emotionally I went to Philadelphia to be with the family, and when I was able to resume work I went to Colorado.

The story was one the *Sunday Times* called "An Experiment in Creative Dropping Out." People were dropping out all over America, and Drop City, all six acres of it, was the oldest and longest-lasting of the communes that were springing up. The inhabitants had built six Buckminster Fuller geodesic domes for living quarters and three large domes that contained community rooms, a kitchen, a workshop, a children's playground and a large lounge. They lived mainly on second-day goods the supermarkets nearby would by law have to throw out. They took local jobs when they ran out of money, and they lived together in harmony. We also visited two other nearby communes, Libre and New Buffalo, and were impressed with the young people who had the courage to live their beliefs no matter how naive.

It was good to see the ferment that was 1968. It seemed a watershed year, though when I look back on it, it's apparent that the water didn't shed. At the time, the youth of the world were in turmoil: there was the student uprising in France, an explosion of protest in Japan, the killing of students at the Olympics in Mexico and wild demonstrations against Vietnam in America.

In the United States there was the civil rights movement as well, so I decided to go to New York, to Harlem, to do a picture essay on "Black Is Beautiful." Black, not Negro, not colored.

There were two advertisements on the bus we passed on the way into Harlem. One said "Black Is Beautiful" and was for a hair preparation. The other said: "Scotch can be Beautiful." Both were put out by giant firms run by white people to sell goods to black people. Farther along were small shops with signs saying "Buy Black." At street corners were stencilled the words "Buy Black." Selling to black people.

I photographed Cicely Tyson, actress—black actress. In 1961 she had appeared in a live TV program about an emerging African nation. She had white-styled, long, straightened hair and didn't like it for the part she was to play. The morning the program was to be filmed she had it all cut off—to the barber's horror. The play was a success, and after Cicely lots of girls dared to "go Afro"—to accept themselves as black and beautiful.

And the barber (his name was Streamline)— the reluctant barber who cut off her hair? The publicity, and the Afro trend, brought him so much custom that he had made his pile and retired. But the hairdressers who specialized in straightening African hair complained that they were losing out.

Then there were Rudel and Walter Fountaine, specialists in hairdressing. They were not losing custom. They ran the most fashionable black beauty shop in New York, called Coif Camp. They had been designing and selling wigs for women, wigs of kinked, woolly hair— African-style hair. (Not, in fact, African hair: that wouldn't kink properly for wigs, so they were importing Chinese hair and kinking it.) "We blacks no longer look on ourselves with revulsion. We are overcompensating now, but it will settle. There will be a choice of wigs, kinked or straight, it will go either way, relaxed or woolly. It's now a cosmetic choice, not a racial one. Three years ago, if a girl cut her hair off and went Afro, her mother would act as though there was a death in the family. Two years ago her mother went Afro, and this year her father."

Every conversation I had with blacks got round to the charitable foundations, the philan-thropists. "They're paying to keep Wall Street intact, paying conscience money, paying for a cool summer."

For a black, to work for one of the foundations is to become a victim of accusations that he's sold out. But some risk it, like Arthur Mitchell, then the only black in the New York City Ballet. He was working with the Ford Foundation, running a ballet school at the Harlem Cultural Center. The classes were held in a church and open to everybody. After only four months, Mitchell was finding gifted dancers. Ballet taught to the beat of drums was exciting—ballet shoes and African rhythms were a fine combination. Black is beautiful.

Another experiment in education in Harlem was the Harlem Prep, which met in a converted supermarket. The school was set up for students who had completed high school but could get no further, or for dropouts who now wanted to go to university. Their ages ranged from sixteen to forty-seven.

James Brown and Jim Brown were two more symbols of the new pride wrapped in the slogan "Black Is Beautiful." James Brown is the American soul singer—"the" American soul singer, Mr. Dynamite, Soul Brother No. 1. He had just finished singing for an hour onstage when I photographed him: he'd screamed his song "Say it loud, I'm black and I'm proud," and youngsters had crowded onto the stage to shake his hand or just be close to him. James Brown was a contradiction—the voice of the underprivileged black who yet had his five hundred suits, his Rolls-Royce and three other cars, his private jet, his own radio stations, his drawbridged castle in New York. He was a militant, yet a peacemaker. At the time of the assassination of Martin Luther King, he was due to sing in Boston. Out in the streets the looting and burning had begun. The mayor got in touch with Brown, and the announcement

Black society debut,
Waldorf-Astoria Hotel,
New York, 1964

went out: "Tonight, TV-JB." It was enough; the rioters went home to watch James Brown. He held them for six solid hours, belting out his songs until the sweat engulfed him—and Boston was saved.

Then there's Jim Brown, actor. Some blacks say he is their John Wayne, which is not quite true, because Jim Brown is nobody's imitation of a white man. He is a remarkably handsome black man. He is also rich, and smart. He's interested in green power. Green is the color of dollar bills, and Jim Brown believes that what's wrong with the black man isn't that he's black but that he's poor; he hasn't enough of the green.

Personally, Jim Brown is clear of that problem. After being an American football hero he turned actor and had a string of good parts. He also had a job with Pepsi-Cola, his own magazine, a nightclub, a record company, a clothing company, a prizefight group. He introduced an industrial and economic union to help blacks set up their own businesses and get more green power.

Perhaps one short conversation sums up the effect of the "Black Is Beautiful" slogan. It came when I was talking with Fountaine and Rudel about hair and race and black problems in general. The phone rang. Fountaine listened, then turned to Rudel and said, "A magazine wants to do something new in ethnic fashion. Rudel, do you feel ethnic today?"

"Not today I don't," replied Rudel. "I feel whole."

Black Is Beautiful,
New York, 1968

I rounded out the sixties by trying my hand at advertising, approaching it with trepidation and respect for the skill it required. If one regarded each advertisement as a problem to solve and as a healthy fee to bank, it just broadened the area of photography in which to operate.

This was not my first encounter with advertising. In the fifties I had photographed an ad campaign for Simplicity Patterns. My brief was to travel all over America taking pictures of one woman in each of the forty-eight states and Alaska; she was to wear dresses made from the company patterns. The copy implied that the clothes were sewn by the women themselves, but to avoid the amateur look of "loving hands at home" they were made in New York by professional seamstresses, and I carted them around with me.

During a meeting with the art director and the "creative" head of the ad agency I asked what the objective of the campaign was. I was gently told in future to refer to the "concept," not the "objective," of the campaign. The photos were to be women enjoying their dresses against the ambience in which they lived.

By way of example the art director said, "If you are in Wisconsin, for example, and you are photographing a farmer's wife and there is a silo, then photograph her against the silo. Your sub-jects should look as though they are enjoying their dresses. They don't all have to smile, but they should look lighthearted and free. Don't worry about showing the buttons and bows. We want illusions, happy reportage. That is our concept, that is our philosophy for this campaign."

It was a brutal schedule to organize and even more difficult to maintain. Every afternoon I would fly into the city nearest the subject, have the dress pressed, telephone to make arrangements for the shoot, work the next day, then that afternoon fly off to the next situation. It was a frantic timetable to keep up: catching planes, sleeping in strange beds, eating hurried meals, photographing and looking for silos, so to speak.

When I returned to home base, the clients loved the pictures, but when they had gone through the process with the research people, marketing people, creative people and top executives (and, I suspected, their wives) in both agency and client company, all the buttons and bows were retouched and the backgrounds were all airbrushed out. There wasn't a single silo in sight.

Advertising had changed radically since my Simplicity Pattern days. In 1959, Doyle Dane, a small New York agency, came out with an ad for the Volkswagen Beetle whose copy simply read: "Lemon." The message it conveyed was that if occasionally the advertisers made a car that was not up to scratch, was indeed a "lemon," they would not saddle the consumer with it; they would scrap it. By not following the usual line of bunkum, Doyle Dane changed the face of advertising permanently.

New small agencies sprang up all over New York. They were slightingly called "boutiques" by the larger entrenched agencies. The way of arriving at a finished ad changed as well. Formerly copywriters and art directors had worked in isolation and separately under a copy chief. Now they worked together closely as a team under a creative head. Irreverent and humorous ads began to appear about formerly sacrosanct products. El Al ran one with the headline "Mine Son, the Pilot." Levy's Bread ran a series featuring photographs of ethnics: American Indians, blacks and Chinese with the headline "You Don't Have to Be Jewish to Enjoy Levy's Rye." Apparently sales responded, and the new advertising came to England along with Doyle Dane. I did a series of ads on Northern Ireland for them showing little-known beautiful landscapes with the copy line "Hardly Anyone Has Ever Heard of"—then the name of the place. By the time the ad campaign was released, everyone had heard of Northern Ireland; the political troubles had started and bombs were becoming part of our daily diet.

The sixties found the new advertising in full spate in London. It was based on the kind of layout and copy introduced by Brodovitch in America in the fifties. It was original, the graphics and typography often amusing and surprising. They fitted well into what *Time* magazine had dubbed "swinging London," which was then the rock capital of the world. It was an outrageous time, featuring sex, drugs, fashion (the mini), and rock and roll. The pill had liberated women, and there were rumors of louche behavior floating about. One such was that Mary Quant had barbered her pubic hair into the shape of a heart and dyed it purple. The buzz words were "peace" and "love" and "psychedelic." The King's Road was the place to go upmarket and Carnaby Street was down-market and becoming known worldwide.

The photographers were up there with the rock stars. Antonioni made *Blowup*, a film in which the hero is a photographer, Vanessa Redgrave appears topless, and the photographer makes out with two models on his studio floor on the bulge of his no-seam paper. In addition to the photographers, the "beautiful people" were the fashion designers (Mary Quant, Ossie Clark, Biba) and the hairdressers—chief among whom was Vidal Sassoon. It was music, pictures, clothes, uppers and downers and LSD for the brave, and pot for the timid.

As I remember it, there was also a feeling at the time that we would soon arrive at an egalitarian society, that the class structure would crumble. The most vivid evidence seemed to be the three working-class lads who made it in photography: Bailey, Duffy and Donovan, each of whom drove his own Rolls-Royce. To meet them in their push to level things out there were the Lords Lichfield and Snowdon. I seem to remember that Snowdon drove a Mini and some of the upper-class lads talked cockney. The mood of the time I think of as generous. There was lots of work around, and the competition was friendly. People seemed kinder to each other than they do now.

From my vantage as a senior photographer at the *Sunday Times*, it was fun to watch the shenanigans going on. The "in" crowd were members of Arethusa, a restaurant club on the King's Road run by a very clever Italian entrepreneur (called Alvaro) who inaugurated the club with a performance by the Supremes. In those days restaurants closed early, so people who wanted to relax after an evening's entertainment would go either to the White Elephant or the Arethusa. There one would see the glamorous ones—visiting movie stars (Britain's studios were working overtime to accommodate Hollywood companies)—and of course the anointed ones—the fashion people, the rock stars, the hairdressers and the photographers. I have tried to figure who their counterparts would be today. Perhaps the media people and the chefs.

Advertising taught me a great deal. It demanded the same concentration and involvement as editorial work, but I had to learn to work with art directors who were focused on selling a specific idea or product. It was a tougher métier than reportage, although I could use my reportorial skills in it. In my editorial work, whether based on my own ideas or the art director's, I had enormous freedom; in the ads there was a very tight brief. The "creative" people at the agency would come up with an idea. Very often, because the slogan or ad copy came first, the idea was not too visual, and was limited in the way it could be executed. The work was really illustration, and often it was made more difficult because, unlike American art directors, most British ones couldn't draw; a sketch artist would have made the layout. If other ideas presented themselves at the shoot, the a.d. and the photographer would have to use words instead of visuals to express their meaning.

I came to feel it regrettable that the photographer was not called in at the inception to help plan the shot, but realized that the creative people would feel that their authority was being questioned. At least I insisted upon working with the stylist, seeing the clothing and props in advance and being in on the "casting."

I spent a lot of time on the various elements of each ad. That way there was a measure of control. I felt sorry for the models who would trudge up my stairs to be vetted by me, then Polaroided by my assistant while they smiled bravely. There might be eight or ten models applying for the single job. I would indicate the one I thought would work best, and then Derek Harman, my advertising agent, would take all the Polaroids back to the advertising agency to be okayed. I particularly liked working with a modeling agency that dealt in ordinary people (not out-of-work actors or professional models). It was called Ugly.

The *Sunday Times* had a splendid daylight studio designed by Snowdon and run by Rose Kendall, which I rented. One could work there by daylight or use the state-of-the-art lamps either exclusively or as boosters. I learned a great deal about photographic illumination in that studio.

As I became more familiar with the work methods of advertising, I started to add my own versions of the original layouts, to depart more and more from them. Most art directors were pleased with the extra choices.

One advertisement (for Pretty Polly tights), used in women's magazines and as a twenty-four-sheet poster in the Underground, won a gold art director's award. It was of a splendid Harley-Davidson motorcycle on which one saw only the booted legs of a man and a pair of Pretty Polly sheer tights on a pair of long elegant woman's legs. She was riding pillion. The ad, although commercially very successful, got mixed reviews from women. The British *Vogue* editor thought it the best picture of legs she had ever seen, but the women in the liberation movement hated it. They felt it was sheer exploitation of women, because the model's body was photographed provocatively showing a great deal of her buttocks; they formed a perfect parabola. It is a paradox that although today the moral climate in England is such that full frontal nudity is acceptable in most editorial venues, the advertising strictures are so strongly enforced by the watchdog committees within the industry itself that it

Pretty Polly advertisement, London, 1969

would not be possible to get away with publishing that advertisement now—even though the model's gluteus maximus was fully clothed in a body stocking.

It was interesting to switch from editorial to advertising and from that to film work. In a sense, the photos of film stars and the situations in which they appeared were really advertising as well. We were selling the film. Very often I would become emotionally involved with the actors and try particularly hard to make sure that Magnum got the pictures placed in magazines with decent space. This would be true if the actor needed publicity—as was the case on my following assignment.

Shortly after I finished the Pretty Polly series, Joan Crawford called me. She was in England, at Bray Studio, making a Hammer cheapie called *Trog*. In it she played a brain surgeon who operated on a hairy simian troglodyte who had lived in

a cave. It was a reverse story of the prince who wakens Sleeping Beauty. Here, the lady wakens the sleeping beast, who sheds his fur, turns into a beautiful prince with an extremely high IQ, and falls in love with his doctor.

It was exactly ten years since I had photographed Joan in Hollywood, surrounded by wealth and fame. Now she was in a schlock studio, and it was hot—there was no air conditioner. She was stoical, even gallant, as she held a small battery-powered fan up to her face to keep her makeup from melting. An actor from earlier Hollywood days, apparently on his uppers, reminisced with her about "the good old days." She was matter-of-fact. There was not a jot of self-pity. It was a bravura performance that broke my heart.

I tried to get some publicity on Crawford while she was in England, but got turned down wherever I suggested it. That saddened me.

At the end of 1968 I was working on a film in Tunisia called *Justine*, with Anouk Aimee. One night after a hot, difficult day I went into the Hilton coffee shop to escape the noisy British crew in the bar. They were good for one drink, but by the second became rowdy, complained about the food and about the "wogs"—to them anyone who wasn't white was a "wog." The coffee shop was empty except for one man. When he rose from his seat (he was a huge man) I recognized Richard Saunders, a colleague from New York. He was with the United States Information Agency, our token black photographer in Africa. It was good to see a friendly face from home. Richard told me that his assignment next day was to photograph President Bourguiba at a rally and to interview him. Why didn't I come along?

At the rally, the president exhorted the women of Tunisia to come out from behind the veil, to come into the twentieth century. My imagination caught fire from this single sentence and led me to a project that was to occupy me for two years. The *Sunday Times* backed the idea and the BBC's *World About Us* and NBC in America commissioned a documentary film. The research was extensive. Every week, Linni, my secretary, would go off to the School of Oriental and African Studies and return with a market basket full of books in exchange for the ones I had read the week before. I read everybody from Doughty to Thessiger to Freya Stark.

Clearly, it could make a fascinating series if I chose right, but the more the research, the more difficult the choice. Where to go? There were, according to the latest census, 493,012,000 Muslims around the globe, ranging from Afghanistan and China to India, Russia and the Philippines. Some Muslim women were still in deep purdah and in harems, with their faces completely masked. Others took the veil upon marriage but walked about with their faces uncovered. Also, the chador—the covering garment and its masks— varied from country to country. All of them either exuded a sense of mystery or inspired horror in the viewer. It was either romantic or terrible exploitation of women, depending upon your orientation.

Although I had labored hard to prepare the material, no decision as to place could be determined until the *Sunday Times* and I agreed on a writer. My preference was Freya Stark, who knew the Arab world, was an extraordinary linguist and adventurer and had written some wonderful books. Godfrey Smith felt she was too old (seventy) and too academic; he preferred a younger woman, a more popular writer. We both pondered the choices and simultaneously came

up with Lesley Blanch, who had written a seductive book called *The Wilder Shores of Love*, about four nineteenth-century women who ride off into the desert sunset with their lovers—so to speak. She was a romantic, I a realist. The idea was that we would complement each other and bring forth provocative essays.

Lesley and I opted for a mix of landscapes and backgrounds: the mountains of Afghanistan, the deserts of Arabia and the waters of the Nile. Lesley was at first uneasy about travelling with another woman. She told the *Sunday Times* that she preferred her own (male) photographer, Henry Clark. The editor explained that the idea was mine and there was no possibility of replacing me. She consented, but seemed disappointed about it. I invited her to London so we could meet to plan strategy.

The meeting left me apprehensive, because we were both strong ladies and I was afraid we might cancel each other out. When I called to ask her to come to London, I asked if there was any place special she might like to lunch or was there any special food she might like. She had just published a cookbook called *Eighty Dishes Around the World* and I wanted to acknowledge her field of expertise. She said she didn't care about the place but she would enjoy a steak and kidney pudding.

I called around to various suitable restaurants, but none of them did the pudding, because it must be made fresh and steam for six hours. If we were to lunch at one o'clock the cook would have to come in at six-thirty in the morning to accommodate us. After drawing a blank from a number of places, I remembered that I was a member of the Wig and Pen Club—an old-fashioned institution that is housed in an ancient building across from the law courts. I called the manager, and he agreed to make the pudding. Great, I thought—this should start us off properly.

Michael Rand and his deputy, Meriel Mc-Cooey, greeted Lesley with vintage champagne. When we were quite merry the chef arrived in his high hat bearing the *pièce de résistance* steaming in the special bowl in which it had been cooked. When he went to serve the guest of honor, she said, "Only a spoonful, please." The cook looked crushed, the others looked upset, and I wound up tripling the gratuity I had intended to give the man.

At our meeting, we decided to go to Afghanistan first. Lesley had a friend, Safia Tarzi, who was a niece of the king. When we arrived in Kabul, she would be there for the celebration of the king's birthday and would help us by introducing us to people and seeing that we were invited to various functions.

Like her heroines in *The Wilder Shores*, Lesley travelled heavy. In her luggage were articles for use in practically any contingency, ranging from a parasol for the sun to a pair of fur-lined boots for the snow. To her luggage she would daily add goods that she bought in the bazaars—brass pitchers, carpets, kaftans she had made to order. Her curiosity was far-ranging. She would dream up all kinds of investigations from an opium den in Kandahar to a spring in the desert where there lived fish of such aphrodisiac potential that people paid five hundred dollars apiece for them. (We later found a man in Kabul who had a freezer full of the very same fish. He offered us a better deal.)

We started our Afghan adventure at the king's birthday gala in full evening attire. But first a panicked call from Lesley. She had brought "enough shoes for a centipede, but only one gold slipper." Come help hunt for the slipper. As the French say, in any combination of two people there is the one who offers the cheek and the other who kisses the cheek. I wound up as the kisser: I was in charge of money, travel arrangements, etc. But

Three widows on their way
to their mutual husband's grave,
Kabul, Afghanistan, 1969

Lesley was such good value, with her sparkling ideas and her charm, that I took on the responsibility without qualms.

The climax of the celebration for the monarch's birthday was a *buzkashi* game. *Buzkashi* is played like polo, but with the carcass of a headless goat, which is placed in the center of a chalked circle. Two opposing teams face each other. At a signal, the horsemen dive down to grab the carcass and place it between knee and saddle. They then race for the goalpost, the man with the goat protected by his team. The other team ride wildly, yelling and slashing away murderously at man and horse with lead-tipped braided whips. Their aim is to get the horseman to drop the animal. The game originated with Tamerlane, who played it with a headless enemy. It is sad to think that this was the last Independence Day festival for the king's birthday before the Russians moved in. There is a media myth that during the Russian invasion the Afghans played the game with a headless Russian.

Safia Tarzi talked about the Independence Day ten years before at which the king had decided to eliminate the veil. Knowing that the mullahs (the priests) would oppose him, he sent four young lawyers all around the Muslim world to confirm his belief that the wearing of the veil has no religious basis. At the Independence Day celebration, all the women of the royal family and the queen herself appeared unveiled before a crowd of thousands. It was, she said, like watching a whole people suddenly strip. The atmosphere was electric.

We stayed in Afghanistan for three of the happiest months of my working life. The country was a photographer's delight and dilemma. The Hindu Kush, with its snowcaps, its brilliant orange deserts, its intense blue lakes that reflected the vivid blue skies, held special problems for photography. How to capture that beauty in color

and not have the images become banal picture postcards? The color that came from the Kodachrome canister was pure prime color, and I had to learn to deal with it so that it didn't come out looking like family snaps that have just been processed by the local drugstore. One way was to work, whenever possible, in open shade; another was to photograph at dawn and late in the afternoon until dusk, during the "magic hours" when the full spectrum of light records fully on film.

The people were an ethnic mosaic: many races and many faces, tribes and subtribes—each sharply defined, for there had been little intermarriage. The men were handsome, strong and virile. I did a series of portraits of the men, feeling that the women would be more clearly defined if we understood their men. With a portrait lens (a 105 Nikon) I photographed the men on the streets, moving in close so that the head filled the frame with bold eyes looking directly at me. When I was editing the pictures later in London, my assistant asked me how I had set up the studio. He was surprised when I protested that all these shots were taken on the street with whatever daylight was available. I just would walk up to whoever I fancied would look good on film and click. My subjects enjoyed it almost as much as did I. The men were friendly; they didn't mug, just looked directly at me. It helped to have an interpreter as attractive as Safia.

The women were more reluctant. Most of them were shy and almost completely covered by the chador. The Afghan version covered the entire body from head to toe, including the face. The women's eyes peeped through lattice-worked cloth. Although the veil had been outlawed in 1960, most of the women were still veiled. The old ones said that no one was permitted to see their faces when they were young and lovely, so why should they remove the veil now that they were old and ugly? Village women were not normally veiled, because they would be hindered in working the fields; they donned the chador when they came to the city in order to look like city women. They thought it sophisticated.

One morning I woke with the idea that we should find a nomad wedding. Lesley was sure I had lost my senses. I assured her that we were approaching autumn, that the nomads would be coming down from the high pasturelands on the way to the Oxus with their animals about now. They faced a long hard winter, so there were bound to be weddings. It was pure intuition, but that day we found four weddings.

First we heard the beat of drums, then we saw the Atan—men dancing their furious dervish, spinning their bare feet, passionately kicking up dust to the passionate beat of the drums. They were accompanying the bridegroom on his way to the bride's tent, stopping at various encampments to pick up other guests who joined the dance.

I photographed quickly, our driver and car keeping pace. When the photos were taken, we took off in our rented Russian Zim to go to the bride's tent. There I hoped to photograph the bride being prepared for her groom. Before the car had properly stopped, I was out and running to photograph the women who were dancing outside the tent. I could hear music, then hysterical barking and then screaming. The driver was out of the car running toward me, yelling, but in a language I didn't understand. What was happening was that the wild dogs belonging to the tribe were loose and coming at me. Lucky the driver

had seen them. A woman gave a sharp command and they slunk away. These were ferocious dogs, taught to go for the stranger's jugular.

We were all shaking. I was scolded, then led into the bride's tent. She was young and attractive, dressed in red silk and covered in jewelry. She stood in a patch of sunlight that filtered through a hole in the roof of her tent. Her veil was drawn back off her forehead by her grandmother's hand. Her eyes were shut tight, to be opened only to behold her bridegroom (whom she had never seen) when he entered the tent.

When it was time to leave Afghanistan, Lesley and I wept. We had travelled intensively in the country, climbed the mountains, lived in the villages and the cities and got to know the people. At first they were wary of us. Who were these strange women who had come from another world to record their lives? The women were interested; the men puzzled that there we were with our exposed faces and our trousers in a land where women wore skirts and covered their faces and, yes, existed to serve men. We puzzled them but also intrigued them. At first they were aloof, but as they got to know us—mainly through an interpreter or through gestures and body language—they began to accept us, to laugh with us and to take us under their protection to make sure no harm came to us.

It had been a challenge to photograph these proud descendants of the men who had refused to be colonized by the British and had driven them out with rifle shot and stones through the Hindu Kush; and it was good to walk where Alexander the Great had walked.

overleaf: Buzkashi game,
Kabul, Afghanistan, 1969

137

We returned home for Christmas. It was hard to adjust to London, to the plethora of goods in the shops, the holiday parties and the manufactured bonhomie after the austere but focused lives we had shared. I needed time to adjust, to make my mind a blank, to wash out my eyes before tackling the editing of the Afghan material. It is always a good idea to take time off after a shoot, to let the experience settle—almost like letting the roast settle before carving it.

The pictures expressed what I felt for Afghanistan. Michael Rand was pleased. But before we left on the second leg of the journey, Bill Cater, the accounts man on the *Colour Magazine*, warned me that we had overspent the budget, used up almost all the money allotted. There was still Egypt and the Trucial States to come. We would have to cut down. This meant not only frugal living but also curtailed time in which to work.

I countered with the fact that we had certainly not been extravagant, that intimate stories required time in which to develop trust, and that perhaps the only costly thing on the expense account was the nightly Coca-Cola in which to brush our teeth; we didn't trust the water, and it was cheaper than chancing illness. But I would try to keep costs to a minimum. The myth has al-

ways been that journalists make money on expenses. I'm always out of pocket at the end of an assignment.

The niggling about money was really a consequence of the fact that although the *Sunday Times* paid expenses, I kept copyright and Magnum distributed the material worldwide. It was an equitable arrangement, because the ideas originated with me. The *Times* tried a number of times and in different ways to get the right to syndicate my stories through its own channels, but it never succeeded.

Egypt was hard work. It was more difficult than Russia and, like the Vatican (but without its charm), demanded daily applications for permissions for each situation. The bureaucratic red tape was beyond anything I had encountered before. The atmosphere was filled with gloom and suspicion. The museum in Cairo was sandbagged and its windows were blocked out—hardly the ambience in which to admire Nefertiti's head. Egypt was at war with Israel.

Whenever one encountered officials their first response was no. There would be explanations and pleadings on my part, obdurate refusal on theirs. Occasionally it was possible to wear them down, but by then all the energy was drained. One instance that typified the malaise and sadness of the country: A new Mercedes which had

A sheikha in her harem,
Arab Emirates, 1970

broken down was being pulled by a donkey at the end of a rope. Before my Ministry of Information guide could protest, I was out of our car and had shot the picture. People gathered and started yelling "Spy!" The police came. The interpreter started arguing. When asked what the trouble was, the cop said I had been shooting on a bridge. No one was concerned with the actual image I had taken. It was just because the car was on a bridge and it was illegal to photograph bridges.

When I returned to the hotel, there was a gift from the minister of information. It was a magnificently produced but dreary coffee-table book published to celebrate the thousandth anniversary of the founding of Cairo. It opened with a two-page pullout of a color photograph of the verboten bridge. In the unlikely case that the Israelis do not have pictures of the bridge in their files, all they need do is buy this commemorative volume.

After Cairo we flew to Luxor, in Upper Egypt. There the women took the veil when they married but did not cover their faces. It was only in the oasis that they wore a mask with colored cloth and gold bangles decorating the black cotton base. I photographed the veiled women in a queue in a hospital waiting for the government-issued pill. Incongruous? Perhaps, but necessary to control the ever-growing population.

Since Egypt was, in 1920, the first Muslim country to remove the veil, it was logical to focus on the progress women had made since then. We featured Captain Aziza al Hasum, an airline pilot who for twenty-five years had trained other pilots (almost exclusively male); on Maître Moufida Abul Rahman, a respected lawyer, who was trying a drugs charge in the courts; on Mme. Amina Said, editor of a women's magazine; and on Oum Kalsoum, the extraordinary seventy-year-old singer. She was a heroine to all the Arab world. On the average of once a month she gave a con-

cert to raise money for the Arab cause. People would come from everywhere to hear her. There would be standing ovation after standing ovation. When she finished, men would fight for the privilege of carrying her in her chariot (a Mercedes) on their shoulders from the auditorium to her hotel a mile away.

It wasn't all hard work and frustration. We went to the Valley of the Kings and the Valley of the Queens, attended a *son et lumière* performance at the Pyramids (with Laurence Olivier's voice), enjoyed the afterglow and starshine on the Nile nightly when we had a picnic sailing in a felucca.

Although we had found over fifty percent of the Muslim women still veiled in Afghanistan, and perhaps twenty percent in Egypt, it wasn't until we got to the Trucial States that we found all the Muslim women veiled and the purdah system of the harem, introduced by the Ottoman Empire, still functioning. And there was one more layer: the burka, a cloak worn over the chador. The mask, which until the end of the nineteenth century had come down past the chin like a beard, had during the twentieth century been whittled away until it ended above the mouth. It had originally covered the mouth because men considered the mouth the most erotic part of a woman. Had the women cut the mask back for the same reason?

It was one thing to read about veiled women, it was another to be faced with the reality: the harem is sacrosanct, the women are in purdah, and photography is against the religion. On the plane I became apprehensive. How to make things happen?

It seems that in every story there comes a time when it can be told. Given the right factors—in our case, the oil boom in the Arabian Gulf and the infiltration of Western influences—the door opens enough for one to make contact. Once that takes place and if there is trust on both sides, things happen.

The Trucial States, the northern fringes of Arabia, were once known as the Pirate Coast. In order to keep the East India Company's ships from being plundered, the British formed a protectorate for the seven states, each with its own ruler or sheikh. The protectorate was to last 150 years. It ended the year after our visit in 1971 when the Trucial States were renamed the Arab Emirates.

We started in Abu Dhabi, then went on to Dubai. We visited each of the seven states and in each were received graciously. The story was pure Arabian Nights—even Scheherazade was represented in the person of Sheikha Fatima, the favorite wife of the ruler of Abu Dhabi. The arrangement established by the harem system is that the husband is to spend one night with number one wife, then the next with number two, then three, then four, then start all over again. It was said that Sheikh Zaid fulfilled his vows punctiliously, but managed extra time each afternoon with Sheikha Fatima, his fourth wife. It was in her harem that we were introduced to him—the wealthiest man in the world—in front of a TV set with five of their joint children. He was captivated with Lesley's blond hair. Was she a movie star? He gave each of us a platinum watch.

Lesley loved it all. Her article wound up with words like "alluring" and "turquoise waters" and phrases like "iridescent ambience of femininity." From time to time we found it expedient to work separately. It was during one of these times that Sheikha Sana, the niece of the ruler of Dubai, invited me to a luncheon at her oasis. It was at this feast that I was offered the sheep's brains (the animal had been royally roasted in my honor, stuffed with rice, raisins, spices and its own head). The sheikha offered me the brains from her own delicate, beringed fingers and made a lit-

tle speech in Arabic, which, the interpreter said, meant I was so bright that I deserved the brains—but the ladies-in-waiting laughed. It was only later that one of them who spoke English told me what had actually been said—that Western women were so stupid that even a sheep's brain might help.

It was over this luncheon that Sheikha Sana and her interpreter and English teacher, Alia Abu Alwan, who was also the manager of the purdah section of the Dubai bank, and I became friends. I asked for permission to photograph Sana in her harem. She was a lady and an aristocrat, so her obligation to her guest weighed heavily on her. She handled it gracefully. "You are welcome to do so, but for your personal album only—not for publication."

I felt my responsibilities, too. I demurred, on the grounds that the temptation to publish would be too great and that if her pictures were published by accident, she would feel betrayed; I was honored to be permitted the personal photographs, but I had to refuse. She leaned over and hugged me. She said she felt she could trust me. I could photograph her ladies in her harem. I was happy to settle for that and permission to write about her. She was a shrewd businesswoman who owned a fleet of taxicabs and much land on which she made the desert bloom, and she had a multiplicity of investments in local businesses. She was a powerful and handsome woman who, covered in mask and veil, drove her own jeep.

I had asked questions about customs, from birth to death. She described the marriage celebrations, which she said were magnificent. We talked all afternoon and I left sans pictures, but plus a friend. That summer she and her entourage came to London. I entertained them outdoors at a beautiful Thames-side inn. It was one of those June days when you can believe the minor poets. She enjoyed the day, and as it ended she gave me a jewelled dagger for my son and told me that she had often thought of the day we had spent together at her oasis and my questions about weddings and marriage customs; if any of her children married she would invite me to Dubai to the wedding.

In my first encounters with veiled Muslim women I had been appalled at the draped bundles of cloth, which looked like giant motion picture film changing bags. It seemed such an insult to womankind. To my Western thinking it meant that women were not to be trusted with their own physiognomy and bodies, the underlying thought being that other men would covet them. I wanted to know how these (to me) barbaric customs had arisen.

The answer I was usually given was that purdah was a loving protection, a forbidden place, a sacred place; that it grew out of desert tribal raids and the need to keep women from being stolen. The men I spoke to would quote the Koran: "The happiness of a woman in Paradise is beneath the soles of her husband's feet."

Some of the women I spoke to shrugged and said that a woman whose husband does not guard her jealously feels herself neglected. The more sophisticated women cited the Western model where often the older wives are discarded in divorce and the men take younger wives. In the Muslim world the older wives are not abandoned but given a place and protection within the harem system. They felt the pattern they had developed was more humane than ours. Also, they said, if a woman was clever she could wield a lot of power with the husband even within the harem system.

Occasionally there would be an emancipated woman within an oil sheikhdom who would be wearing a Saint Laurent mini under the shrouds. The daughter of the ruler of Dubai, who was the wife of the ruler of Bahrain, was one such. She would be (like Joan Crawford) covered in matching sets of jewels. (Piaget and Cartier had salesmen with suitcases of precious bijoux travelling through Arabia.) The legend was that she would wear the gems for a brief period, then tire of them, and you would see a lady-in-waiting wearing the discarded sets of emeralds or rubies and the sheikha would have an entirely new assembly.

It had been a mind-opening experience to get within the harem and behind the veil to photograph a forbidden world. And it had been a difficult photographic assignment to reveal shrouded figures as women. I had to depend on design and form, the occasional peeping eye, the gesture of a hand or body movements to make the picture. It was a unique photographic problem.

The Monday after the harem story appeared in the *Sunday Times* I received two telephone calls: one to ask me to make a film for the BBC and the other to ask me to make a film for NBC in America. I was flattered but said I had never made a film. The callers both said the same thing: they had tried to get into a harem, but to no avail. I had done so, they had not, therefore they were willing to gamble that I would be able to make the harem film. Whom had they sent to make the films? Oh, their best men. So now they would like to try a woman. The NBC man offered me the newest handheld 8mm equipment. I refused. If I were to do it, it would have to be on the best 16mm equipment, on tripod, and with the best crew of women possible. But first it would be necessary to think about it. I'd let them know.

In the end the decision to make the film depended upon being able to put together an all-women crew. There were lots of leads, but they all turned out to be assistants or assistants to assistants. Whether this was due to the weight of the gear or the tradition of using men only, or because the unions didn't want women, was hard to tell. Things are different now, but in 1970, while my more militant feminist friends were clucking about my going into the benighted medieval world of women of the East, I couldn't find four

skilled experienced female technicians: lighting camera and assistant, sound and clapper loader.

I checked in London, then New York, then Paris. In the end I found a sound woman and a clapper loader in London, both of them beginners. I settled for a British cameraman, and a French woman to assist him. The idea was that the man would be in charge of lighting the empty harem, and when he was done he would leave, the ladies of the harem would come in, and my women and I would film.

In the end it worked, because to our surprise the lighting cameraman was permitted to light and photograph the ladies in the harem. What we were to learn is that to an Arab, if you are not an Arab, then you are not a man, therefore not a threat to their women. The ladies of the harem were accustomed to being served by non-Arab male servants.

I had planned to call Sheikha Sana when everything was ready—crew, storyboard (which was based on my still story), contracts with BBC and NBC, equipment, film and the endless preparation necessary for making a movie abroad. But Sana forestalled me. One midnight, returning from interviewing the cameraman's assistant in Paris, as I unlocked the door to my house a man stepped out of the shadows. He was a Palestinian who had been sent from Dubai to London

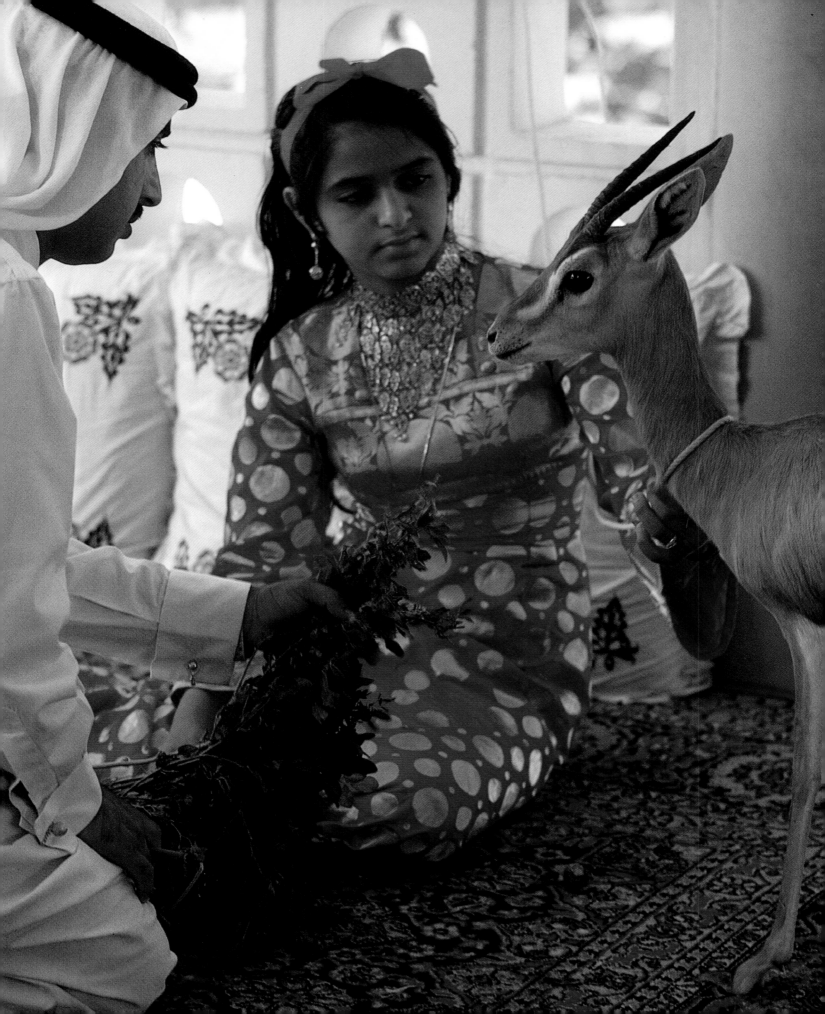

to bring me an invitation to the wedding of the sheikha's daughter Alia to the crown prince of Dubai, HRH Maktoum bin Rashid. The dancing in the desert would go on for three weeks. Would I be their guest for the entire time to enjoy and savor it all? Enclosed was a first-class round-trip ticket.

Next morning I called Sheikha Sana at a time of day when I knew her interpreter would be with her. The operator in Bahrain, through whom the call was routed, refused to put me through. My husky morning voice sounded like a man's. I waited until the voice rose a few tones and called again. This time I got through. The sheikha was pleased at my accepting the invitation, but there was silence and then consternation when I asked about a film crew. Absolutely forbidden, but do bring the little cameras and long dresses—no trousers. Gifts? Lingerie for the bride. It would be an insult to the groom to bring things for the household.

Filming in a harem seemed impossible of achievement. The women were in purdah, veiled, masked and hooded against the world and the evil eye. I mourned the lost chance to make the film, went to Harrods and bought the lingerie, but took the precaution of giving the BBC the names and phone numbers of the crew I had hoped to hire. I called the crew and told them about the latest development. The wedding was in ten days. My hope was that when I arrived in Dubai there might be a way to reverse Sheikha Sana's decision.

Before I left, there was a problem to solve. The union refused to okay the women I had chosen. The male was fine but the females not, because they were not members. Well, give me female members. We haven't any. Then make these four (including me as writer-director) members. This wrangle took days, but the union finally broke down and we were made the first female members of the Association of Cinema and Television Technicians.

The city of Dubai was in high excitement over the wedding. I was met at the airport and piped into a suite in a new hotel on the river overlooking Sheikha Sana's house. With a long lens I could see all the goings on and either shoot from my balcony or go down to shoot.

I was unhappy about being forbidden to make the film and managed to convey that to my hostess when I called on her that evening. She sent a message next morning for me to see Jack Briggs, the British officer in charge of military affairs. I was not to say I had spoken to her. In her elliptical way she was saying that she had spoken to him and cleared the way for the film crew to come in. And indeed it was all right. Invitations were issued by the ruler immediately. When I called the BBC people to tell them the good news they said that the contract had not been signed, so they couldn't issue money to the crew for air tickets. I settled that by having Magnum issue the money on my behalf and guarantee payment to the company that was supplying film and equipment.

It took almost a week for the crew and equipment to arrive, a week I spent replacing the old storyboard based on my stills with a new one. This one had to be changed constantly, because we were at the mercy of fluid events. Nightly the crew and I were invited to a party at which we would be told the plans for the following day. The crew went the first night but refused to go again, so there I was, a woman alone with the government bigwigs—all men. The inexperienced women in the crew were disgruntled because they wanted a hard and fast script, which even if it had been possible would have been a mistake—it would have meant missing the incredible things that were happening. Filming was a perpetual struggle. All I could offer was the armature on which to build the film.

Hint Bint Maktoum
with her brother in her harem,
Dubai, 1971

147

I wanted to use the device used in *The Thousand and One Nights*: a woman storyteller based on the idea of Scheherazade. She would be the link to bind the various episodes in the film together.

I cast Noura, who was lady-in-waiting to the young princess Sheikha Hint Bint Maktoum, the fifteen-year-old cousin of the bride, as the narrator. We would see them first when Hint is dressing to go to the wedding. They are in the harem. Through their lives together we would get a sense of the way the harem functioned. Noura says: "When Hint was born, I was assigned to her, to protect her, to teach her the ways of women, to keep her pure."

Through the voice of Noura, her relationship to Hint and their point of view, the film processes through the wedding, revealing its preparations, including the feeding of two thousand guests daily. All are welcome, from the desert tribesmen to the rich oil sheikhs. We show this against the background of Dubai, the Arabian Venice. In addition to the daily dancing and joy-shooting on the desert there was camel-racing and horse-racing on beautiful white Arabian steeds. On the final night, when the bridegroom went in to his bride, the fireworks, the chanting, the wild ululations and the booming of cannon went on until daylight, acting as a serenade to the groom and bride.

The bride was not to put on the mask at marriage, thus breaking a tradition of centuries. It seemed right in the film, after dealing with this fact, to go on to changes that were taking place for the women of Dubai. First, there was the pill (the women said they didn't know why it didn't work. They took it *almost* every day); then there were the small businesses women were undertaking on their own; and of course education. Formerly the injunction was: we must teach our women to read the Koran, but we must not teach them to write because they will then write love letters to young men. Now literacy classes had been set up for women and they were being taught to write.

There are three images from the wedding in Dubai that are indelibly imprinted on my mind. The first is the camel race to end all camel races. It was a contest between Sheikh Zaid's camels from Abu Dhabi and Sheikh Rashid's camels from Dubai. The two sheikhdoms are traditional enemies. In 1948 they had been at war, so the race was a true contest. It was held over many miles of desert. The two teams of camels were followed at fierce speed by a flotilla of vehicles: jeeps, trucks, taxicabs, an ambulance and all manner of private cars from the rulers' Mercedeses (with the rulers in them and with flags flying) to Volkswagens. The race had become a participant sport, with the racing cars riding practically up the camels' rears to make them run faster. The noise was deafening: screaming camel jockeys, blaring horns, yelling spectators and into the middle of the mêlée suddenly a running sheep. Where it came from nobody knew, but it was game and kept up the pace until the finish.

We were amused by the ladies in the harem, who would wait until we finished shooting and as soon as the lights were extinguished hold out their hands to us. At first we didn't understand. We finally did understand: they mistook our equipment for professional Polaroid cameras and they expected us to give them Polaroid prints. No matter how many times we tried to explain that we were making a film, we never got through to them. Each time we finished filming they held out their hands.

Another thing that intrigued us was the meeting of all four wives of one of the sheikhs at a party given in one of the harems (each of the four had her own establishment). They were convulsed with laughter. The interpreter translated. They were comparing the nightly performance

Prince Maktoum,
younger son of the ruler of Dubai,
Dubai, 1971

(he visited each wife in turn) of their mutual husband.

I worked for months in London with John Nash, the BBC editor, to complete "Behind the Veil." We engaged Janet Suzman to do Noura's voice. She sounded good, the film looked good, and it was well received. The BBC liked the idea of women making films and offered me a contract to make other films about women with a women crew.

At first I was enchanted with the idea; the experience had been a rewarding one in terms of the film itself. When asked at an interview how it felt to work with film as opposed to stills, my reply was that it must be like a celibate's suddenly discovering sex. Out there, all these years, had been luminosity, sound and motion, and I had worked on the opaque silent flat page.

But despite my euphoria about the film, when I started to consider the possibility of becoming a filmmaker the idea of working in a group worried me. I am essentially a loner, enjoying the fact that my work depends upon my own ability to pull it out of myself. The dependency upon others in making a film troubled me: in an *équipe*, a crew, the whole is interlocked, and the end result no better than the weakest link. The chance for error seems to multiply geometrically as each component person is added. And making films meant becoming (in addition to all the other duties) an administrator. I remembered the endless problems when working on the film, the questioning looks when I decided on a necessary move the crew didn't like, the anarchy when the sound woman took the jeep with the equipment to go shopping when we had to shoot the sunset that wouldn't wait. Then there were the personal problems: the clapper loader was pregnant; one of the women fell in love with another who didn't return her ardor. All of it piddling, but it affected the work.

Perhaps it would have been different with experienced people. Still, it would be necessary to train a crew. We would have to learn together, because I was a beginner in film. The first time around I had been lucky. Who knew about the second time around? I was not willing to chance it. I was reminded of a story told me by Bennett Cerf many years ago. Voltaire spent a riotous evening with homosexual friends. When they invited him again, he refused. They said, But you had such a wonderful time. His reply was that indeed he had, but—once a philosopher, twice a pederast!

The actual filming of the harem movie had been a much more trying experience than a stills assignment. I was green, the crew difficult, and when it was finished I sighed with relief. Still I was tempted by the BBC offer. I spent months dithering, seeing documentary films and talking to technicians, scriptwriters, cinematographers, sound people and editors. I was contrasting what life would be like as a filmmaker compared to being a stills photographer. I would be scriptwriter, cameraman and director—as such I would also have to be able to supervise sound and editing and be conversant with how the money was allocated and spent.

I now began to examine my role as a photographer. How much of what I knew could be applied to film? Originally I had made the mistake of looking on film as a compilation of thousands of stills. Now I learned that even though the components for both are the same, they differ in the way the frame is composed. In the photograph (unless there is a design reason for it), the standard is to straighten the lines of the picture against the horizon. In film the lines go off at a tangent in order to achieve dimensionality. In still photography the image is frankly two-dimensional; in film there is an effort to give the illusion of three dimensions.

Film is an entirely different art form. It depends on the juxtaposition of images, upon luminosity, sound and the illusion of motion. A still, on the other hand, is an entity unto itself, an opaque object one can hold in the hand. All of this, of course, is elementary, but I had to go through it to define it for myself. Paradoxically, in spite of the differences between these two mediums there were skills of seeing I had acquired over the years as a photographer that would apply to film if I could unlearn some of my more rigid self-imposed training and branch out to learn a new visual language that would be handmaiden to a new technology for me. Photography and cinematography shared the same aims. To paraphrase existing definitions, they strive to capture and reproduce reality, to enhance the familiar and, by isolating it, transform it into dramatic impact.

What troubled me about the possibility of my directing film was the distance between me and the final film—the intervening people and the intervening technology. The way documentary films were made then was too complicated for me. I sought a more direct technology and worked with an expert in optics at Manchester University to try to design a handheld 8mm camera with built-in sound that 1 could handle all by myself. I wanted to be a one-woman band. This assembly would permit me the same way of working that I used for stills and get me closer to the optical reality I sought. To work the way I had on "Behind the Veil" meant that by the time a crew had set up a shot we would have lost the actuality. I was not interested in the illusion of reality; I wanted to get close to what was happening.

I didn't fool myself that I could achieve pure reality without distortion; that isn't possible. The camera's presence changes the atmosphere and people's reactions, but there are degrees of change within the process, and obviously the single person with small equipment and no lights, tripod or other gadgets can move faster and get closer than can a crew with stationary equipment and lighting.

I was a couple of decades too early for the new, light, handheld video and sound equipment. (My friend at Manchester came close, but we had to abandon the idea because it became too complicated.) After all the research and indecision I found the thought of ensemble work daunting; I decided to go back to my first passion, the still camera.

I love the chance for personal expression and spontaneity photography gives me. I love the idea that I can go off with a single camera and a few rolls of film unencumbered and find instant response to a mood, a need. I abandoned the idea for what the Chinese call electric shadows and opted for the corporeal—the printed image.

It was all so contradictory. Returning to still photography should have been a breeze after the complexity of working on film. On the contrary, I found the still page the toughest discipline imaginable. It was confining and demanding after the latitude of sound, motion, space and time. It was a struggle to settle down, to think and work in comparative miniature, but therein lay my chance to express myself without restrictions other than my own ability to make things happen.

It helped me to ease back into reportage photography by doing two series of ads and some editorial portraits and small stories for the *Sunday Times*:

1. "Manhood," a group of portraits in action of men at various jobs, their identities defined by their work. We used a ship being built in Newcastle to show a number of skills.

2. "The Royal Veterinary College," to depict veterinary training and the relationship of doctors and students to the animals, everything from a budgerigar to a percheron.

3. "J. Paul Getty"—at Sutton Place, Anne Boleyn's ancestral home, where she met Henry VIII. There, Getty, the billionaire, for the fee of one dollar ($1.00), spoke a thirty-second commercial as a favor to an investment broker, who was the son of a onetime partner.

4. "François Marie Banier"—a cover story on a twenty-five-year-old author of two slim volumes who was the darling of the French critics. Of him James Fox wrote: "He leads the social life of a Paris *mondian* more frantically than Cocteau can ever have done, recruiting admirers, infuriating people with his insolence, delighting with his drolleries."

In early September I went to Munich to photograph and write an account of the making of the official Olympics film.

Here is the account, based on my diary:

It was all very gay—the sun shone, the flags flew, the crowd roared periodically, and then the national anthems were played and medals were distributed. It was a spectacle to be enjoyed visually, aurally, mindlessly. I shot an occasional picture, waiting for the oblique, the amusing, the unexpected. I had wanted for once to be unassigned—to be free to shoot for myself, not for layout—and so had come four days before my first subject, John Schlesinger, arrived.

The Olympics have come a long way from the days when Greek men competed in the beautiful nude and women were put to death if they were caught watching from behind a bush. I thought this as I saw the battery of 500mm and 1000mm lenses lined up in the photographers' pit that ran all around the stadium, then to the field where

Welder,
Swan Hunter shipyard,
Newcastle, England, 1972

153

crews of TV, film and sound people awaited the beginning of the 10,000-meter race. All over the field were clusters of people in blue corduroy suits, cameras at the ready; the blue uniforms identified the makers of the official film.

Oddly, I felt compassion for all those camera-toting characters who had to shoot this winner or that one, this national or that, while I could miss the jump or the run or the toss and feel like an amateur.

I noticed that practically all the professionals were using high-speed Ektachrome and exposing at 1/500 second, some of them pushing the film two stops when the light started to go. I went back to watching the filmmakers in the blue suits. They were an impressive lot. David Wolper Productions from California had won the right to shoot the official film. You knew him immediately for the producer he was by the size of the cigar he smoked. He was really making ten films, it seemed to me—not one. He had convinced ten of the world's top directors to come and each make a ten-minute segment of the final film.

"We do things different from our parents in 1936," said the liaison man from the Olympics Committee who stood beside me. "Here is joy and happiness, and is modern. And all these thousands of press people see it and never again do they write about Germany the same way."

Yes, I thought, it is different. The producer of the official film is a Jew. One of the directors, John Schlesinger, is a Jew, Ousmane Sembene is a black, and there is even one of my own repressed minority—a woman, Mai Zetterling. There is also a Russian, Ozerov; a Czech, Milos Forman; an American, Arthur Penn; a Japanese, Ichikawa; Lelouch, a Frenchman; and a German, Michael Pflegher.

If we are lucky, I think, as I pack up and start back to the Olympic Village, where my hotel is,

perhaps the blood spilled in Bavaria will all be expiated.

I slept well and happily that night. At nine o'clock in the morning in the elevator on my way to coffee I heard the news. Arab terrorists had penetrated the Olympic Village and killed two Israelis and were holding others hostage. Rumors flew. It was hard to sort out the facts: there were twenty-six being held hostage, not twenty-eight; there were five guerrillas, not three.

There was a ten-o'clock deadline (what a word to use in this context), then a five-o'clock deadline.

I went out as planned with the black director, Ousmane Sembene, to shoot some blacks from Senegal competing in the canoe races. With us were his Senegalese cameraman and his interpreter-cum-unit-manager, "Ossie" Raghob, an Egyptian born of a German mother—a charming man. He was deeply distressed. Why, he kept asking, do the headlines keep saying "the Arabs"? It's the Palestine guerrillas.

I felt his pain; he was an Arab in an alien land. I asked Ousmane and the cameraman, Georges Caristan, to have lunch in the *Bierstube* near the judo hall, where they were to shoot next. We were all angry and unhappy, and the men started to talk about girls. Our guard was down. I asked Ousmane if he preferred black or white. The herd knows no color, he said.

I felt ashamed and anxious. We had been getting the news on radio and it told us nothing. I returned to the Olympic Village. I had expected protests from the athletes—a demand for cancellation of the games. Not a bit of it. I photographed from my window on the fifteenth floor, which faced the back of Number 31, the building where the horror was going on. There were the national flags flying over three ambulances, a fire truck, hundreds of police with guns, the bus that eventually took the hostages off to the heli-

Student,
Royal Veterinary College,
London, 1972

copters and their deaths. All this on the left-hand side of the frame—the right side showed a rectangle that was the play area, and there in bouquets of color were athletes playing Ping-Pong, chess with giant wooden chessmen, miniature golf; people sunbathing, and laughing. It was surreal.

I was furious with all of us. Show biz as usual, while people were at gunpoint, and with the dead in the same room. All the time the bleating of TV. Would the games be continued? It was a fair guess they would be, since the gross income was $250 million. The horror was the inevitability of it all. It was not a matter of politics, but of simple humanity.

What, I asked myself, is my responsibility as a reporter with a camera? Did not all of us just by being there create this forum for desperate men to tell their story? Doesn't the fact of the camera's presence bring on the drama? I remembered a discussion at the Magnum office during the Hungarian uprising when we had argued about whether the photographer had the right to photograph men being put up against the wall and shot—and Cartier-Bresson's comment that I have never forgotten: "At the moment of death and at the moment of love, one should turn away." Someone brought up Robert Capa's famous picture of the soldier dying in Spain. That, I was told, was a symbol of death—and therefore part of our heritage—but the other, a reality and an intrusion.

Enough of these philosophical arguments, I told myself. I must go to work. I can decide afterwards whether to publish. I dragged myself and my cameras to the front of the building. On a hill in the growing dusk stood hundreds of photographers with long lenses and black-and-white film that could be pushed to 2000, 3000, 4000 ASA. Like so many vultures, we waited. Then we all ran down the hill to photograph the bus into which shadowy figures were being placed, all roped together. By this time, I was too disturbed to think. And besides, it was too dark to see anything anyway. I was surprised, two days later, to find that there was a clear image that was as good (or as bad) as anything else shot from that space that night. I returned to the hotel to the news that all the hostages were safe, drank a glass of wine in gratitude and went to sleep.

Next morning I dressed to the strains of music-to-mourn-by coming over Radio Free Europe (American Army Network), "Whistling in the Dark"—and facing me on TV there were some beautiful African athletes trying to get a ball into a basket. This was interrupted by the news that indeed the hostages were all dead, along with three guerrillas and a German policeman. Then I wept for the dead, Arab, Jew and German, and for us, the living, who had stood by so helplessly.

I went to the memorial service and sat and watched the various filmmakers and photographers, hoping that in so doing I could learn something about this benighted profession I belong to, not to mention something about myself. I shot with a long lens and comforted myself with the thought that I was not invading anybody's private grief. The speeches droned on—translated three times each—and suddenly a mayor of an obscure village in Israel had a heart attack. Through my long lens I photographed a photographer running beside the stretcher carried by the Red Cross men. He was obstructing their work. My gloom was complete.

It was in this mood that I dined that night with John Schlesinger. His reaction to the murders was perhaps the most humane, the most intense, of all the people who had planned a simple, pleasant job only to have it changed into something vile and terrible. At first he refused to come, because he thought the games should be

156

stopped, and then he consented only if his part of the film, the marathon, would include incidents of this terrible day. He talked of various technical ways to use still images and film to intercut while the race went on—a sort of subliminal reminder.

We talked about Lelouch, who had simply grabbed his camera and his crew and gone off to the airport to shoot when he realized that that was where the action would take place. Lelouch was doing the losers, and someone commented that we were all losers in this debacle. Later, Lelouch said he had been trained as a newsman, and that his running off to shoot at the airport had simply been reflex. I was still reflecting on photography and photographers when I went to bed. I was sleepless, and instead of counting sheep found myself trying to count the amount of film that had been used for the Olympics film . . . a million feet, I thought (I was wrong, it was only three-quarters of a million), which will wind up as eleven thousand feet in the final cut.

Other statistics jumped across my consciousness like sheep. Samuelsons, the equipment-rental experts, had masterminded the whole scheme of the film (Michael Samuelson had also done the Mexican Olympics) and had worked on it for six months. Arriflex had built five 35mm blimped (for silence) cameras that could be comfortably hand-held. Samuelsons had built a special prism so the weight lifting could be seen from a worm's-eye view. On the scene were also two of the world's only four 35mm 20-to-1 zoom lenses. Two hundred and fifty people were involved in the making of the film.

Wolper, the producer, had made a reciprocal deal with ABC for the use of their footage. He had been in luck: on the morning the killers got into Number 31, ABC dressed a young British cameraman in a track suit and put his gear and film into a sports bag; he ran into the building opposite 31 as though he belonged there, and

from upstairs filmed the entire scene, complete with hooded men, negotiations, food brought in, etc.

My wakefulness continued, and the statistics stopped. Now I started seeing some of the film that had been shot. A sequence Arthur Penn directed of the pole vaulting—purposely shot way out of focus, and giving lovely vague pastel abstract images.

And a sequence by Milos Forman, who was doing the decathlon. He has always tweaked the nose of authority, and now he was being hassled by the officials—so he shot them at four frames per second. They should come out looking like the Keystone Kops.

Oh, yes. And then there was Ichikawa, who did such a marvellous job shooting the Tokyo Olympiad. His subject was the 100-meter race, which lasts ten seconds, and which goes to ten minutes on film. Although he was probably the most organized of the directors, he started with a script that was sheer poetry; it was written by a Japanese poet. Ichikawa shot half a million frames for the ten-second run, used ten high-speed Mitchell cameras, each with a 1200mm lens and each running at 120 frames per second.

It was beginning to get a bit lighter outdoors. Still no sleep for me. Early in the evening, we had been locked into the village again, and there were rumors of the Moroccans trying to shoot up the Russians. Hell, it was like living in a concentration camp. I poured myself some wine and went back to contemplating the film.

There was the German director, Michael Pflegher, who was doing the girls. Most of the cameramen were bored with the muscle-bound athletes and wanted to shoot the girls. And thinking about girls brought me to Mai Zetterling, the only woman director. It was a joy to watch her work and to see her with the huge weight lifters. She was particularly concerned with their obsession for lifting weights—and I was interested in her obsession with their obsession. I was disappointed to find that she wasn't obsessed—just interested. Hers was the happiest crew around, friendly, relaxed. She and Rune Erickson, her Swedish cameraman, worked closely and without words—he trying to realize what was in her mind and give it to her.

Now I was getting sleepy and must have dozed off. A knock at the door. Breakfast. Another day. My mind was still ticking over. . . .

Yes, Ozerov, the Russian director with his two Russian crews. He was doing the starting line. The drama of the lonely man who faces himself before the moment of truth—so said last night's publicity handout. A story had been told last night that Ozerov had gone to the little church on the Olympics grounds where the athletes came to pray. He had seen a few at prayer, and had brought his crew. On that day there was no one there, so he dressed up his crew and shot them at their devotions.

Breakfast over—so to work. Today was the final event, the running of the marathon, which was Schlesinger's job. He had sixty-five camera positions and fifty-five camera crews and was covering the forty-two-kilometer race, for which the world's record was two hours, eight minutes. Trying to keep up with John Schlesinger was like following a bouncing rubber ball. His energy was formidable, his briefing to his multilingual crews done almost totally in pantomime. He was runner, orchestra leader, whole orchestra, spectator, and member of the Olympics Committee awarding medals. I was worn out before we started.

John deployed the crews, waited at the start line with his two personal cameramen, and—secure in the knowledge that the helicopter crew was gone, the three electric cars on their way and all other crews at camera position—himself filmed the electronics system which kept him informed of the location of the man he was following in the race. (He had picked Ron Hill, an English chemist from Manchester.) And so he filmed audience, press bar, television screens, commentators, the press and the events going on in the field, and waited for the runners to come through the marathon gate. His man came in sixth, but Ron Hill's questionable glory should be that his run and his part in the Olympics was photographed by more camera crews than had ever focused on one man before.

Then it started to rain and the stragglers started to come in. The drill was for them to go once around the track after coming through the gate. One poor devil was stopped halfway round by an official because a national anthem was being played, and he was made to stand still. Can you imagine training for four years, running forty-two kilometers in two hours, thirty minutes, and then being stopped halfway round the track?

Well, I thought, now it is over. I saw John Schlesinger, excited, laughing, his marathon over, sweat and rain pouring down him in equal proportions, and photographed him. Come and have a drink, he said. But on the way to the press bar we passed under the marathon gate, and there in the semidarkness was a black man on a stretcher with a Red Cross doctor working over him. John looked about for his film crew. They were all gone. I'll get you a still, I said. I picked up my camera and started to shoot in the dark.

By the time I returned from the games, the worry about whether I had made the right decision to forget about a career in film seemed to have evaporated. It may have been seeing the massive equipment and money needed for moviemaking. I compared filming with stills: the comparative weightlessness of a few rolls of film and small cameras; no tripods, no lights. Perhaps that swung the balance for me. It might, on the other hand, have been my cussed sense of independence asserting itself. Whatever it was, I felt free, and anxious for a difficult reportage assignment to prove to myself that working on my own, on stills, was best.

The *Sunday Times* assigned me an essay titled "Black in South Africa." The editor, Magnus Linklater, and I discussed the advisability of my going in on a tourist visa. We decided it was too dicey: if I was caught masquerading as a nonprofessional it would raise serious problems.

At the South African embassy there was a form to fill out before one was given the application form. The initial paper asked, Are you a writer, a photographer? What will you write about? Photograph?

My answer: I am a photographer and my subjects are people, landscape, animals. The consul himself came out to handle my request. He said some complimentary things about my portrait of Lady Spencer Churchill—he had seen it in the *Colour Magazine* and said he would process my application soonest. Then he gave me the second form to fill out. The consul's office called within days to say that Johannesburg had granted me a two-year-multiple-entry visa.

I was elated at my good fortune, congratulated myself on my cleverness, packed on a dark miserable day in February and set off for the sun and further adventures. What the consul had not told me, and what I hadn't the foresight to envision, was the way the authorities handled journalists and photographers once they arrived in South Africa. I had been outsmarted. In order to go to the Homelands, or wherever blacks lived their segregated lives, it was necessary to go to the capital, Pretoria, and there apply for the permits necessary for each area, then wait six weeks for the papers to be issued—clearly a delaying tactic meant to discourage the press.

It was off-putting but not sufficiently so to deter me. I travelled and listened and tried to learn. During my first week, eight black students were banned and eight white students were banned, four films were banned, and one T-shirt was banned. It read: "Lo, though I walk through the Valley of the Shadow—I shall hear no evil, for I'm the meanest son of a bitch in the Valley." In most countries the law gives at least lip service to breaking down social prejudice and racial discrimination. But in South Africa the rule of law was used to smash every possible bridge between black and white, to maintain a slave-master relationship. It was the legality and cool, reasoned approach that was most chilling.

Even after the permits came through it was a battle of wits to stay ahead of the police, but I managed. The drill when working in the Homelands was to present one's permit to the local white police, who would then issue their own permit. Their office opened at eight a.m. and shut at five, so the trick was to come in to photograph after five and leave before the police office opened at eight. This worked well in Zululand, where I had gone to photograph Chief Gatscha Buthelezi, the Zulu prime minister, with the blessing of the police. It also gave me cover to sneak into the Charles Johnson Hospital at Nqutu to see the malnourished mothers and babies who were dying of kwashiorkor. There was a sign on the wall that read:

> The Labor Bureau will be here in early January to recruit 1,000 laborers for work in Emandini. Please refer depressed, despairing pellagrous men to us so we can discuss this with them.

One of the days I reported to the police in Zululand, the senior white official, Commissioner General Torlage, took me to a ceremony to install an acting chief. The ceremony ended in tragedy. The tribe had been split into rival factions over the succession since the death of the former chief in 1971. It was decided, after two years of wrangling, that the uncle of the chief's fourteen-year-old orphan be acting chief until the boy came of age. The boy was then removed to his mother's kraal to avoid possible assassination and to allow the split to heal. (The chiefs were paid by the government. They were administrators for the Labor Bureau, where every African must register

for work. Thus the government had effective control over the tribal area.)

At the ceremony, Torlage spoke in Afrikaans, English and Zulu. He presented the acting chief with an attaché case as the symbol of his office—it was known locally as the "dignity bag." He joked about the bag, saying that he knew it was intended to hold official papers, but it really was just right for three bottles. There was an uneasy titter from the crowd.

There were prayers and readings from the scripture, singing from a school choir and tribal dancing. Two thousand guests then wound their way up the hill to kill the cattle for the celebration in the sacred grove where dwelt the spirit of their ancestors. It looked as though the delicate compromise worked out with the authorities had worked, but fighting between the factions broke out at the feast. I read in the paper next day that on his way home, the headman, Mr. Jabula Shange, was axed to death by a rival gang. His enemies said that it was because he had helped the government install the man they could manipulate as acting chief. I began to understand the anonymous phrase used throughout the country: "There is only one thing worse than being black in white South Africa—that is being black in black South Africa."

The worst iniquity was the breakup of the black family. Nqutu could feed perhaps ten thousand but was forced to support eighty thousand. The men would therefore have to leave their homes and their families behind to go into the mines or the cities to work to support their dependents. By law, they were forced to leave their families behind to struggle for survival. Zulus lived on R1.60 per capita per month (forty-five cents).

What would the life of a young wife be whose husband might be away for forty years, returning only once a year, until finally he returned to the

Child suffering from kwashiorkor,
Nqutu, Zululand, 1973

160

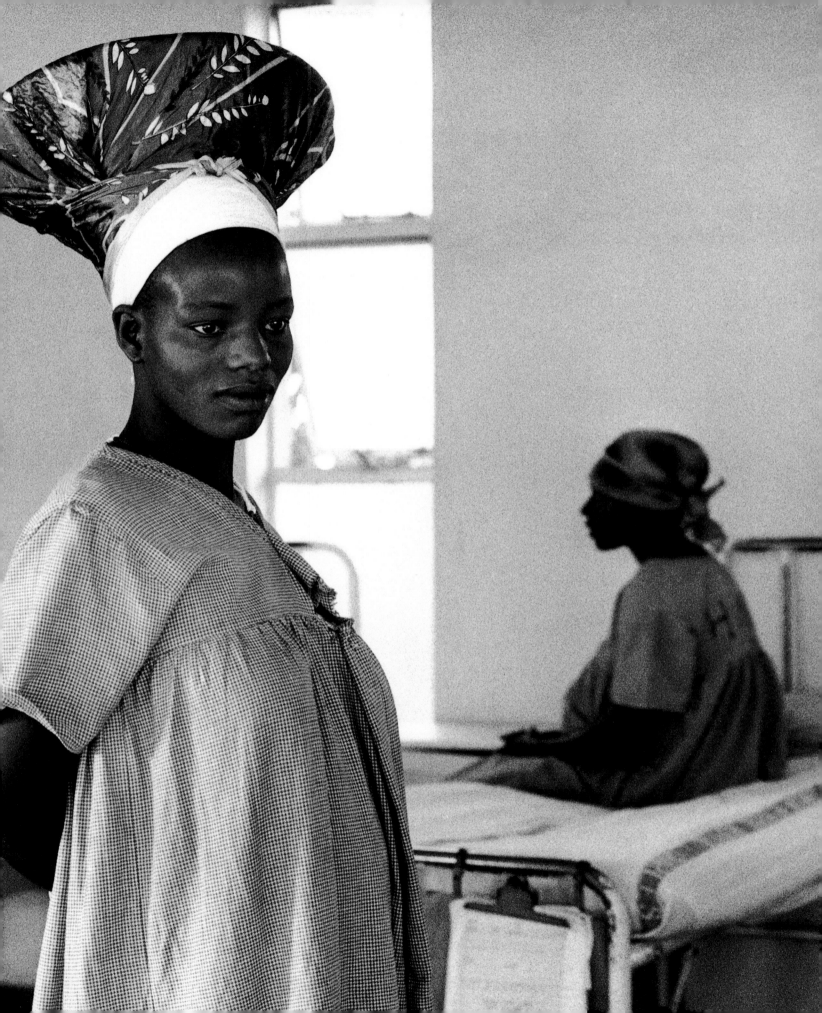

kraal either ill or too old to work? Usually on his annual leave he would make her pregnant. She would remain behind with her children when he returned to the mine or the city. She would not know where he worked or what he earned. He, too, would be lonely, and perhaps take another wife—it was permitted by tribal law.

My initial plan had been to record a single separated family: the women and children in the kraal thousands of miles from the husband, and the man in either the mine or the city. But it proved too difficult to try to present a single family as an example, so I settled for a general story on the women in Zululand and a separate general story on the men at the Val Reef Mines in the Orange Free State. The men in the mines had been reared on tribal discipline. The elders made the decisions for them—"elder" to them meant "wiser." The mining companies exploited this cultural pattern to achieve obedience on the part of the blacks and control by the whites. By setting up the compounds where the men lived on the "boss boy" system and keeping tribal units intact, discipline could be handled at the mine with police chosen from among the men.

I did a series of small stories: a witch doctor, a black literacy class, meetings of the Black Sash Society (middle-class white housewives who boldly had set up to help blacks in trouble with the authorities), a school for black children. It was hard to pin down the figures, but the estimate was that forty percent of the children between seven and fourteen did not go to school because there were no classrooms, and those that did exist were hopelessly overcrowded. Children roamed the streets while their parents went out to work. Education was neither compulsory nor free for the black child. His parents paid special taxes, paid for books and helped pay for teachers' salaries, school construction and maintenance. It was easy to see that schooling was a luxury that few parents living on the breadline could afford.

By the time my permits came through in Pretoria, it was almost time to go home. I had worked for almost three months on the material—in the beginning without a writer, then when he came I turned over notes, information, and introduced him to my sources.

On the day I was to leave I was ill, shaking with chills and fever. The hotel doctor diagnosed tick-bite fever, gave me some tablets to take on the plane, and advised me to go to bed immediately upon arrival in London. The illness went on for months. Mainly I was confused, totally without orientation, totally run down, and my chest ached. My GP was concerned lest I had suffered a heart attack. He sent me around to various consultants, but there was no physical problem with the heart. One doctor, after questioning me about my time in South Africa, said the illness was my reaction to what I had seen in that benighted country. It was not scientific, but his opinion was that I was suffering heartbreak.

The tick-bite fever continued to trouble me for some months, but the heartache, although it diminished, never left me. All I need do is think of people I met and conditions I saw at that time, look at the photographs or think of the worm in the apple in that beautiful Paradise, and the pain is back again.

Miner,
medical examination,
Val Reef Mines, South Africa, 1973

The *Sunday Times* editor waited months for the writer to deliver the South Africa text. When it arrived it was all wrong. The writer had written an essay on the daily lives of white South Africans, not black. He had spent his time dining in white people's houses. His only contact with blacks was when they served him at table—the dish extended in one white-gloved hand, the other gloved hand placed neatly behind the servant's back.

The text was back in my lap and I was too ill to deal with it. When I had recovered sufficiently to write it, we ran into small summer issues of the magazine—too few ads to yield the necessary fourteen pages of continuous editorial space. So Michael Rand decided to hold the essay until the autumn, when we would have the necessary pages.

When autumn came, the whole country was in a gasoline and labor crisis, reduced to a three-day work week, and the miners were on strike. Toilet paper was in short supply, and the street lights were dimmed to half illumination. There were daily electrical power cuts. We lived by candlelight. The poor had their smelly kerosene stoves, the rich had gas heating, and those of us who had electric heating were out of luck. When the power was cut off, I would light the gas cooker in the kitchen, then—huddled in sweaters and blankets, and with freezing fingers—would try to write my article by candlelight. When the power *was* on we were endlessly exhorted to turn off our individual heating systems to conserve electricity. I would fluctuate between a cold ass and a bad conscience.

That dread autumn of 1973 and winter of 1974 were not without an occasional small compensation. In the *Guardian* of January 31, there was the following item:

> A marriage bureau at Bradford is holding a winter sale for would-be marriage partners. To counter the effect of falling wages due to the three-day week, men over the age of sixty and all women are being offered introductions at half the usual fee.

The *Sunday Times* decided to publish every other Sunday. This gave me more time on the article, which finally appeared in the autumn of 1974. Apart from the physical problems, there were the difficulties inherent in the story itself. I had promised to protect my sources, so I could not name people or even adequately describe them. Working on the layout was even more difficult, because there were holes in the story. There were people I should have photographed but didn't, because if their photographs appeared in the paper their lives were at risk. I decided that if there were holes in the story, so be it. I had no choice. I had concluded that one picture may be worth a thousand words, but a thousand pictures are not worth one man's pain.

For years there had been offers from publishers to do a book on the women I had photographed. One such came from a new small firm called Matthew, Miller & Dunbar. They suggested a triptych of women: Marilyn Monroe, Joan Crawford and Marlene Dietrich. I was uneasy about it, but signed a contract and then tried to find a format to fit these three powerful ladies into a single volume. It didn't work. All I kept coming up with was three separate picture essays that looked suspiciously like three magazine articles. We finally agreed that it would be better to have a picture anthology of many different women photographed in various parts of the world.

At that time I wrote to a beloved friend, Marcia Panama:

> I face a year's intense look into myself. My pictures, motivations, and experiences are all bound up here. I am understandably apprehensive—at once excited and anxious; but pleased that it will be done. I feel that until I have understood, no matter how imperfectly, this part of myself, I cannot develop further in my work. I must just stop and take stock. It isn't easy.

In fact it proved to be quite traumatic to go back into my work, which was a large part of my life. In the beginning I was sensitive to every error, every indecisive moment (to paraphrase Cartier-Bresson). Then I became more accepting, more philosophical: that is what I was and that is what I did during whatever time I was examining. It was hard to dismiss my initial reactions. (If I had stepped six inches to the left or a foot to the right the picture might have been a masterpiece—yeah, yeah.) If . . . if . . . if . . .

There is no profession I know that is so fraught with uncertainty as photography, each component of which depends on the way the other components are used. For instance, the aperture of the lens and the time necessary for exposure are reciprocal with each other; if one is changed the other must of necessity be changed. This also applies in processing, where time and temperature are interdependent. These are only indicators of the technique, which, like driving a car, becomes reflex action.

It is the uncontrollable elements like the light, the people before the lens (and the way they relate to each other), the chemicals, the location, the photographer—all metamorphic and interchangeable—that are the creative forces that make the difference between the banal and the wonderful. It is the *photographer* who chases these imponderables around the world who is central to the result.

I've begun to question whether photography is different now from what it was when I started some forty years ago. Certainly there have been radical technical changes: film and lenses are faster, and the speed has increased many times, thus making it possible to photograph a black person in a dark room without adding light; color has come into its own; zoom lenses are in standard use; there are both automatic focus and automatic exposure on practically all professional cameras. The equipment is light, and can be hand-held. The multiple exposure system is established so you can knock off a dozen exposures with one flick of the exposure button. The picture practically takes itself.

But it is still the photographer who has to press the exposure button; it is still the photographer and not the camera who makes the choice of the elements within the frame and the time at which these elements should be exposed. On the other hand, we have gone from photos being about people to photos being about photography, and we are now hanging on museum walls.

When I started, *Life* magazine dictated the style: black-and-white human-interest pictures. Now, Josef Koudelka, Sebastião Salgado and many others have joined Cartier-Bresson in working solely in black-and-white, their pictures being mainly about people. Salgado's tea pickers (in black-and-white) are not very different in content and approach from Dorothea Lange's (and mine) of migratory potato pickers. We have come full circle.

Putting the book together was harder than anticipated, and as the book began to take shape it became clear that the new publishers were as inexperienced as I was. We all began to have cold feet about the project. It was just at this time that Connie Bessie, an American friend, brought Ed Victor, a superb literary agent, to meet me. We clicked immediately. He was (and has been for almost two decades) friend first and agent afterward.

We had a careful talk with the publishers and all agreed to amicably go our separate ways. The advance money was returned, the publishers gave me a celebratory champagne lunch, and I was free to have Ed find me the right editor-cum-publisher. Here I was fortunate, indeed. His choice was Alfred A. Knopf of New York, with Robert Gottlieb as publisher-editor. Over the years Bob Gottlieb has shepherded me with affection and understanding through six books.

Before beginning work on the woman's book, which we called *The Unretouched Woman*, I had to gather negatives, transparencies and various papers from where they were lodged in the Magnum offices at New York and Paris. For the next two years (the book was published in 1976) I was in and out of both cities preparing the new book. It wasn't possible to devote full time to the book because I was doing various ad campaigns, as well as fulfilling my *Sunday Times* contract.

I went to Paris with Bruce Chatwin to do a profile of André Malraux. It was our first assignment together. Malraux sat among his paintings, his African sculpture and his drawings of cats, and talked.

Bruce was splendid in this setting: face animated, tongue darting, green pen flashing on notepad. His French was faultless. Malraux talked, Bruce listened, occasionally asked questions. They covered a lot of ground that winter afternoon: D. H. Lawrence, de Gaulle, the British monarchy, the English gentleman, Malraux's political career, the Russian approach to art, Spanish cafés, Orwell, Hemingway ("Hemingway thought Malraux a poseur, Malraux thought Hemingway a fake tough"), French intellectuals, Afghanistan and Tibet. I sat by, and when there was a lull in the conversation (which was seldom) I would take a picture. The reason for my being background to Bruce's interview was to make it as painless as possible for M. Malraux. He was shaking with what looked like Parkinson's disease and kept propping up his chin and jaw with his hands, so the fewer demands on him the better. Before going to see him I debated with myself as to whether I should bring along a photograph of him taken by Robert Capa when Malraux was a political activist in France in the thirties. He was young, vital and handsome then. The question was, would it sadden him now that he was old or would it please him to be reminded of how young and dishy he had been? I did bring the picture and he was pleased.

My next story was in Rome. I had met and photographed a very pretty Russian model when I worked in Moscow in 1966, Galya Malovskaya. She had talked about her need to leave the USSR, and I had promised to see if there was anything that could be done for her in the West. I showed her pictures to Alexander Lieberman at

André Malraux,
Paris, 1974

Vogue. He then made a deal with the Russian authorities to send in a fashion photographer and crew to do a fashion feature using Galya. *Vogue* paid the usual Western rates (low by today's standards) of one hundred dollars an hour. Galya received her usual seven rubles a week. Typical of *Vogue*, they arrived in Russia with magnificent sable, chinchilla, caracul and special mink garments made by Madison Avenue craftsmen. Galya was posed in all this opulence against a background of various statues and posters of Lenin, and since it was during the October celebration of the anniversary of the Revolution, she was also posed in front of the marching Red Army in Red Square.

The authorities pocketed the money, Galya went on with her abysmally paid job, and five years went by. Then she was called into the office of whatever commissar handled fashion. She was spat upon, called a whore and told that posing in front of Lenin's statue was a treasonable act. After that she was harassed badly from time to time. She decided to leave the USSR—but how? She invented a Jewish grandmother and managed to get one of the Jewish aid societies to sponsor her. She fetched up in Rome.

Galya called George Feiffer, the writer who had introduced us, and asked him to help her; he called me. I called the *Sunday Times* and dreamed up a story on her. My friend Pierluigi, who had what was probably the best state-of-the-art push-button photography studio in Rome, agreed to give Galya a model's photography test if he could be named and featured in the article. Pierluigi and the rest of us hammed it up, the *Sunday Times* did a cover and four pages, and Galya was launched as a model. She didn't stay with it, though. She went to Paris, met one of the world's few politically gauche bankers and married him.

Sweeper,
Castle Medina-Celi, Madrid, 1977

By the end of 1974 I had seriously embarked on preparing material for book publication. I was lost in a wood of black-and-white negatives, a wilderness of contact sheets, a jungle of workprints. There was over twenty years of work to research—and I hadn't even touched the color.

Since I had to mine my entire archives I realized I could do the initial preparation for three books rather than one with very little additional labor. So full steam ahead: *The Unretouched Woman*; a book on America in the fifties, the time between Joe McCarthy and Malcolm X (later named *Flashback! The Fifties*); and a book on the British, whose working title was *A Loving Look at the British*.

My life in London seemed to be lived on various levels: the painful pleasure of looking at myself through my pictures—because my photographs were really fragments of my self. Towards this end there was the routine of identifying and numbering negatives, which acted as a sleep-inducing agent, so that when I went to bed my tired brain continued the numbering. A good replacement for sheep jumping over stiles.

I set up a small darkroom in my living room and hired an assistant. By making prints myself I invented the structure for the pages as I went along, adding and subtracting pictures and get-ting ideas as we printed. It was exhausting but rewarding. We printed steadily in the dark for six weeks—six-day weeks working from ten to six. When my assistant left, I would work for another six hours to prepare the next day's stint. Only when I was ready to drop did I get off to bed.

Another level of my life was what was going on in London while I was immersed in printing in the darkroom. When I surfaced on my day off it was to an awareness of rising tempers and rising costs. People were hoarding sugar and salt, but as compensation toilet paper was available again. People were buying as though this were to be the last Christmas of the world. The theory was that if money was devalued and prices could not be held, the least people would have is this gadget or that, this garment or that. It was depressing to sit in people's houses, gorging on roast beef and vintage wine, and hear the fear in their voices as they complained of rising costs and of a disappearing world.

I escaped to Morocco for Christmas and New Year to join John Huston in Marrakesh, where he was making *The Man Who Would Be King*. We stayed in splendor at the overelegant Mamounia Hotel, ate pigeon pie sitting on ornate gold-embroidered pillows on the floor while being served by beautiful black-skinned men in wide trousers and white turbans. The sun shone. I was a tourist a million miles from London. We shopped in the bazaars where lean-to makeshift hovels had signs that read "American Express cards accepted."

For thirty years John Huston had wanted to make Kipling's *The Man Who Would Be King.* The short story was in the same audacious male tradition as other films he had made: *The Maltese Falcon, The African Queen* and *The Treasure of Sierra Madre.* It had a great yarn and high adventure and would be challengingly tough to make. He not only talked about it over the years, he wrote and coauthored three scripts. Four other writers tried their typewriters on it. John went to Afghanistan, Bhutan, Iran and Turkey in search of locations. First he cast Humphrey Bogart and Spencer Tracy in the principal roles, then Clark Gable and Montgomery Clift, but somehow the picture didn't get made.

Finally it was being made in Morocco, with a cast closer to Kipling's characters: a cockney, Michael Caine, and a Scot, Sean Connery, playing the parts of the two rogues who were former British army sergeants on their majesty's service in India in 1880. They make a wild and dangerous trek from Lahore through the Khyber Pass, the Afghan plains and the Hindu Kush to Kafiristan, to a mountain enclave where live descendants of Alexander the Great. There they plan to set themselves up as kings. The story was replete with brigands, battles, an avalanche, impassable rope bridges, narrow escapes, a beautiful girl and finally death.

What particularly interested me was the tribesmen in the Atlas Mountains who were the extras being cast for the film. Most of them had never seen a film. The tribal people looked close enough to the people I had seen in Nouristan (formerly Kafiristan) to be brothers. I had gone to the villages on a casting mission with Boaty Boatwright, the casting director, and Mahomet

Abassi, her interpreter aide. He was a Moroccan out of the drama school at Berkeley University in California. His job was to test the tribesmen to see if they could act. There was a scene in which they had to become enraged enough to kill. Abassi tried several ploys. First he taunted them, saying their daughters had been abducted. No reaction. Then he shouted that their wives had been raped. No reaction. It was only when he bellowed that their landlords had taken their land that they raged and screamed obscenities.

One day we went in search of a man to play a hundred-year-old high priest. We found a splendid man. He was taken to John for a screen test in which he was photographed wearing only a loincloth. I still remember his vertebrae that seemed to pop like knuckles through his dark skin. This was the first time in his life that he had left his village.

John decided to show him the rushes. Again he was brought to Marrakesh. When he was flashed on the screen there was a great gasp from him. When the lights came on, tears were flooding down his cheeks. His friends surrounded him and asked him questions while he wept. Finally he stopped weeping. "I shall never die," he said.

In August, Bob Gottlieb came to London. For days we sat on my living-room floor shuffling pictures and working on the editing and pagination for *The Unretouched Woman.* I had looked at the photographs too long and was beginning to flag. His fresh eye, quick decisions and light touch got me back on track. When he left I prepared for two assignments: a cigarette campaign in Switzerland (the brief read: shoot 35mm color film, only vertical pictures of middle-class men and women between twenty-four and thirty-five with strong Swiss character in the face—smoking a cigarette) and a trip to the USSR to document the first non-Russian (British Airways) tourist flight. Its itinerary was Moscow, Leningrad,

Kiev, Tashkent, Samarkand and back to Moscow.

The cigarette had to show a glow of half an inch at its tip. The art director and my assistant kept lighting and puffing away to produce exactly the right glow from the cigarette, with which the model was then supposed to look relaxed. The fumes bothered me so much that I gave up both smoking and cigarette campaigns.

I returned to London for a week to clean my cameras and my clothes, get injections against tetanus and cholera and prepare for Russia. One evening a bomb went off at Trattoria Fiori, an Italian restaurant across the street from my flat. It had been engineered by the IRA. I had been scrunched into the corner of a sofa writing—trying to find the right lead sentence to begin *The Unretouched Woman*. The impact was so strong that I was thrown off my seat.

Only minutes later the police, the fire department, ambulances and TV crews arrived in a dead heat. The whole thing was instantly on the air. Then my phone began to ring. Newspaper city editors had looked up the area. Was I Eve Arnold, the photographer? Please go across the street and take some photos. The answer was no. I couldn't bear to photograph the mayhem visited on my neighbors. Through the night, friends and family called from as far away as Australia. When they asked how I was, I replied I was fine, but you should see the windows of the pub next door. Actually, I was badly shaken.

The Russian fortnight was difficult, because British Airways had lost my bag, which contained both summer and winter clothes. I spent the entire two weeks—through sleet, snow, rain and ninety-degree temperature—in one pair of brown trousers.

I roasted in Samarkand and froze in Leningrad, where I bought two cotton shirts I wouldn't normally have considered for dishcloths. In Samarkand I bought a shapeless jazzy peasant ersatz silk dress that had screaming red and yellow stripes. This was my evening attire. When we got back to Moscow my bag had been found and was returned with its contents intact.

There was still the layout to do on *The Unretouched Woman*. I chose Barney Wan, art director of British *Vogue*, to work with me. Evenings and weekends we got together to try to make disparate color and black-and-white pictures come together into a cohesive whole. The photographs ranged from a birth in Haiti, a betrothal in the Caucasus, a divorce in Moscow and a nomad wedding in Afghanistan to women mourning their dead in Hoboken, New Jersey; from the queen of England to Joan Crawford to a mother in Zululand with her starving child. I lost all perspective on the individual pictures, but as a document of a generation of women seen through one woman's camera, it did seem to work.

I had an elegant bag made to hold the layout and prepared to go to New York to deliver it. The morning of departure, Ed Victor came for coffee and a goodbye hug. Immediately the doorbell rang and a special-delivery parcel of negatives and contact sheets arrived from Magnum in New York. I looked at the negatives, said they weren't mine, put them aside, then picked up the contact sheets and burst into tears. These were pictures of my mother I had thought lost and since her death had been seeking. It was a benediction.

So to America, text still to be written, dust jacket to decide on, production schedules to meet and book to be published in the autumn of 1976. But I was tired and jittery, and went first to Mexico, to Cuernavaca, to my sister-in-law Gertrude and my brother Jack for Christmas in the sun. Somehow, the worry that I had been nursing about whether to have someone else write text for the book or do it myself seemed to solve itself. Since I had been at the scene, why not tell it myself? Why a secondhand view? I wrote the text for *The Unretouched Woman* sitting on the veranda in Cuernavaca. Early in the morning I would rise (only the peacock was awake) and take up my legal pad and ballpoint pen and start work while watching the light over the twin volcanoes, Izzy and Popo. I would work for a few hours, then back to bed.

I wrote a short text, Knopf accepted it, and I returned to the London doldrums. The pound was down (against the dollar, the yen, the mark) and the cost of living was up. We were still on a three-day work week and gas was still rationed. There were those who predicted the end of the motor car as we knew it. They had never really believed in it anyway. There was a general feeling of letdown, a sense that the party was over. There were few assignments, few ads, and I was too involved in thinking about books to think up story ideas. To keep sane and to try to allay the nervousness about my first book and how it would fare, I started work on the two other books I had in mind.

Meanwhile, plates for *The Unretouched Woman* were being made in the States and forwarded to me in London. It was the beginning of the switchover from plates being made by people to plates being made by machines. A good platemaker (a man) could correct by eye, heighten a highlight, put a bit of life into a shadow—but the laser could only read densities; it still lacked the sensitivity of a practiced eye and hand. The men handling the machines were still unfamiliar with the technology. Ellen Mc-Neilly, the superb head of production at Knopf with whom I worked on six books, kept the platemakers at it until she got really good work out of a firm in Atlanta.

We were late for publication. When we got to the plant in Chicago for the actual printing of the book, there were further delays—somebody had forgotten to send the formula for the inks—so there were all-night sessions trying to match inks without proper formulas. Finally formulas were sent from Atlanta, and we lost two more days while new inks were ground.

I have now been in on the printing of seven books. Usually the work took the same form whether it was taking place in America or Italy. The presses would be kept going on a twenty-four-hour basis, usually with three separate crews. This meant that a signature might be ready for Ellen's okay at any hour of day or night, depending on problems encountered at press. For the days or weeks (depending on the size of the run) that the book was being printed, we would get little or no sleep. If there was a technical problem, like changing the inks or putting down a new blanket on the machine, I would stretch out for a while on a sofa or on a skip used for loading paper.

The people at Lehigh Cadillac in Chicago were kind and thoughtful to us. The Polish pressmen brought us flowers from their gardens, bottles of homemade wine and fresh cakes their wives had baked. The supervisors took us to elaborate meals, and when we could spare the time, to the movies. Occasionally a macho character (the crews were always male) would try to get away with something because Ellen was a woman, but it didn't work; she handled herself and her work with the authority that comes from knowing your stuff, and the guy would back down.

When the printing was finished I went East to take up an assignment for *Life* on the bicentennial of the United States. *Life* had deployed one hundred people across the country to document the celebration on the Fourth of July birthday. I went to my hometown, Philadelphia, the birthplace of the Declaration of Independence, and photographed President Jimmy Carter, parades, protest demonstrations, fireworks and a fifty-thousand-pound birthday cake six stories high and housed in Memorial Hall, which had been built in 1876 to celebrate the centennial. (The cake contained two million calories. The day after the celebration, the chocolate-flavored edifice was cut up and distributed to city hospitals and jails.)

I had been through a patchwork of problems and experiences, but the one I returned to London to partake in was the most trying. The BBC wanted to make a twenty-five-minute film on me called *The Unretouched Woman*, to be aired in Britain when my book was published. Work on it started out badly, with the director going through my wardrobe. He dressed me in an elegant hand-woven Tunisian silk kaftan, which had been designed for me by Irene Sharaff, the Academy Award–winning designer. I was made up and seated in the center of my living room. When the lights and the cameras were trained on me, the director, who doubled as interviewer, said: "Now tell me about yourself."

It would have frozen an experienced subject, let alone someone all of whose experience was on the other side of the camera. Even though I objected violently to this kind of talking-head portrayal, we did film this situation. By contract I had right of veto, so we started over again. The director agreed that we should do a reportage of me at work photographing as I normally did (in trousers). The first subject we chose was black immigrant aging women living in a black ghetto in a recreation center where they came daily for a hot meal, companionship, exercise and to pursue a craft like dressmaking. There were also to be pictures of a women's cricket team, and a glamorous woman: Shakira Caine, Michael Caine's wife. When I finished photographing, the BBC followed me to my apartment, where I was shown working with the processed material. I was being fed a double dose of what I put my own subjects through. I described the experience to Bob Gottlieb in a letter:

> The BBC lunacy drags on. Imagine me being followed with close-up lenses, brilliant lights and a great penis of a microphone, which is shoved at me to show an intimate me at work. It's enough to put me off photography for life— except that I have to produce professional photos under these circumstances to be used in the film to show how clever I am. Since my way of work is a low-key approach based on establishing contact with the subject, and since I do not light at all but use whatever light is available, you can imagine my frustration. I am also expected to talk to the subject, to lull her into a sense of security so she becomes unaware of the crew of five guys.

To replace the talking head in the elegant kaftan, I was photographed in my apartment projecting color slides, editing transparencies and dictating captions in a checked red-and-white cotton shirt and a pair of trousers.

When the film was finished it was okay. It served its purpose, which was to promote the book. I felt a bit the way Mary Hemingway must have when Mr. Gottlieb told her he wanted her to promote her book on Ernest. She went out and had her face lifted. I didn't do anything quite that drastic. I settled for a beautifully cut grey flannel suit.

The Unretouched Woman was published in the autumn of 1976 in America and the spring of 1977 in Britain, where there was a great deal of publicity—the BBC film, a twenty-minute interview with Mary Parkinson on Channel 4, a six-page excerpt in the *Sunday Times Colour Magazine* and interviews in the *Times*, *Vogue* and *Cosmopolitan*, as well as numerous reviews. I was learning to deal with reporters both press and electronic and beginning to lose my reticence. Interviewers were sympathetic, because they realized that it wasn't easy for me to come out from behind the camera.

I was learning, too, from watching Margaret Thatcher, whom I was following around for a cover story for the *Sunday Times*.

In the beginning of her drive to become prime minister she was an object lesson in how not to behave toward the press. She was abrasive and tried to impose her will by toughness. When I photographed her she would tell me where to stand and what to do. I resented it, as did most reporters, but as she felt more secure with the new persona forged for her by her advisers—new dentition, new hairdo, smart clothes, softer, deeper voice—she used her personal authority and style as well as the power of her office to gain whatever ends she sought.

It is interesting to contrast the powerhouse she became with the woman I met for the first time in the Orkneys: badly dressed, badly coiffed, grim smile. She was doing what Americans call "pressing the flesh"—shaking hands. She was fierce in her dealings with people. We went into a grocer's shop, where she clutched an Orkney cheese. She indicated to me where I was to stand, and she became the grocer's daughter she was.

At the Conservative Party Conference in Blackpool she scared me with talk of law and order. It had echoes of the Joe McCarthy days in America, but when she started electioneering hard she didn't concentrate on that theme but started in a grandiose way to try to create an image of herself in people's minds which was coupled with Winston Churchill. Her adviser responsible for press and TV relations, Gordon Reece, called me to arrange for photographs that would show her in Churchill's footsteps—or at least posing with statues of Churchill, to try to create that illusion. I thought at first that it was some kind of joke, but realized that she and her mentors were dead serious. There was a sculptor friend of Churchill's named Nemon who had done a series of statues of the great man, and it was with these vast heroic (still uncast) objects that she wanted to associate herself. My colleagues at the *Sunday Times* thought it was a joke, too. We couldn't have been more wrong. We found out at election time that voters had taken her seriously and that we at the paper had helped with our mite to get Mrs. Thatcher elected.

Mrs. Thatcher was a difficult subject for me. I felt a personal antipathy between us that made it difficult to work. I have since spoken to other women who knew her or who worked under her who felt that she was tough on her own sex. It didn't help that I found the direction in which she was leading the country reprehensible. No matter how much my sense of fair play demanded that I mustn't let our political differences stand in the way, in the end it was she who revealed herself as the strong, hectoring woman she was.

I find it is impossible for me to dissociate myself from the situation—inevitably and often unconsciously, my point of view injects itself, so that when people in front of the camera show interesting aspects of themselves I click the shutter. In that sense Norman Parkinson was right when he said the camera is a scalpel.

It was interesting to go from the election of a prime minister to another British institution, the queen's Silver Jubilee. When the celebration of the twenty-fifth anniversary of the reign of Elizabeth II began, there was a so-what attitude on the part of her subjects, but as the week progressed, London began to sprout with neighborhood parties: battered upright pianos were wheeled out onto sidewalks, voices were raised in song, and the dancing in the streets began. Sidewalk artists drew messages of praise in chalk, people's faces were painted (for a small fee) with the Union Jack, and overnight there was a countermovement called the Anti-Jubilee that held its own

festivities—all in good humor. Throughout the city, celebrants—young and old, black, white and yellow—joined the fun. I was assigned to photograph the preparation for the trooping of the color, and it was a hoot. When the adjutant inspected the troops before their departure for performance he was followed by a little man who painted in with black paint all the bald spots on the black horses.

Even the cynical *Sunday Times* got carried away and decided to do a special newsstand issue. Toward that end, Michael Rand brought in fifteen prestigious photographers (including Cartier-Bresson) and we were deployed around the city. On the anniversary day I found myself caught up in the hoopla racing after gilded coaches and drum-and-bugle corps on horse, photographing various private parties, and as evening drew near rushing from the queen's procession to St. Paul's to a river regatta in which the Dunkirk boats (tarted up in bunting and lights) passed the queen's barge in salute. The boats were so small, appeared so gallant, that perhaps that was the most appealing part of the entire Jubilee.

The mood of the photographers, reporters and editors was so jolly that it was reminiscent of the old days at *Life*. The material produced was in keeping with the pleasure we derived from the group effort. It was so good that Harry Evans decided to do a Silver Jubilee book. Nobody noticed that we had all missed the one expected picture of the queen. We were told that as her gold coach moved down Pall Mall she would be to the right of Prince Philip because he should be protecting her with his sword arm (his right) free. Of course, these instructions were wrong—and the photographers were on the wrong side to get the definitive picture of Her Majesty on her special day. Nobody noticed, nobody cared. We, the photographers, had had a field day.

The last week in July I went to Paris with Joe Losey, the film director, to do an assignment for French *Vogue*. Triannually the magazine turned over forty pages to a personality (they had used Alfred Hitchcock, Marlene Dietrich, John Huston) to create whatever he or she chose for publication. When asked, Joe (with whom I had worked on *Modesty Blaise*) said he would do it if I would. We chose as our theme "Backstage at the Collections." Together we planned layout and strategy. We were to shoot eighteen collections in five days: clothes, models, designers, audience, the lot. In one day there were seven showings, each in a different part of Paris. We were to move from place to place by motorcycle escort. I was at once delighted and terrified of the responsibility. If I failed, what would they say on those forty blank pages offered me? "Compliments of a friend"?

One thing neither Joe nor I anticipated was that if he took time to direct me during the actual event, I would miss the crucial moment. So we would discuss the possible situation beforehand and then I would try to give it to him. It was adrenaline-producing!

We had decided to tell the story of *haute couture* collections backstage so that people who had never seen them would know what they were like. As we travelled from one collection to another, a car filled with lights followed us. I never once used those lights. I wanted the raw reality, not the photographer's illusion. Joe was a bit nervous about this. When we were photographing a black model in a dark hall at Maxim's where there was just a single bare bulb, Joe asked about the lighting. I said, "Don't worry, Joe, just light a match." The picture was used as a stunning double-page spread, the model's dark eyes glittering through the shadows.

Each evening after a dinner discussion with Joe about the next day, I would return to my hotel

Margaret Thatcher
with Churchill statues,
London, 1977

179

to check over the day's work, which the Magnum Paris office had processed. We had to keep up so Jocelyn Kargere, the art director, could plan his layout. The time pressure, the work pressure and the designers' egos that had to be satisfied (Saint Laurent, Marc Bohan, Pierre Cardin) left me tingling with excitement.

Another problem arose about retouching. Mme. Grès, who was then in her seventies, had always refused to be photographed except briefly on her runway after the presentation of her collection. I wanted her creating her splendid sculptural dresses on her models, but through official channels she had graciously refused. I thought that her work was splendid and that she herself, when she appeared small, authoritative and understated in a pale-blue-striped cotton shirt, blue flannel skirt, white turban and chatelaine's belt on which dangled scissors and various implements of her trade, was too good to miss. I was lucky. At Mme. Grès' atelier I was greeted by François Marie Banier, the French writer I had photographed for the *Sunday Times*. When he said that Mme. Grès was one of his closest friends, I asked him to speak to her on my behalf. When she came forth to receive congratulations on her splendid work, François brought me forward to be introduced. He pleaded my cause, told her that he loved my pix, etc., etc. She was shy and demurred. She said, "I am not young, I am not pretty." I said, "No, Madame, but you are beautiful."

She threw up her hands in a Gallic gesture of defeat. "Ten minutes," she said.

An hour later I had pages of color and a black-and-white portrait of her. When Jocelyn Kargere had made up a lovely separate little section on her featuring her portrait, I warned him that under no circumstances was it to be retouched. This was the real woman and should remain as such, in contrast to the artificiality of the milieu

itself. I offered to go into the *Vogue* darkroom to make a kind print—but absolutely no retouching.

The editor came to me herself. She loved everything I had done—wouldn't I do her the one small favor? Just touch out a few lines. I had forewarned Joe, so both of us were in absolute accord: kind printing but no retouching. In the end we won the battle. French *Vogue* turned the whole thing to its advantage: it sent out a press release (and got lots of space) that said: "Joseph Losey— Eve Arnold: La Mode Sans Retouches." *Match* ran a picture of Joe and me photographing a topless model. We ended up with forty-six pages in *Vogue*, and on Christmas Eve I received a cable from Mme. Grès thanking me for her "lovely portrait."

When I returned from Paris there were adjustments from high-speed reportage to the continuing editing of the books, and the occasional ad (like a pair of stunning legs on a motorbike for the *Grocer's Annual*). Life was slow and easy. I was turning down assignments to go abroad because my grandson's birth was imminent and I wanted to be on hand to welcome Michael.

My cloudless summer was disturbed at four a.m. one morning. It was a breathless call from a reporter in Durban: *The Unretouched Woman* had been banned in South Africa. What did I have to say about that? The reporter said it was because of an obscene picture of Vanessa Redgrave's bare bottom. My foggy, sleepy brain tried to make sense of the information so I could make an intelligent comment. What emerged was the following facts. The book had not been banned, but an excerpt from the book in *Fair Lady*, a women's magazine, had. And as was customary, the magazine was then temporarily unbanned under appeal. This meant that in some crazy way it could be sold for the entire time the periodical was on the newsstands. It also gave the publisher time to print even more magazines, which would increase sales enormously because readers' curiosity would be piqued.

I found the whole situation pathetic and ludicrous. Here is my reply that was carried in the press in South Africa.

LONDON—The reaction of photographer Eve Arnold to the banning—and subsequent temporary unbanning under appeal of a magazine containing her photograph of Vanessa Redgrave's bare bottom—is characteristically blunt—"sheer lunacy."

She says:

"Shall I tell you something funny? My book, which contains the same picture, is on sale in South Africa—unbanned. But in that book, in the South African section, there are pictures of children dying of kwashiorkor. Now those photographs are *really obscene*. Vanessa Redgrave's fairly innocent bottom is the subject of all this waste of energy and money, and yet the pictures of those children dying of malnutrition go unquestioned. This situation makes the comment I want to make. I'm tired of the silliness; really, I feel violated that something so trivial can take on such proportions alongside the real problems that exist in South Africa."

I have a huge folder of clippings about the banning. There is one full-page article that pleases me. The page is divided in half. On the left, in three-inch bold type, there is the word NO and with it a picture of the celebrated bottom and the words "this picture is not . . ." On the right, there is the three-inch word YES, and with it a wasted child's dying face and distended belly and the words "this picture is obscene."

B ob Gottlieb and I had agreed that for my book *Flashback!* I should write about the color and the flavor of the fifties, but also give the facts. It should be a personal account through the camera's eye but avoid the with-gun-and-camera-through-darkest-Harlem on the one hand and the precious elitist jargon that was becoming current in the seventies with the general acceptance of photography as a fine art. It was a tough brief, but eventually I managed acceptable text and was free to get on with the layout, working with the production people and setting up an exhibition to launch the book.

Meanwhile, Lee Gross, an agent Magnum worked with, came up with *The Great Train Robbery*, a Michael Crichton movie to be filmed in Ireland. (Coincidentally, Bob Gottlieb was Michael's editor, too.) Lee also introduced me to Toiny Castelli, Leo's wife, who had a print gallery and whose director, Marvin Heiferman, offered us an exhibition. Then I flew back to London to work on a series of ads and from there to Ireland to begin work on *The Great Train Robbery*.

Michael Crichton is a polymath of a man: a doctor, teacher of anthropology, best-selling novelist, screenwriter and film director. He was interesting to photograph because of his height—six feet seven inches. The challenge was to show him with his cast—Sean Connery, Donald Sutherland and Lesley-Anne Down—and not have him overshadow the others. But the hero of the film, as far as the locals were concerned, was the replica of the 1855 train they saw chugging through their countryside sixty miles from Dublin. They would come in their hundreds to watch the filming: wives and girlfriends, husbands and boyfriends, children and dogs—on foot and by bicycle, driving cars and pushing baby carriages. On days when the helicopter was filming the train, there was an even larger crowd.

Now they watched Sean Connery (007), in his black stovepipe hat and his elegant black-caped coat, walk across a field and stoop to look at a man's body with blood oozing from one ear. "What's this then," asked the sheep farmer who had heard the train whistle and come running. "Is it a fillum?"

Yes, it was a "fillum," based on a true story that Michael Crichton embellished with fantasy—a mastermind (Sean Connery), a master lock picker (Don Sutherland), a beautiful woman (Lesley-Anne Down) who played a lady, a bawd, a serving maid and a beggar woman. The story was about how millions in gold bullion were stolen on their way from London to Folkestone, where they were to be shipped to the Crimea to pay the army. The film was a period frolic. The producer (John Foreman), the actors, everyone

Vanessa Redgrave
dressing for the role of Anne Boleyn
in *A Man for All Seasons*, England, 1966

183

seemed in good spirits. There was the occasional worry, like the day Sean Connery was being filmed trying to escape on the top of the train and almost didn't pull his head in fast enough when he went into a tunnel.

We had worked flat out through six-day weeks when we were given a long weekend during a bank holiday. We had the choice of returning to London or spending the time in Dublin. I opted to go home. I remember having a beer with Sean Connery in the plane, and that is the last thing I remember. What comes next is my being aware that I'm in a hospital bed, with an intern asking me who is president of the United States.

What had happened was that I had been met at the airport by a chauffeur-driven Bentley, courtesy of the film company. Two blocks from home, the driver, who had a blemish-free thirty-year record, and I, who had practically circumnavigated the globe without mishap, were hit by a taxicab. I had a concussion, a brief amnesia, a four-day stay in hospital and a holiday with Michael, my grandson, who burbled and gurgled at me for a week. During my loss of memory, when I couldn't recall the president's name (the standard question to establish amnesia), a consultant was called in. He started to reassure me, telling me not to worry about my equipment. I became indignant—I wasn't worried about equipment. The intern who had seen me in the emergency room said, "Lady, you came into the hospital screaming about your cameras and your exposed film." They assured me that the security people had locked up my bags. "Where then," I wanted to know, "is my smoked salmon?" The intern and the consultant looked at each other as though I were bereft of my senses. When they left, I prayed that the Irish salmon bought in Dublin was still in the camera bag; otherwise they would wonder whether my brains were scrambled. Although it was midnight, the doctors

woke the security guard, who got out the camera bag, and it was brought to me intact. Hallelujah! When I unzipped it, there, wrapped in layers of plastic, was a pound of rosy-pink Irish salmon. Oh, yes, the exposed film was okay, too.

When I was well, I went to India with Bruce Chatwin to do a cover story on Mrs. Gandhi. The *Sunday Time*s had decided to do a miniseries on two women in pursuit of power: my Mrs. Thatcher pictures to be followed the next week by Mrs. Gandhi. Mrs. Thatcher, as head of the Conservative Party, was trying to become prime minister, and Mrs. Gandhi, who had lost the election after the disastrous emergency, was trying to come back as prime minister.

Since we had last worked together, Bruce had published *In Patagonia* and was now a successful author, a little touchy about being thought a journalist. He seemed to think that the more prestigious title of writer would yield not only more respect but more time with his subject. We started on the campaign trail with Mrs. Gandhi through Uttar Pradesh. She was electioneering for a Muslim woman, Mohsina Kidwai, whom she was backing to win a seat in Parliament in the Congress I Party. This was a trial balloon to see if a woman and a Muslim could win. Mrs. Gandhi had been defeated by the Muslims. If her candidate won, she herself would run for office.

We travelled in a convoy of cars with about a hundred press people, both foreign and domestic. Mrs. Gandhi's relations with the press were maternal: she always made sure there were tea and cookies. With Bruce she was concerned because he requested more time than she gave others. Why, she wanted to know. Because he was a writer and his work required more time, he insisted, and would be more lasting. She gave in graciously and saw him privately whenever he requested extra time.

With me she was considerate and anxious that

Indira Gandhi,
speaking engagement,
Uttar Pradesh, India, 1978

Audience for an Indira
Gandhi rally,
Uttar Pradesh, India, 1978

I get whatever I needed. She would send for me to come sit on the platform with her wherever she was speaking. Except for impromptu whistle-stops where she would speak extemporaneously, there were hours of waiting for the huge audiences to gather to hear her. They would come from hundreds of miles around: by bus and by oxcart, by tonga and bicycle. They would gather slowly and wait patiently by the hour until the hundreds of thousands were in place. Then she would speak—in English, usually. She was an indifferent speaker—and when she began to speak, the crowds would begin to melt away.

Her kindness to me was almost embarrassing. We travelled in the pre-monsoon heat, which was at its worst at midday. We would start early, by seven a.m., make a number of local stops, then pause for lunch and a siesta. When the heat of the day lessened, we would proceed to a huge rally and a late supper.

On one of the hottest days she sent for me after lunch. She was in her bedroom in a hotel. She said it made her tired to watch me working so hard—in and out of the car, running to keep up. Did I have an air conditioner? (She knew that she was the only one who travelled with a transformer and an air conditioner.) She pointed to her own air conditioner, whipped the counterpane off the bed and insisted that I rest—she was going off to an interview. I tried to refuse, but she wouldn't listen, and left for her appointment.

I was acutely uncomfortable at being in her bed in air-conditioned comfort. As soon as she left I got out of bed, put on my shoes, covered the bed and started to leave. Standing guard on the other side of the door was one of her three-hundred-pound turbanned Sikh bodyguards. (He might even have been one involved later in her killing.) He told me that I couldn't leave, that Mrs. Gandhi had left instructions for me to rest.

He had his orders. I went back to the air-conditioned room.

This pattern continued for a full week. We talked about our children (she said her son Sanjay was to be arrested when she returned from a trip we were to take to Benares), about her chances for a comeback, about India's insurmountable problem with birth control, and about Mrs. Thatcher. She was a bit disconcerted when she found out I was photographing Mrs. Thatcher. She said that when Mrs. Thatcher had been on a trip to India she had been so nervous that she (Mrs. Gandhi) had felt like warning her that if she was that tense she would never make prime minister!

I was interested in Bruce's reaction to Mrs. Gandhi. He started out with a sort of boy's crush on her. He saw her as a romantic figure. But as the weeks passed and we listened to people's reports on her handling of the Emergency, the beatings, incarcerations, inhumanity, and her condoning her son Sanjay's mishandling of the birth-control problems, and the lack of compassion she expressed for President Bhutto of Bangladesh, who was under sentence of death, the glow faded and Bruce seemed like a child from whom a dream had been snatched. I, too, felt disillusioned and sad after our work in India.

As another woman, I had desperately wanted Mrs. Gandhi to be a heroine. Unlike Bruce, who had difficulty blocking out the hard facts of her reign, I managed somehow not to let them enter my mental computer too deeply.

When I think of her now it is as I saw her those weeks in India: offering me her cool bed for a rest, reading to her grandchildren, talking of the poverty of the women of her country who when she came to power were in such miserable tattered saris that they were ashamed to be seen at political rallies. Now they came in their hundreds of thousands in new saris, in a rainbow of color.

Much that we know about her is too unpleasant to contemplate. Let her rest in peace.

I returned to New York to publish *Flashback!* and to print the exhibition that was to accompany it. The thirty prints for the Castelli exhibition were made to be ready for framing and hanging to kick off the exhibition for the fall season beginning September 9. I talked with Toiny Castelli and Marvin Heiferman about what we should charge for prints. I was a populist and would rather sell prints cheaply at a price students could afford. After all, photographs are endlessly reproducible cheaply, so why give them an artificial value that only collectors can afford?—collectors who normally put them in drawers to accrue in value. At that time my prints were selling (depending on size, whether they were limited editions, whether I printed them myself, etc.) for between five hundred and one thousand dollars. My idea was to sell twenty prints at twenty-five dollars to students instead of one print to a collector at five hundred dollars.

Castelli argued that that was going counter to the market, that at my reckoning we would have to sell a lot of prints to break even. But they would try an experiment and sell prints at fifty dollars. Thinking back, I see that my pricing didn't allow for rent, light, salaries, the wine-and-cheese offering at the opening, and a profit. We were all, however, enthusiastic, and went ahead at fifty dollars per print.

I felt (with tongue in cheek) that we had struck a blow for photography by pricing photographs at a folk-art level so that students could afford them. That is not what happened. What did happen was that we sold out the show, but not to students. It was the dealers who bought them. Even now prints from my "student" edition often come on the market for a thousand dollars. It's no wonder that at my next exhibition (*In China*), Castelli politely told me to get lost and let him deal with the pricing.

From the very beginning of my becoming a photographer, high on my agenda was a plan to go to China. It seemed impossible of achievement because Red China and America were sworn enemies, and as an American I could not get a visa, but this did not stop my dreaming about it. When I began working for the *Sunday Times* of London, it started applying annually for a visa for me. This was during the Cultural Revolution, and although we never even got a reply, we persisted.

I read voraciously about China for fifteen years. Beside my bed there was always a high pile of books about that fabled land, and at the bottom of the pile there was always a book called *Away with All Pests* by Joshua Horn. One sleepless night I started on Mr. Horn's book. The title was from a quote from Chairman Mao. The book was fascinating. It told the story of Horn himself, a courageous English surgeon who had taken his family to live in China in the 1950s. It was a moving tale about the country, its people and their struggle to find a decent way of life. I read the book through and at dawn sat down and wrote Joshua Horn a fan letter—something I had never done in my life. I addressed the letter to his publisher, with a request to forward it. I assumed the author was still in China. Then I packed my bags and enplaned for New York.

Mr. Horn had returned to England in the late seventies to seek medical help for his wife, who in her early fifties was suffering premature senility. My letter was forwarded to him in London just as he was about to embark on a trip to America. He called me in London, and my assistant gave him my address in New York. When he called me there I was too busy working to make time to see him, but we met in London when we both returned home. Through him, I met the Chinese ambassador to London and various other Chinese dignitaries. I also learned a great deal about present-day China. It was indirectly through him that I finally fetched up in China.

His son had married Sirin, a Thai girl who had been brought up by Chou En-lai. Her father was a Thai revolutionary who had been jailed by the Thai government. While he was imprisoned, Chou En-lai sent for one of his sons, whom he planned to bring up in China. Sirin, his eight-year-old sibling, demanded to go too, so both children were sent to China to be educated, and lived there for ten years.

When I met Sirin in London, she had been through hell during the Cultural Revolution, had been beaten by the Red Guards, and had eventually been sent to Europe by Chou En-lai, where she became the eyes and ears in the West for her benefactor. She was teaching piano in

Retired worker,
Gwelin, China, 1979

London at the time we met, and I took her to the Festival Hall to hear Rubinstein—she was ecstatic. We formed an instant friendship. She came home with me after the concert and we had supper and talked most of the night. From then on, we would meet from time to time, and Sirin would give me the latest news whenever she returned from Beijing. Then, in 1979, America and China established diplomatic relations. Sirin was in Beijing at the time. She called to tell me to go to the Chinese embassy in London—there was a visa to China awaiting me.

Within five days of her call I was in China. The Chinese were issuing three-week visas at the time. I had received one for three months.

I called Michael Rand, my editor at the *Sunday Times*, to tell him the news. He announced that he was coming to take me to a Chinese luncheon to celebrate. The magazine was deep in an industrial dispute and not functioning—in fact, it was not to publish for eleven months—but Michael arranged money and letters of introduction and backup for me. It was all done with great speed and good humor. When I asked him for words-of-wisdom-in-a-hurry, he said, "When you are in Peking, do a story on Peking duck. The rest I leave up to you."

I called Robert Gottlieb. He too was pleased, said that he wanted a book and would work out the contract with my agent Ed Victor. When I asked him how he saw the book, he said he would like to see a book that a hundred years from publication would show people how the Chinese had lived a century before.

I had to move quickly, because I wanted to take advantage of Sirin's presence in China. There was equipment to check and clean, film to purchase, injections to get, packing to do and gifts to buy. I had asked Sirin what to bring, and she suggested that her Chinese foster father (she had been brought up under the aegis of Chou En-lai but in the household of Vice-Chairman Liao Ch'eng-chih) would enjoy a filet of beef and some *dolcelatte* cheese; he had spent many years in America and was nostalgic for good beef. I had Allen (the great butcher on my street) freeze and pack a filet of beef against leakage. I had Harrods pack the cheese properly. I bought the usual scarves, books and toys for adults and children and bought myself a fleece-lined coat, fur-lined boots and heavy gloves. I hoped for a trip on the Yangtze and wanted to be prepared for freezing weather.

Sirin met me at the airport in Beijing along with an interpreter and a senior member of the Tourist Bureau, under whose auspices I had come to China. Although it was nine o'clock at night when we got to the Peking Hotel, they all came up to my room with the itinerary they had planned for me. I had been travelling for twenty-four hours and was numb with exhaustion, and begged their indulgence to meet in the morning instead. They seemed worried at my asking for this change in plan but were satisfied when I suggested we meet at six a.m. to photograph people in the public squares doing tai chi. This was the first item on their agenda. After accomplishing it, we would meet for breakfast to go over the rest of the itinerary.

Sirin and I had a light supper and a long conversation in which she filled me in on conditions in China: the mood of the people was pure euphoria; they were thrilled with the pact with America and determined that their country be industrialized by the year 2000. The slogan being used for the New Long March was "Mobilize the masses to make contributions for the Four Modernizations: Agriculture, Industry, National Defense and Science and Technology." She said that as an American photographer I would be given top-priority treatment. After she left, I was so excited I couldn't sleep.

The Beijing winter was severe, and I was glad for my heavy clothing when the interpreter called for me at six sharp the next morning. I photographed the graceful tai chi and wushu (a form of shadow boxing performed by the young) at Tungtan Park and then returned to the Peking Hotel for my briefing. It was agreed that I would use the hotel as a base, taking only what was necessary for each leg of the journey. I would return from time to time to leave exposed film and pick up fresh, get messages, have clothes cleaned, etc., etc.

My hosts had stuffed my itinerary as tight as a Christmas goose. They had taken literally my request that I wanted to see as much as possible of daily life in China. The general plan was to start at six every morning and stop only for meals and an hour's siesta after lunch. The evenings were all organized for me to photograph whatever entertainment was available. The diversions ranged from the most sophisticated operas in the cities to the most naively sweet children's plays in the factories or communes.

The first day's work was a sample of what was to follow for the next ninety. To get a feel of the city we drove around Beijing, stopping for the interpreter to make a speech about what I was seeing and for me to take notes. It was considered bad form to interrupt her set speech. I would then photograph, and it was only after this that I would be expected to ask questions. The pattern would vary when we were travelling. Then we would be joined by a local member of the Tourist Bureau who was familiar with the local terrain and situations. Often the interpreter would need an interpreter. So in Canton it would be (if I was speaking) English to Mandarin to Cantonese and then back again.

That first day, in addition to the morning tai chi and the conference about the itinerary, we visited the Temple of Heaven, where the emper-

ors used to go to pray for an abundant harvest; a playground; the Pai Hai Park, where people were ice skating; and another playground, where there was a slide in the shape of an elephant.

The next day we visited markets, photographed in Tiananmen Square, and went to the Forbidden City, but the highlight of the day was lunch with Vice Chairman Liao, Sirin's friend, the beef eater. He was seventy, round, and had a wicked combination of wit and humor. His father had been Sun Yat-sen's adviser and had been assassinated. His mother was a classical painter: she did landscapes, animals and flowers on beautiful scrolls, he filled in the human figures. His curriculum vitae was special. He had lived in San Francisco, spoke fine literary English, had gone on the Long March, and was head of the Japanese/Chinese Friendship Society, which he had founded.

When I photographed him, he was impressed with the fact that I used "no frash." He then described a Chinese photographic session: the first man carries in the camera, the second man carries in the tripod, the third man arrives with the "frash," the fourth man fits the whole assembly together, the fifth man carries in the photographer, and the sixth man comes in to tell the subject to "smire." All this was told with a wicked grin. Of course, he said, it was a gross exaggeration. But could I teach their photographers to work with available light to ease their burden of heavy gear? I said I would try. Accordingly, a directive went out asking local photographers to offer me any assistance they could, and to watch me at work and try to learn.

Wherever I went, delegations of photographers would show up. A comedy of errors would ensue that would leave me spent with laughter and lucky if I could get pictures in focus, I was so busy trying to keep a straight face. They would appear in droves, all the sub–Irving Penns with their sub-rip-off Hasselblads, their "frash," their assistants and their Fuji color. They were still shooting fifties-style, did not know the 35mm miniature camera had been invented and were still retouching heavily.

From me they wanted an easy formula—what my father would have called learning the Torah standing on one foot. Their questions drove me to distraction. To ease my burden I came up with various basic tips like "Focus on the eyes," "Know that a lens is at its sharpest between f5:6 and f8," and so on.

My charges became instant experts. They would point out where I was to stand to get the best picture and correct me when I chose to shoot into the sun. Then when in despair I would stand with the sun on the subject, carefully angling myself to get my own shadow out of the way, they would come and stand next to me and put their shadows into the picture. When I was working in the Electric Shadow Factory (film studio), whenever I found a bit of splendid murky shadow area to shoot in, someone would instantly bring a lamp to light up the shadows. Of course, they were just trying to help me. On the film set there was a wonderful slapdash democratic attitude to their work. Everybody from the sweeper to the cameraman got involved and offered suggestions.

It wasn't only the additional burden of handling the photographers that made work difficult, it was the cultural differences. In the cities, where tourists and their cameras were the norm, there were few problems, but as soon as I got outside Beijing I would gather crowds, mainly children, who would close in so I couldn't work. When I moved they would follow after in queues, until on some days I felt like the Pied Piper of Hamelin. In areas where people had never seen a white woman or a street photographer there were always difficulties. Once I started photographing an herb seller. The government had just declared

that there could be a free market, that not everything had to be sold through government channels, and that as long as the seller didn't exploit another citizen, commercial transactions were encouraged. This was a historic change in the Chinese brand of communism. Everybody in the tiny market in the country village near Beijing where I had gone was excited. But when I started clicking away, there were screams from my subject. She tried to stop me by yelling and flailing her arms at me. My interpreter came running and tried to explain that I was a friend of China and a fine photographer. "A fine photographer," hooted the lady. "How could she be a fine photographer? She doesn't even have a studio! All she can do is get in the way of honest people who are trying to earn a living."

Although the plan set for me by the Chinese was demanding to the point of exhaustion, it was actually the best way to keep the fresh impressions coming. They piled one event on top of another: kaleidoscopic, colorful and immediate. It meant calling into play enormous stores of patience, forbearance and tact. It meant keeping notes and interviews up to date before the vividness could fade. To do this I would wake at five, have a cup of tea from the thermos at my bedside, review the previous day's events and prepare whatever data would be needed for text and captioning.

I tried to set up a routine, but it wasn't easy. The endless markets, handicraft workshops, schools, sanatoria, museums and scenic spots were hard to differentiate after a while. The different sounds stemming from different dialects, the smells, the varied peoples (there were fifty-six separate minorities) and their varied physiognomies kept me in a state of bewilderment.

As I visited communes and factories, hospitals and schools, theatres and film studios in cities and in the countryside and talked to workers and

Family in alpine forest,
Sinkiang, China, 1979

194

cadres, peasants and city dwellers, people high in government and ordinary citizens, what struck me most forcibly was the people's faith that they were part of a grand design to build a better China for their children and their children's children and for "ten thousand generations to come." It was that faith that literally moved people to move mountains in China. What a sadness that it all was to culminate in the horror of Tiananmen Square.

Looking now at *In China* I am impressed with my audacity in trying to tell the story of so vast a country in a single book. My two books before it had been compilations of existing material tied to a theme: *The Unretouched Woman* was about women, *Flashback!* was about America in the fifties. They had both been photographed over a period of twenty years in a country that I knew well and whose language was my birthright. Now in six months (there were two three-month trips) I was taking on an assigned book in a land whose culture and language couldn't be more alien to me. The only theme that I thought might encompass the whole was the daily lives of the people, and the only familiar constants were my skills or lack of them as photographer and journalist. I was high on the knowledge I had acquired in fifteen years of research and the fact that I had managed to get the go-ahead from the Chinese for a three-month visa while they were doling out three-week visas even to famous writers.

Another motive that drove me was anger brought on by being patronized by the grandmother of my friend Michelangelo Durazzo, the Baroness Garnier Caetani, who as wife of the Belgian ambassador to the court of the Celestial Kingdom had spent three years in China in the early part of the century. She had been slighting of my travels—Europe, Russia, Afghanistan, the Caribbean, America, South Africa, etc.

Have you been to China? Not? Then, my dear, yours is *pedestrian* travel. It infuriated me. I would show her—she hadn't been to Tibet or Mongolia. I'd notch up more Chinese miles than she had. In fact, my tally for the six months was forty thousand.

After a week in and around Beijing, I took off for Chungking, a journey down the Yangtze, Wuhan, Shanghai, Soochow, Hangchow, Gwelin, Foochow and Canton.

I had the sniffles when I left Beijing. They turned into a light cold in Chungking. On the ship carrying us down the Yangtze I developed a serious chill and a hacking cough. When the frigid Siberian wind struck in Shanghai, I got bronchitis. In Soochow I was taken into hospital, where X-rays showed pneumonia. The X-rays also showed old tuberculosis lesions. I thought they were the kind of old battle scars everybody had, but the doctors were nervous and decided to treat me on the basis of tuberculosis—a chronic disease that would take six months to treat on ordinary medication. So they decided on twice-daily streptomycin injections.

Every morning and every evening a doctor would come to my hotel to give me an injection. They kept me in bed for a week. After a few days, the fever receded in the mornings and I would be permitted out for an hour or two to work.

So, bundled to the eyes, I would venture forth. It was on one of these forays that I photographed the magnificent Chinese lady who was used on the cover of my book. I saw her in a doorway. She withdrew into the shadows, so that only the ancient face, with seams like the pleats on a Fortuny dress, shone forth. We looked at each other through the lens and then after a beat I clicked the shutter. It is said in China that a beautiful young woman is a joy to be expected, but a beautiful old woman is a work of art.

Bottler in a beer factory,
Tsingtao, China, 1979

I knew the instant I saw her how remarkable that face was, and I sent my interpreter, Kuan Sui Hua, back for vital statistics. I was shaking with fever and excitement. All the information she returned with was that the woman was a retired worker. Name? Age? Marital status? Children? The interpreter thought she shouldn't pry. When the book was published I sent a copy to the lady, asking Hsinhua, the news agency, to find her. I never heard whether they did. It might have been nice for her to know that her picture appeared on the cover of *In China* in ten countries.

I continued my trip around China at a slower pace. I could get all the pictures and information I needed by cutting down on duplications in the form of factories, workshops, schools and other institutions. I had realized that the Chinese were very proud of the progress they were making industrially: every machine, every tractor factory was an achievement, and they wanted them all photographed and documented.

I asked to move from workers' quotas to concentrate on medicine, education, living conditions, birth control and old-age homes. There were trade-offs, and occasionally handling these matters was ticklish. I realized just how important it was for Chinese self-esteem to show what advances they were making when a senior cadre we met on the Yangtze pointed out the industrial waste floating on the river. "Look," he said, "we're industrialized." I thought he was being cynical. Not at all. He was proud that the Celestial Kingdom had joined the twentieth century.

On another occasion, a senior editor at Hsinhua pointed out a statistic on a production sheet from one of the communes: the production and sale of tobacco had doubled in the year 1978. I couldn't help mentioning that then the Chinese could expect more lung cancer. With a perfectly

straight face the man replied, "Yes, but we're catching up with the West." He wasn't joking, either.

We returned to Beijing to see Mme. Sun Yat-sen. She received me sitting under a photograph of her husband. She was tiny—barely five feet tall—and her little feet hung just above the stretcher on an impressive high chair. She lived in the palace where the last emperor of the Ching dynasty last lived. It was snowing, and she said she longed to go out in it, but sadly her health did not permit it.

She said she had heard that I was a longtime friend of China, and she wanted to thank me for that. Did I know Cecil Beaton? He had come to China and photographed her during the war, but she had never seen the pictures. (When I returned to London I located them in the War Museum archives and ordered the four that were on file—for all of seven pounds forty-one pence—and had them sent to her.)

I had brought her a photograph of mine, the baby's and mother's hands immediately after birth. She asked me to inscribe it. "Do I address you as Madame?" "No, no, we are friends. Either 'Soong Chieng Ling'"—she did not like the new spelling Sung—"or as 'comrade.'" What I wrote to that indomitable spirit I do not remember, but I do know it began with "comrade." She had touched me deeply. When I returned to my hotel there was a box of candy from her. Her note to me began, "Dear comrade . . ."

China was much at the forefront of Western news at this time, and corporations were vying for permission to come to China to display their wares. Pierre Cardin was one, and the Coca-Cola Corporation was another. They would cloak their interest in the guise of cultural events.

Pierre Cardin, who was consultant to the

China silk industry, brought in his models and his Paris collection and gave a fashion show in Beijing with the French ambassador to China as host. Next day he took the models to the Great Wall and the Ming Tombs. It was snowing at the Great Wall. The Chinese tourists couldn't contain their laughter at the chiffon-clad models disporting themselves for the cameras. The pictures were, of course, being taken to garner international publicity for Cardin. When he went to the tombs, the models posed against elephants (couchant, marble). Just then a farmer driving a horse-drawn wagon full of hay drove past. His expression as he saw the scantily chiffon-clad goose-fleshed models was one of shock, then he shook his head and drove on. One wondered how he squared this apparition with all he had been told (in another era) about the decadent West.

The Coca-Cola episode was different. The Chinese were invited not only to drink the product but to come and listen to the orchestra—the Boston Pops, with Osawa conducting—that Coke had sponsored and brought to play with the Beijing orchestra. It was an emotional evening. The Beijing orchestra had been disbanded during the Cultural Revolution, and many of its members were jailed or put under house arrest. Some of them had not played an instrument for years. It was touching to see Chinese instruments onstage with Western instruments. When the combined orchestras played the Beethoven *Fifth* there were tears and sobs, and when the program ended with "Yankee Doodle Dandy" there was prolonged applause and a standing ovation.

After the concert, my team—interpreter, local interpreter, Hsinhua representative and I—went up to my hotel room to wash up before attending a party for the orchestra. Waiting for us was a gift from Coca-Cola, a full case of the stuff. When I asked my guests whether they wanted tea, beer or Coke, they laughed and all asked for Coke. I

watched surreptitiously as they took a first sip. Each one sort of gagged, smiled politely and put the drink down, not to be picked up again. It was just as well they weren't enamored of it—it sold for a dollar a bottle, a day's average wage in China.

After the concert I kept wondering how people in the arts had fared during the Cultural Revolution and how they were being treated now that it was over. I was taken to meet a leading painter, Huan Yung Yu, who was preparing an exhibition that was to open the following week.

His story would serve, he said, as an example of the horrors experienced by people in his field. A friend had asked him to draw a picture of an owl. He drew a black owl in the standard pose—the bird asleep on a perch with one eye half closed. Black in a painting is considered sinister. He was nonplussed to be accused by followers of the Gang of Four of making a drawing that attacked socialism and showed hatred of the socialist system. He was also accused of lampooning Chairman Mao—his critics said that the owl was Chairman Mao. (In fact, the bird *did* look like the Chairman, who had a lazy right eye.) For four years he was forced to go to three or four meetings a day, at which he was castigated and forced to listen to endless speeches accusing him of treachery. He was asked for his paintings. He said he had none, the leaking roof had spoiled them.

Meanwhile, he painted at night in a room so small that if he sat with another person facing him, their knees would touch. Friends had formed a network and built him a room within a room which could be closed off if he heard anyone coming. There he painted huge pictures on paper stretched on the wall. There were eighty of these at his exhibition.

The support of friends as well as of others

Nursery in a cotton mill,
Beijing, 1979

he did not know sustained him through the daily harassment and the hounding of intruders throughout the night. He received money and expressions of encouragement, but perhaps the most touching gift was a pine bouquet with the message "Like a pine tree that is never afraid [of cold and wind], be brave and straight."

He said to me, "Something blossomed in my heart. When they oppressed me I never gave in. Now, how do you want to photograph me?"

"Painting?" I asked.

"An owl," he said. With sweeping sure strokes he drew the owl. When it was finished he picked up a smaller brush and wrote something vertically in exquisite calligraphy in the right-hand corner. He placed the drawing on a table to dry. I asked him what the writing meant. He said, "This line says, 'The owl is a beneficent beast,' and this says, 'Given to Eve Arnold.'"

I shall always treasure both the experience of that afternoon with Huan Yung Yu and the drawing. As I left he shook my hand and said in what was translated idiomatically for me: "Once get known to each other, twice become friends."

It was time to go home. Before leaving, I went for a checkup of my lungs. My chest was clear. The doctor with kindness and consideration asked whether I had any other ailments she might help with. Nothing except back pains from carrying equipment, but that, I said, was incurable. Not so, she said. Let us try acupuncture. So there were the needles, moxibustion (the heat treatment with burning herbs) and cupping. It felt wonderful when she had finished the treatment, and I thought, Great—at least there will be surcease from pain today. But I was pain-free for seven years. How or why not even the Chinese know.

It was with a light heart that I approached the final day's photography. Finally—Michael Rand's Peking duck assignment, at the Front Gate (Chien Meng) Restaurant in Beijing. At the top of red-carpeted stairs there is a very large gold plaque. The inscription is a facsimile of Chairman Mao's handwriting. It reads: "Serve the People." Here a staff of 160 serve the people between twelve hundred and two thousand duck dinners daily. It seemed fitting that not only my last day's shoot but my last banquet in China should be Peking duck. I had invited the people I had worked with and their immediate superiors to celebrate. It was a festive occasion, with many compliments all around, with many bottles of Mao-Tai, with many toasts, and with many questions and answers. What was my opinion of China? Had I enjoyed the trip? Would I like to return? I would indeed. When and for how long, and where would I like to go next time? We discussed possibilities.

I told them that it was necessary for me to return if they wanted a book on China. They agreed in principle and said they would notify me before the first of May. I was elated when the plane took off for London, certain that I would be returning.

Art class,
Chungking, China, 1979

202

My sense of accomplishment about the China trip lasted until I stepped across the threshold in London, then a fury of anxiety assailed me. Would the pictures be in focus? Well designed? Tell the proper story? Be good? As always, I was a case of suspended animation—okay until it was time to send film to the processors, then apprehension and anguish would take over with such force that there would be no rest until the processed film was returned.

Why this pattern of behavior? I have never been able to fathom it. During my three-month stay in China I never had a moment of concern about the quality of the work I was producing. Why then the sudden intense worry? It was as though I were holding my breath until inspecting the first finished roll of color. Then, if it was all right, I superstitiously knew that the entire "take" would be fine.

Somehow I got through the two nights and a day until the film was processed, and only after the developer's courier had left and I had inspected a random sampling of the first roll and found it good did I relax. Although I hadn't slept properly for days, I stayed up all night and looked at the entire take. Then I let out a deep breath—the structure for the book was there, and I could project what was needed for the rest.

I fell into bed and slept the clock around. My beloved friend Marcia Panama, who was familiar with my mad way of handling my reentry into my London life, organized a picnic for us. We went to Regent's Park to sit in the sun, drink champagne and eat lobster-salad sandwiches. When we were walking back to her car I heard a screech of tires and a yell—"Eve, Eve!" It was Bob Gottlieb. He had thought I was still in China, and I had no idea he was in London. We made a date for breakfast next day to look at the China material. In his quick decisive way he summed up what was needed to finish the book. It was exactly what was necessary.

The pictures from the first trip were a compilation of the more expected and familiar places and situations: major cities (Beijing, Shanghai, Chungking), and the daily lives of people as they were lived under the Chinese brand of communism (in communes and factories and in the army). There were four major classifications in the book: landscape, people, work, living. So far so good. We had the expected. Now what was needed was the unexpected, the rare and the exotic which had kept me reading and intrigued for fifteen years. I wrote and thanked my Chinese hosts for their consideration and cooperation. And I repeated the request I had made while in China—for permission to go to Tibet, Inner

Folk song group,
Inner Mongolia, 1979

204

Mongolia, Xian and Urumqi, and another trip on the Yangtze. (I had been ill while on the river and had not done it justice.) Could I please have a four-month visa? It seemed fitting that on my birthday I received a cable from the Hsinhua News Agency, my new sponsors, offering me a three-month visa. Could I come in June? They were sorry not to be able to arrange a four-month stay, but I could negotiate a third trip for an additional three months upon arrival.

Perfect. I had been there in the winter, had photographed in the snow; now there would be the blessed summertime and a chance to get away from the Han people whom I had photographed abundantly and who composed ninety-four percent of the population. It was the other six percent, the minorities, whom the Han had pushed to the borderlands, that would spice the book. They still wore their own tribal clothing, spoke their own languages or dialects, followed their own cultures and practiced their own religions. With typical generosity the Chinese had added Hsishuang Panna, a region close to the Burmese border, to add yet another dimension to the mix.

The second trip was easier than the first, because my health was good and I fitted better into the lives of the people I met. I began to know what was expected of me and to behave accordingly. Also, Liu Fen, my interpreter, had been more exposed to photography than had been the people on the first trip. She wrote picture captions for the Hsinhua News Agency and was married to a photographer.

There was an easy camaraderie between us. We wore the same size clothes, and people often took me for her sister recently returned from abroad. She spoke in parables and was avid to learn idiomatic English and American. She would say things like, "We have crossed a thousand mountain peaks and ten thousand rivers" and

wind up with "and we are on the last leg of the journey."

She characterized my three-month mad dash through China by saying, "It was like looking at a flower from the back of a galloping horse." She was right, but in a way it was wonderful to garner all those instant impressions in the mind on film and to unravel them at leisure when I returned to the West. It worked because the camera is the instrument for the immediate image, the fleeting experience, the whole implied in the fragmented moment and the luck of being in the right place at the right time.

In the introduction to *In China* I wrote:

Within China I travelled by plane, by ship, by train, by car, by air-conditioned bus and on foot: I walked on the "Roof of the world" in the rarefied air of the thirteen-thousand-foot Tibetan plateau, hand held by a Tibetan lama who steadied me as we climbed to the top of the gold-covered Potala Palace. In Sunkiang I descended to the Turfan depression—426 feet below sea level—the lowest spot in China. I roasted in the Gobi in July and froze in the snow in Peking in February; was soaked by the monsoon in Hsishuang Panna and was almost blown off my feet in a predawn gale on a boat on the Yangtze while waiting for sunrise over the three Gorges. A water buffalo I was photographing tried to charge me because he did not like the smell of my perfume, and a yak that was being milked by a Tibetan maiden grew restless because she did not like the click of my camera.

Even though I still was shooting some of the more obvious situations the Chinese requested—the army, an engineering university, a carpet factory, a department store, endless clinics and hospitals—what was marvellous was to see the quotidian against the exotic background of the extraordinary terrain, and oh! those wonderful faces.

The most pleasurable part of the trip was the

photography. There was a great sense of fulfill-ment in knowing that what one saw with the eye would be transmuted into an object that could be held in the hand. The hard part was the end-less briefing when all I wanted to do was see and photograph.

I find my notes tell graphically just how irk-some, by the end of my second stay, information pumped into me became. I had been in China three months and had worked and travelled every day without a stop. We were at the Victory Oil Field. A senior cadre was briefing me, the local Hsinhua man was translating. I was writing in my notebook:

—"In the past decade we repaired one million and sixty-two meters of pipe" (my God I'm dying—a combination of the abyss in boredom and the heat).
—(here we go, kids) "Established 1956, four workers to a machine. . . . Our glorious etc." (drone, drone, drone—go ahead, Baldy, beat your breast).
—"I am factory supervisor and only had three years of primary school" (will wonders never cease and my brow never stop running sweat?).
—"Our glorious workers—thirteen million, two hundred thousand yuan saved for the state" (I'm afraid I'll faint, please, Baldy, please).

It was fortunate that my patience waited until the last week to go threadbare. Which reminds me that Liu was beginning to unravel as well. She started worrying about my photographing people who were wearing old and patched clothes. I pointed out that in the West people did not put on their Sunday best to be photographed running a lathe. She understood, but she still worried about dignity, so we struck a bargain. It was okay to photograph people at work in tatters, but out-side the workplace they had to be neatly dressed.

Liu and I had enjoyed a particularly harmo-nious working relationship. She had been tour guide, interpreter and schlepper. She was friendly, she was meticulously careful about keeping to our time schedules, and she had a sense of humor. She was central to the entire en-terprise, but although I was grateful to her, I re-sented my dependence.

I began to be angry at her failure to respect my privacy (she would do things like coming into the bathroom without knocking while I was in the tub). I failed to recognize that in her life, where six people shared a room, privacy didn't exist. (I was told that her language didn't have a word for privacy.)

From her point of view, I was a rich foreigner accorded privileges she could never expect for herself or her family: she earned so little; she was rationed to one egg a month. Travelling with me she lived luxuriously by any standards.

As the journey neared its end, it all became al-most too much for both of us. After a frustrating day of hard work, heat and travelling in a train with sealed windows and no air conditioning, we were both cross. I wanted to sit quietly and work on my notes. Liu's social sense told her that I should be entertained. When she started to chat-ter I snapped at her. I tried to apologize, but I choked up—then we both burst into tears. So there we sat in the steaming train, tears pouring down our faces and with our arms about each other for comfort. We, such very different people from opposite ends of the world, had come to-gether to share many unforgettable experiences, and between us we had produced a book. I tried to express this—my gratitude, and the fact that she, Liu, had been central to the scheme and that without her it could not have happened—but I was blubbing too hard. It struck both of us as funny and we began to laugh. Then we started to reminisce.

We spoke of the highlights: Soochow, Tibet, Inner Mongolia, Hsishuang Panna, Chungking.

Horse training for the militia,
Inner Mongolia, 1979

We remembered the interesting people we had met. But it was the great meals that we slavered over: the Peking duck, the fifteen-course dinner given in my honor by the mayor of Wanxian, where dozens of children had raced ahead of us chanting, "She's here, she's here." We relived the color, the fragrance and the taste of the food, and we smiled over the names of the dishes that four chefs had labored over: Snow Lotus, Goldfish Nests Prawns, Phoenix Tail Heavenly Pleasures, Twin Peaks on a Snow Mountain, Emperor's Paradise, Maiden's Delight, Warrior's Reward, etc.

But it was the meals at the Golden River Commune in Inner Mongolia that brought out the guffaws. We were given (among other things) a dish of wild mushrooms (it only rains in August there—so the mushrooms were a luxury). Next morning at breakfast we were offered what I took to be more wild mushrooms, and I remarked that the mushrooms we'd had last evening had been more tender. Our hosts roared with laughter when they saw my face as I was told that it wasn't mushrooms but the inner pads of the hooves of the camel that I had eaten.

Before leaving China I was invited by Hsinhua to address its editors, photographers and technicians. To minimize the boredom of the audience having to endure my speaking in English and Liu translating into Chinese, I had Liu translate the speech I wrote and read it directly. I did, however, answer questions.

One man who had seemed asleep during the reading suddenly came alive. "What," he asked, "do you think of Chinese photography?"

I was not prepared for this but decided I must tell the truth. Nervously I said that I hadn't seen enough to give a full critique, but I was familiar with the propaganda publications the Chinese sent abroad. I would offer an example, a genre photograph: "Your people are all dressed up in their Sunday best, they are singing, the sun is shining, and they are bringing in the harvest. We cannot help comparing your idealized image with our own farmers at work in their worn work clothes and their sweat pouring down. It is backbreaking work and they haven't either the time or the inclination to sing. However, one thing we do share: we both need good weather for the harvest, so the sun is shining in our photo too. But you show too pretty a picture, so we do not believe you."

The man who had asked the question looked relieved. He said, in English, "And we do not believe us either." There was a sharp intake of breath from those who spoke English and then they started asking technical questions.

I thought about that question on my journey home. It was a loaded question, one no Chinese would have dared to ask during the Cultural Revolution. Of course, so much were foreigners hated during that period of civil strife that it would not have been possible for me to be in the country at all. I couldn't judge if the question showed a shift in the party line, but the man's honest reaction was a hopeful sign. All over China there were slight breezes of what one hoped would portend a "wind of change." In fact, it was interesting to compare the first trip with the second. On the first trip, people were given walls on which to write any criticism they chose on "democratic posters." One could damn and castigate anyone from the local party apparatchik to the leader of the country. All day long there was an endless queue (mainly of men) lined up to add their comments. When I returned for the second trip three months later, the posters and the queues were gone, replaced by twenty-four-sheet posters advertising Bulova watches, Lucky Cola, and heart medicine that could be bought over the counter.

There were other changes. On the first trip the young men were playing guitars and dancing

Buddhist monks studying sutras,
Inner Mongolia, 1979

211

in the streets. There had been no dancing for thirty years in public or even in private places. Wherever one went there was joy, and a shy abandon. This too had disappeared. Instead, on the same street the young were demonstrating against unemployment and against being sent to the countryside to bring in the harvest. These were just minor indices of the repression to come. Although I noted the differences between the two journeys, they were certainly slight. The dominant feeling was a lingering glow from the euphoria that pervaded the country on my first visit.

The book was a happy book for the most part. It included pictures that revealed China's problems, but they were not stressed. I wanted the book to reflect the reality, which was that most people were happy and hopeful that they would indeed be industrialized by the year 2000.

I edited the transparencies (it was an all-color book) down to a manageable number and went to New York to work on the text and pagination with Bob Gottlieb, the layout with Bob Scudellari, and the production with Ellen McNeilly. It was a fruitful time. We wound up with top awards for best book cover and best-designed book; we were a book club choice; we launched the book with an exhibition at the Brooklyn Museum which travelled throughout America for three years (thanks to Exxon). The book was published in America, England, France, Germany, Australia, Canada, Japan and New Zealand and plagiarized in Taiwan. There it was printed half-size, horizontally, and the thieves added a few pictures that were not mine of Taiwanese Chinese, to distance themselves from the Communist Chinese.

When *In China* was published in the United States at the end of 1980, the American Society of Magazine Photographers gave me a Lifetime Achievement Award.

In my acceptance speech I cited the fact that this was the first time in the thirty-five years of the society's existence that it was honoring women—both Louise Dahl Wolfe and me. Heretofore it had been men. It reminded me of the treatment of Arabic women.

1. After the birth of a female the days of a woman's purification were doubled.

2. For the birth of a boy in Saudi Arabia a midwife was paid twenty dollars; for a girl it was ten dollars.

3. In law two female witnesses equalled one male witness.

4. A man's inheritance was double that of a woman's.

5. For a woman killed the blood money was half that paid for a man.

Now by choosing two women I hoped they weren't equating two of us with one of them— just trying to catch up and make amends.

So thank you for the award.

The evening had a blight cast on it by the death of Gladys Hill, John Huston's assistant and a good friend. Even so, John insisted upon coming to the award-giving, and in his speech about me he was at his most Irish. The least praising phrase was "She is an adornment to this earth." Even now I blush when I think of it.

Television,
Shanghai, 1979

Photography, text, production, exhibition and promotion of *In China* had consumed two years. It had been an exciting time of travel and work. I didn't begin to settle down until the end of 1980—then I felt deprived. When I tried to return to the usual diet of editorial magazine stories and the occasional advertisement and film assignment, it all seemed diminished and without flavor. I felt without enthusiasm and drained of ideas. I missed the sustained effort of making a book.

My publisher-cum-editor, Robert Gottlieb, suggested a book on America. My instant reaction was no. America was too difficult, too familiar, and there was the fear that after China it might be an anticlimax. I dithered a bit, spoke to my agent Ed Victor about it, and finally we agreed that it was a very good idea and the next logical book for me.

Perhaps I shouldn't have plunged immediately into another major project, but I was restless and anxious to get back to the camera. Unconsciously I feared working in America. It was much more difficult than working in China, where the exoticism and unfamiliarity of the country were a natural goad. Part of the visual interest of China stemmed from not knowing the language. A poster would look wonderful because I didn't know that the beautiful calligraphy read "Lucky Cola." In America a Coke poster was just a Coke poster. Also I worked in China during a very happy and hopeful time, whereas America was now going through a troubled period.

I was apprehensive about the undertaking. The more I questioned the advisability of tackling America, the more ambivalent I became, but also the more interested and the more curious. I began to think that perhaps I could turn the very familiarity into an asset which might produce insights that another might not know to seek out. The logjam in my brain loosened and ideas began to trickle in.

I spent months researching, talking to people, and planning strategy. Then for two years I crisscrossed America. I worked intensely but seldom felt the quiver of recognition that comes from knowing that this is a special assignment, a special picture, the way I did so often in China. What I did feel was a sense of guilt for not responding excitedly to my own country. Looking back, I think it was the concern of not showing America to advantage. I loved the people and the landscapes, the energy and the humor, but was deeply distressed at the destruction in the cities, the bag ladies and bag men sleeping on the streets, the people spaced out and talking to themselves as they ambled along. Many mental hospitals had turned their patients into outpatients; they were treated with drugs, but frequently neglected to come to the clinic for their supply. Unemployment was high. Mortgages were being foreclosed. The AIDS virus was beginning to hit.

The photography was further complicated by the fact that Bob Gottlieb and I approached America from totally different angles—not eye to eye, but toe to toe. I was on the spot, seeing the detailed reality; he had an overview in which he saw a broader perspective that was not all gloom and doom. There was no right and no wrong—it all depended upon one's point of view. Inevitably there was a struggle between us. It was like being at odds with the midwife who is going to deliver your baby.

In essence, he was prodding me to be careful not to emphasize the downbeat, because that was only part of the whole. (But photography is about time, and if you hit a rough period, then it is dishonest not to show people within that time frame.) Since only part of America was in difficulty it was essential to try to balance the rich as well as the middle class with the poor, the good with the bad, the ugly with the beautiful, the young with the old, the commercial with the cultural life. The whole project would be in danger of becoming didactic if we weren't careful—yet photography flourishes on the absolute; the quotidian is hard to make interesting.

In order to help us come to a closer understanding, Bob suggested he come with me on a junket to photograph. We eschewed inner city scenes, where I seemed blind to all but poverty, drugs, prostitution, unemployment and decay. We headed first for Queens, then Asbury Park, for small family decencies and a sense of middle America. The trip helped clear the air. I began to understand his approach to America, and he became more tolerant of mine. But that book was never easy for either of us.

There was yet one more hurdle to consider. In the beginning, the book was to be in black-and-white. My reasoning was that we saw daily a plethora of color images in magazines and on television, so perhaps monochrome would look fresh. But on observing so much sadness about me, I realized that black-and-white would be too depressing. I opted for color, which would be used to emphasize the incredible ethnic mixture of the people. And I was happy to find my thinking reinforced the following year when I photographed a sampling of the population at the Pike Place Market in Seattle. In one hour I photographed the following— and I have the pictures to bear witness: Hungarian-Cherokee, French-Irish, Swedish-Norwegian, Austrian-Polish, Scotch-Albanian, Afro-Indian, Dutch-Spanish, French-Sioux, German-Canadian, Italian-Russian, Chinese-Jamaican, Panamanian-Latvian. However, the wonderful combinations of people simply pointed up the difficulties of trying to impose any artificial structure on the book. It seemed that the only way to approach it was as an organic entity; to let the people and the landscape emerge; to let them be themselves. It was a mistake to compare America with anything but itself. Finally, the only stricture I set upon the book was a physical one: the decision not to work in each of the fifty states but instead to work in each of the nine regions in which the country is divided for the census. In the end, I photographed in thirty-six states.

I knew images would come easily; what would be difficult would be to make a cohesive book that expressed the whole—the whole was made of so many diverse parts that no matter how good the pictures, there was the danger that the whole might become a kaleidoscope whose fragments it would be difficult to contain in finite space.

Physically, America is the most varied and possibly the most beautiful country in the world: the Rockies are more majestic than the Alps, the Mississippi is more impressive than the Nile, New York is in a class by itself. I would need pictures of landscape, cityscape, seascape, but it would be the people that would challenge me and become the subject of the book.

I remembered John Steinbeck's proposition in his book *Travels with Charley*—"We do not take a trip. A trip takes us." So it was to be with me, too. It would be an adventure; each day and each place would lead to the next. I hoped to chart an unexpected America.

I started photographing in the Southwest. Like so many other photographers, I had always had a strong desire to do an essay or even a book on the American Indian. I flew to Albuquerque, New Mexico, where the streets seemed to be filled with cowboys and Indians. The cowboy myth had spawned a living prototype. The whole state was in blue jeans, cowboy boots, fancy belt buckles, bolos with silver ornaments and ten-gallon hats (many of them in straw). The pickup truck had replaced the horse.

My brother Jack, who is an economist, put me in touch with a client of his, Rio Rancho Estates, which was building low-cost housing in an area twice the size of the Bronx—91,999 acres. There was a new migration: from the frost-belt to the sunbelt ("Every time there is a blizzard we get a few more buyers"). It would make an interesting contrast with the original Americans—the Indians—if I were permitted into a reservation.

Thus it was I met my first two American Indians, Chico Gomez, with his green headband, and his companion Roseanne Tootsie, with her braids—two young, attractive itinerant carpen-ters, nailing uprights to frame a house. They were on the construction site just long enough for me to photograph them and for them to intro-duce me to Chico's brother, Gregory, who opened doors that eventually got me into the Navajo reservation. So began the most singular three weeks of my professional life.

Gregory Gomez was a professional social worker, a child-welfare specialist in the Depart-ment of Health and Human Resources in Texas. He agreed to take me to the Navajo reservation and appropriately rented a red Bronco pickup truck. We covered 583 miles in two days, stop-ping to photograph a fair, a flea market and a carnival. We broke the journey in Window Rock, Arizona, at a supermarket to pick up food for lunch. There Greg ran into Valerie. She was a whiter-than-white registered full Navajo who was assistant to the chairman of the Navajo Nation.

We agreed to meet next day for a picnic and carried on to the glorious Canyon de Chelly among the sacred mountains. I tried to photo-graph them but knew without seeing the results that the pictures would be beautiful picture-post-card clichés and gave up in despair. Instead, I concentrated on a lucky find—a Little League baseball game that was a mixture of white kids, black kids, Indian kids and that numerous minor-ity, girls.

We waited around for a ravishing sunset that never came, had a fleabag dinner of stony-hard green chili omelet that burned going down it was so spicy and a cup of cold tea and then set off in the dark in search of shelter. There was no room at the inns, and the motels and the hotels were full. It was Memorial Day weekend.

Greg drove us to the Navajo College, which was dark, and we settled down to sleep in the freezing car. He gallantly sat up in the front pas-senger seat. I tried to keep warm bundled in the larger backseat with Greg's down jacket over me.

I slid around on the plastic seat and the jacket slid around on me.

We were chilled, cramped and miserable—just on the threshold of sleep. About midnight there was a bang on the car and a flashlight in my eyes. The school security wardens were making a routine check. Who were we? What did we want? Greg explained our predicament. The school was officially closed for end of term, but Greg was offered a sofa in the warm lobby. I was lucky: there were still two female students in their dormitory, so I was offered a bed.

Next morning we joined Valerie and her party at Birland Lake. It was interesting to see the Indians making camp with fire briquettes, Aladdin lamps for light and aluminum struts to hold pre-fab tents.

Gregory and Valerie explained: "We have chosen to acculturate to survive. No, we do not want to assimilate. To do that means to buy the system—what Indians call red on the outside, white on the inside. We do not want to buy the Coca-Cola, French fry, hot dog society. We enjoy a plane ride, driving a four-wheel-drive vehicle and seeing a film. And, yes, all these little conveniences you see here."

We parted from Valerie with her promise to help me work on the reservation. I would return in a week. Greg and I set off for Albuquerque to return the red Bronco and for him to enplane for Dallas to report for work.

On the return trip we saw written in the dust on a pickup truck: "Cowboys make better lovers—ask any horse." We then started watching out for comments on bumper stickers and found:

We gave them an inch, they took 3,000 miles.
America: Love it or give it back.
Custer died for your sins.
Fried Bread Power.
Custer got Siouxed.

But perhaps the most eloquent words encountered that weekend were Gregory's before we parted:

"I see my brothers and sisters on drugs, alcohol, fat bodies, bad skins, but I see the inner beauty. I want to live as though this were the first moment and may be the last. I have so many dreams and fantasies of so many tomorrows. I may never reach the stars—perhaps the clouds. As I go into the spirit world I want people to say of me as they did of my grandfather: he was a good man, a staunch friend, a gentle man."

The logistics for the way to work on *In America* were arrived at through trial and error on the first trip to the Southwest. The plan was to use New York as home base and do basic research there. Then when I arrived on location I would find a researcher-cum-driver who knew the area to help me get at the specific stories planned for the book. The assistants came recommended by friends, by other photographers, through a list of people Magnum used from time to time and by chance. When finished with the particular region I would return to New York to transcribe notes and edit pictures. In this way section by section would unfold (I hoped) until the whole was finished. By focusing on the individual character of each region I hoped to arrive at a vivid picture of the whole. It was a deliberately loose plan to allow for the unexpected, the adventitious.

I hired a driver—Ted Sudal, an escapee from New Jersey who had come seeking a better life in New Mexico. He took me to the Navajo Reservation to meet with Valerie. Ted was deeply pessimistic about the economy. He told me that people had come to a point where they had to shoplift and live on dog and cat food. But that wasn't what I wanted to hear. I wanted to know about the American Indians.

The reservation of 25,000 square miles was located on parts of four states: Utah, Colorado, New Mexico and Arizona. The Indians were being ripped off in all directions, because the land when given to them was considered worthless, but actually had thirty-seven percent of the world's known deposits of uranium. There was also coal, oil, and timber. It seemed that no matter where you started a conversation it ended on the economy.

Valerie had assured me that Angela Barney—Miss Navajo, 1976—would be a perfect guide for me; she had access through her family to almost anything I might want to photograph. But when we met, I felt a chasm between us, our worlds were so very different. She was twenty-eight years old, brought up in a Catholic boarding school, a full-blooded Navajo and a member of the military reserve. She seemed skeptical about whether she could trust the white woman.

On that first day Valerie invited me to spend the night at her house, taking Dana, her five-year-old daughter, into her own bed to make room. It may have been that which caused Angela to look on me with less mistrust, or it may have been Larry Yazee, a young Navajo lawyer, who changed her mind.

By way of introducing myself and my work, I showed them *In China*. Angela, Valerie and Larry looked at the book seriously and asked questions about China, about me and about my purpose in coming to them. What did I intend to show about the reservation and about their lives? I told them honestly that it was a search, and that I hoped not to impose predetermined ideas on the pictures. Larry excused himself and left. When he came back he said he had brought something for me—a gift. We then all sat in Valerie's kitchen and he described in simple terms something about his life, his tribe and his beliefs. I don't remember his exact words (it would have been rude to record them), but I can still hear the cadence of the beautiful voice, which I seemed to have completely absorbed into myself. Although none of it remains on a conscious level, I have only to close my eyes to recall the sense of oneness Larry evoked among us. He had brought me a magnificent turquoise-and-silver ring that had been made by a member of his tribe and that belonged to his family and so to him. He wanted me to have it as a token of esteem and friendship. He then told me that when his family wanted to put him into a white boarding school at the age of six, they took him to the nearest trading post and told him to go inside and buy some candy. When he returned, the family was gone and someone from the school was waiting for him. He said he had never recovered from that blow.

The following day when Angie started to take me around Navajoland there seemed to be no barrier between us. In the pickup truck we rented (Greg, too, had a loosening of the tongue and the spirit in the cab of a truck), she talked of her childhood. When she was seven she was sent to a Catholic boarding school, where she was forbidden to speak Navajo. Every Saturday she was taken to see a movie about cowboys and Indians. The cowboys were heroes, the Indians savages. She was a Navajo. By no stretch of the imagination could she consider herself a savage. She was a Navajo—she did not identify with Indians. It took her years to realize that she was indeed an Indian. The experience was shattering.

She took me to her parents' ancestral summer place at Narrow Creek Canyon in the Chuska Mountains of New Mexico. We arrived at dawn to witness the raising of a tepee in which a peyote service was to take place that night to celebrate the high-school graduation of Angie's nephew. The service was to begin at sunset and last through the night.

Donabah Barney
baking bread for peyote ceremony,
New Mexico, 1982

219

All day long, preparation for the evening went on. Donabah Barney, Angie's mother, made the bread for the feast to break the night's fast. A younger son, Evans, who was a Marine in San Diego, set up an altar in the tepee: a semicircular band of sand five inches wide that was set in the exact center of the tepee. It represented the sun, which, like all things in the altar area, was referred to as female. In this space a mighty fire of cedar logs would be kept blazing through the night, tended by a special group of young men. In the center of a raised half-circle representing the sun the sacred peyote was placed. (Peyote, the sacred drug, is a mescal derivative. At the service it was used as a powder and as a tea. It is illegal for general use but legal for ritual purposes within the Native American Church.) When the sun set, fifty people from infants to great-grandmothers sat down in a ring within the tepee.

Angela had arranged with the medicine man (also called the road man) to permit me to photograph. Alas, it all went wrong. The original medicine man suffered a death in his family, and in the confusion the substitute misunderstood about me. He was openly hostile. He announced that the stranger would make a million dollars from the pictures and was there for one reason only, and that was to exploit the Indian, a very poor people.

Angie indicated that I was to keep silent and not remove my camera from its bag. The service started. We were to celebrate the elements: fire, earth, the sun and water. The mother of the graduate spoke, part Navajo, part English, saying that Angie had brought me, a stranger. Angie introduced me, then her mother spoke, in Navajo, pointing to me. Because I had to sit rigidly still and could not question Angie in this tepee church, I spent twelve agonizing hours wondering whether she was in deep trouble with her family because she had brought me. We sat cross-legged and straight-backed on cushions, but there was no place in the sloping tent to lean the aching back and we were not permitted to stretch out our legs.

The service started with everyone in the congregation smoking a big cigarette which each of us had rolled ourselves and which was lighted from a faggot from the great fire which passed from hand to hand. The fag ends were collected and placed symmetrically against the altar. After this, peyote, the green powder that had been ground from cactus buttons, was passed around. The participant took as much as he or she wanted—but whatever was taken had to be eaten. Because I was uncertain of the effect I took only half a teaspoonful. It was bitter. This was followed by a gleaming pail of peyote tea passed from hand to hand. We drank. Again, it was bitter.

My reaction to the drug was a sense of clarity and serenity I had known only once before in my life—when I was kept on purple hearts after an operation. As the night wore on, the excruciating pain in my back and legs lessened and the sense of gentle happiness increased.

The most sacred moments were when the pail of clear water was passed and drunk. There was a deep reverential silence. Then the singing and the chanting started, accompanied by the beating of the water drum. Only the men sang and beat the drum, and each time four songs were sung. At the end of each song there was a turn of the drum, the slosh of water, and a new song begun. Evans was the head drummer.

Sometime before dawn we went into the night to stretch our legs. Against the cobalt-blue sky the tepee lighted by the fire within stood silhouetted. Against its white walls were the moving figures of the medicine man, the drummers and some of the worshippers. Through a hole in the roof the sparks from the fire flew upward to the brilliant stars. I caught my breath. This scene would defy photography. Was it as beautiful as I remember it or was the effect heightened by my intake of peyote? Perhaps there are things that should be kept sacrosanct in the mind and not recorded. The image of the whole episode stays more vividly, more tenaciously in my mind because it was not photographed, and I could experience it fully, without the barrier of the camera at my eye.

Soon after we reentered the tepee, prayer started. First Angie's mother prayed for her fifteen children, their spouses, her grandchildren and her tribe. As she prayed, she wept. When she finished, a daughter took up the prayer. Her words were part English, part Navajo, so I could piece together what was being said. She was accusing her fourteen-year-old daughter of unseemly conduct—of neglecting her schoolwork and mixing with bad companions. She had been picked up by the Navajo police.

The girl sat quietly beside her uncle Evans. The mother's accusations and appeal to the congregation for understanding were in Navajo. This was interspersed with her calling on the Almighty in English. "Heavenly Father," then Navajo, then again "Heavenly Father," then more Navajo. When a fire-tender opened the tent flap to get more wood, we could see the sky lightening. The fire blazed, the driving beat of the drums became more strident, the chanting rose higher and higher as the people called upon the Heavenly Father. At the end Evans spoke in English to the accused girl—movingly and eloquently about the world outside the reservation. He was twenty-two years old. He then addressed the seventeen-year-old graduate whom we were honoring that night. He spoke of how hard it was for an Indian, of the need for education and training. Later Angie was to say: "Our parents urge us

into the white man's world to be educated and to learn his ways. Then when we return to the reservation, they say, Now wait a minute. You are forgetting traditional ways. Do you wonder that we are torn, that we are confused? Do you wonder that we take to alcohol and drugs? We seem to have trouble in both worlds."

At the last hour many testified. Men wept, women called on the Almighty. Then the mother of the graduate, a beautiful woman in dark blue with a crimson shawl, went out of the tepee to greet the dawn. She returned, then knelt straight-backed in front of the fire and prayed to the Almighty.

A last drink of water from the shining pail was passed from person to person. The medicine man came and blessed the congregation by touching each shoulder and each forehead. He passed me by. Then a token feast arrived: a bowl of corn, a bowl of mutton, a bowl of single grapes. We took a teaspoon each of corn and mutton and a single grape and ate. Then the road man emptied the water from the drum into the earth with incantations.

Thus ended the peyote service.

We passed into the daylight, and Angie and her sisters went to prepare the real feast. They grilled mutton and steaks over a huge grill, made coffee and cut up their mother's bread, baked the day before.

I suddenly felt deeply hurt. I had come with a clean heart to document what I saw, and I was not wanted. I understood their rejection of me, but this did not ease my unhappiness. I felt the way they must have felt many times in my world, but this didn't help my pain. But I understood that they were right to question me, the intruder; just being there with my white face I had changed the atmosphere.

They had given me a great gift that I had hoped to repay with my photos. I had wanted to transmit what they experienced, had hoped in my small way to forge a link between them and the white outside, but I had wound up as an interloper. Maybe it was the peyote that loosened me. I sat in the truck cab weeping and shaken.

Then Angie came to me with her brother-in-law Leland, a medicine man. He said, "We understand you, the old do not." (He was thirty-two.) "I would like to bless you." He took me to the outdoor fire where the steaks had been cooked, built up the fire and waved a feather-beaded wand over it. Then he touched my shoulder and forehead with the wand as he chanted a blessing in his language. I felt restored.

I returned to home base, New York, to process film, transcribe notes and captions, absorb what I had experienced and plan the next trip. Also, I found it expedient while all the above was going on to keep photographing in New York and vicinity. There was always something happening on the streets: a fair, a parade, a protest march. In the summer you could almost believe the city's claim—that New York is a festival.

It was a personal festival for me as well. My son and his family came from England to visit me, and we became tourists in New York. I started seeing the city through their eyes. Michael, my grandson, who was four, loved it all from the vantage point of his father's shoulders. There were dancers and musicians, booths that sold posters, ice cream, homemade jewelry and hot dogs. And there was a festival to celebrate the second anniversary of revolution in Nicaragua. People were nervous about being photographed on the streets, because the CIA was known to be out taking pictures to target dissidents for its files. We were still close enough to the McCarthy days for people to remember that era of repression and questioned patriotism. After all, we were attending political events. Even so, a handsome black man asked if I wanted his face. Indeed—he was great-looking: dreadlocks, two sets of glasses, one on his nose, one on the dreadlocks. He looked sharply at me. "If you're a member of the CIA, then the U.S. is down the drain for all of us. Anyway, go ahead and shoot."

We toured the city for a week. It felt good to look on the good side, the outside: the jewelled towers, the dazzling skyline. We went to the World Trade Center and observed the cityscape from 107 stories up. Eventually I would have to confront the problems of the slums, the hopelessness of the poor, the drug-addicted—but not yet. Now we would look at the gateway to America. It is brash and vulgar, beautiful and touching, a monument to man's dreams and a monument to man's greed.

I asked my son, Francis, if there was a single image that he thought of for America—was it a melting pot to him? No, to him it was a tree nurtured in its own soil. Like a living organism, parts of it are growing, parts are in bud, parts in flower. There are spores and fungus. And parts that are ageing, rotting, dying.

When the family left for Mexico I felt refreshed, and branched out to New Jersey and Pennsylvania. My researcher had found a male strip joint—Sneaky Pete's—for me to photograph. They didn't call the men "strippers" at the club, though; they called them "dancers." Strippers remove everything (illegal in New Jersey), dancers strip to the G-string. Patrons were instructed that tips—paper money—must be folded and hung on the G-string, not stuffed into the spangled pod that held the dancers' crown jewels.

There was an audience of about three hundred. Mainly, the women were young. They looked like clerical workers, telephonists or housewives out on the town. And there were two brides with their female guests who were celebrating a stag night the way men do before marriage.

There were three rooms, with a dancer at work in each of them. There were three more dancers spelling them, and three amateurs who were trying out. The men started dancing slowly, removing their garments as they danced and moving more and more suggestively. The screaming women, many of them standing, became more and more frenzied, yelling, dancing along with the performer as his pace became wilder and as he pushed through the crowded rooms. They would brush against him, moving rhythmically, practically masturbating to the music. It was like a scene from Hieronymus Bosch with its abandoned writhing, its rutting smells and its wild dancing. After a while, lesbian overtones crept in as the women began clutching and touching each other. It was illegal to exclude men, since that was considered discrimination and sexism, so they were admitted but charged double the rate for women. This was done to limit the number of men so as not to inhibit the women, to leave them free to act out their fantasies. But this didn't stop men from gathering at the bar next door to wait for what one described as "hot women," when the club closed at midnight. It was strange to see the reversal of roles, with men as sex objects. My poor assistant—as he moved through the club assisting me, his bottom was pinched black and blue by the women. He was afraid he might be raped.

I went to the New Jersey marshes to photograph the industrial landscape, the petroleum-cracking plants, the containers of goods, automobiles and chemicals being loaded onto trains and ships. It was all so magical in shape and color and composed so well into photographs that it was only afterward that I remembered the lethal poisonous muck we were breathing and the pollutant noise that broke the sound barrier from the planes overhead. As though to mock me, everywhere in this phantasmagoria were sunflowers, Queen Anne's lace (the British call it cow parsley) and goldenrod, and there were pigeons and gulls swooping down and coming to rest on bollards and pilings.

I was overwhelmed with the endless choice of subjects available. Although I tried to narrow it down to the scale necessary to fit between book covers, still the magnitude of the task depressed me. Luckily, the depression didn't last long. It was blown away by the pressure of the picture taking. And the sheer variety kept me engrossed. I rode the subways with the Guardian Angels, walked the streets of the barrios (the word means literally "dustings," but has been transmuted to "neighborhood") of Spanish Harlem with a reformed dope peddler. He took me in hand, and we walked the streets where addicts were "nodding out," and went into clinics where desperate people were trying to kick their addiction.

The expected pattern had changed. It now cut across class barriers and was a middle-class problem. By way of illustration, Tony said that a major department store chain was worried about how many of their employees were heroin-addicted.

Uptown on Lexington Avenue we came to a row of small shops with signs in their windows. The first said "I ♥ New York." The other said "This shop protected by guard dogs" and had a

Male stripper,
Sneaky Pete's,
New Jersey, 1982

picture of a vicious, snarling dog as its focal point of interest. The next few shops looked fairly innocuous: a newsstand, a candy store, a dry cleaner—just neighborhood stores. Tony told me they were all fronts for the numbers racket. Down the street he pointed out a block-square abandoned, windowless apartment building. This, he said, was a crash pad where floating groups of youngsters (from ten to sixteen) who had left home took up residence. It was padlocked. Tony said there was nobody home; they were all out on the street, hustling.

What is hustling?

We are talking about three-card monte (the old shell game), shoplifting, burglary, prostitution (male and female), selling drugs.

We are talking about marijuana.

We are talking about cocaine.

We are talking about heroin.

We are talking about Quaaludes (a muscle relaxant downer originally intended for women with menstrual cramps).

We are talking about Black Beauties (diet pills that are a stimulant like Dexedrine and keep the taker running all over the place).

We are talking about acid (it is coming back heavily).

We are talking about a new drug, not as heavy as LSD, called Christmas Tree.

We are talking about PCP (angel dust)—originally designed as a tranquillizer for huge animals, elephants and the like. This drug is dangerous. It embeds in the fat tissues and may stay there until the taker is burning up great amounts of energy. Some can control the drug, but many go berserk—jump out of windows, kill their parents or whatever.

We were talking in a restaurant. I was suddenly totally exhausted and distressed by Tony's tale. I stopped taking notes and asked for a glass of milk—perhaps going back to the nipple, where all was pure and untroubled. I sipped my milk and listened to Tony describing his life during his drug period: We had our own society. It was structured. It had its own levels and its own classes. I would put the "shooting galleries" (drug addicts) at the bottom. They didn't do anything. Above them are the "takeoff artists," the ones with guns, the ones who could blow you away. Above that are the B&E men—breaking and entering. Then there are the con men, who live by their wits. At the top there are the dealers.

Pimps? No, pimps were not into that. They were into fancy cars, high life, girls. We didn't have time for cars and high life and girls. I asked who could possibly turn things around. He said: youth, only youth has the energy and the insanity to get involved. I didn't ask about age and experience. They had failed flagrantly.

After all the spadework I didn't photograph the New York drug addicts. Was it because it was too difficult or was it (as I would like to think) consideration for those bedevilled creatures who had enough trouble in their lives without exposure to my camera? Or was it all suddenly too much to deal with? I don't know.

For a change of pace from the unresolved problems in Harlem it seemed a good idea to check out a group of people who felt they had some definite answers for their lives. These were a fundamentalist group of Hasids in Brooklyn called Lubavitcher.

I found Pinchas Schecter, a twenty-three-year-old side-curled, bearded, brown-belt-judo diamond cutter in a dusty building on 47th Street. When I offered my hand in greeting he looked shocked and ushered me out into the hall so his boss wouldn't witness my disgraceful behavior. In his world, men are not permitted to touch women who are not their wives.

We sat on the stairs twelve stories up. Behind

each office door there was a fortune in gold and diamonds monitored by a bank of closed-circuit TV sets and security officers. We negotiated. If I waited until his boss went to lunch and said in my caption that Pinchas was the third-best diamond cutter on 47th Street, then I could have his picture.

When the boss had gone to lunch and Pinchas had been photographed I asked him about taking pictures of other Lubavitcher. He reminded me that in his religion the graven image was strictly forbidden and also that because I was a woman I would be prohibited from being on the floor of the synagogue. Nevertheless Mr. Schecter promised to help, and a few days later called to say it was okay and for us to come on the celebration of the festival of Succoth. And he also mentioned that there would be a surprise—a succoth-mobile.

When we arrived outside the synagogue it looked like a giant carnival. Men were wandering along Eastern Parkway in their prayer shawls, and there was nothing to prevent my photographing them out of doors. But when I went to talk to the public relations man who was also the rabbi's driver, he was appalled and said that Schecter had gotten permission from the wrong man. When we found the original man he disowned the whole thing and crazily kept repeating the same phrase: "Wherever in the world there is Coca-Cola, there you will find Lubavitcher." I asked him what he meant. He shook his head and said it was a parable and walked away.

We were told that the Succoth-mobile would arrive at ten a.m. When it arrived at one-thirty, I was refused access because I was a woman. Men could not ride with me; it would create a *shande* (a scandal), they said. Lee Falk, bless him, tangled with them—in Hebrew. He was a good man to have around. In Harlem, his Spanish had come to the rescue. Somehow he managed to get permission for us to go on the mobile.

We started for Brighton Beach. The whole structure of the truck shook. Each start and stop hurled the benches inside (and the sitters) from side to side. Bamboo poles dropped from the roof onto our heads. The fifteen or so young men held on to the sides of the structure lest they collapse completely and toss us into the streets. Also, it kept them away from the possibility of being thrown in the direction of a woman—and thus, heaven forbid, touching her. Through all this, Lee held on to me, and I held on to the cameras and kept shooting.

When the nightmare ride ended, we stopped at a predominantly Jewish shopping center under the elevated train. The young men, holding a citron and palm fronds, stopped people on the street. Question—are you Jewish? If the answer was yes, the person had the citron and the palm fronds thrust at him and found himself repeating the blessing in Hebrew after the young men.

The Lubavitcher are missionaries, and had set up the Succoth-mobile to proselytize other Jews to partake of the ritual and thus earn redemption for themselves.

Shaking only slightly less than the palm fronds had been shaken in the hands of the celebrants, Lee and I made for the subway and Manhattan.

Just as I had reached a point of diminishing interest in New York, I was invited to the Chinese Culture Center in San Francisco to open the exhibition of my travelling show on China. My show became a community affair in the heart of Chinatown. The opening was wonderfully colorful, with Chinese ladies in ancient embroidered silken robes, and with lanterns, firecrackers, dancing lions, a Chinese orchestra, champagne and dim sum. The mayor of Chinatown and the Chinese consul general were there and many friends from all over the West Coast.

There was a splendid banquet after the opening at which the consul made a flowery speech about what good friends we had been when he was the Chinese ambassador in London, and of how we had played Ping-Pong together at Harry Evans'. The truth was that we had never met, and that he had for years ignored the newspaper's applications for visas for me to visit the Middle Kingdom.

It had occurred to me that I was beginning to enjoy the plaudits and the tributes, and it was becoming hard to differentiate the real from the commercial. I told myself to guard against believing the publicity. It may sell books and prints but it eats up time better spent on real work. Yet

this packaging, too, is America—perhaps a large part of it—and something that can't be totally ignored. The important thing was to get back to work. After an excursion photographing John Huston, Billy Pearson—the tiny jockey who had twice won on *The $64,000 Question* for his knowledge of art—and the painter Morris Graves for French *Vogue*, I spent a week trying to set up an itinerary for northern California. I find an entry about those days in my diary: "Promises, possibilities all very boring. I keep telling myself I edit and control by doing my own research—but oh, it does swallow time, rot the mind, dull the enthusiasm and use up what little money I have."

The diary was a great place to unload frustrations. When I moved back from the camera viewfinder to consider the adventure on which I was embarked I would become apprehensive and highly critical. The only way to ease back into the book again was to write out my fleeting moods, which ranged from slight irritation to strong exasperation. Putting all of America into one book was a job that seemed all too big and too contradictory. The major problem was (and always is) how to keep pictures fresh. Sometimes a change of technique—a new lens or a combination of filters—can act as a change of

pace and start the photographer on a new track, but it can easily become a gimmick. For instance, many people are now using an extreme wide-angle lens because they think it makes their work look different. Alas, all these different-looking photos are now becoming clichés; with endless use the changes become old hat and the search continues for the "new."

I haven't taken that path. Rather than seek the sensational for its own sake, I try to be true to the subject and let it dictate the treatment, the angle of approach, the point of view. These will emerge if one comes to the picture with humility and integrity. But there are fallow periods when nothing seems right, and when that happens I take time off from photography. I read, I cook, I walk—and I try to divert myself by staying away from the camera. It usually works.

I went back to trying to deal with events on a day-to-day basis. To help me I hired Marina, the daughter of my colleague Paul Fusco. She was a young photographer who was to drive me around northern California in her piebald Alfa Romeo. We roller-coastered through breath-catching red-wood country, staying in old inns in the woods or at the seashore.

We travelled and photographed intensively for two weeks, dealing with an odd amalgam of subjects: a woman wine taster who had taken a university degree in the subject; migrant grape pickers who were illegal immigrants; people who raised llamas for a living; a couple who travelled by burro and lived in a tepee; and fiddlers at a country fair.

We had been hearing tales of layoffs at the lumber mills, small businesses folding and general unemployment. It was said that 78,000 people in Mendocino County were unemployed. We tried to check out the figures, and also the rumor that the local cash crop was marijuana, but this was harvest season, and the state narcotics officers were about. It all had the flavor of the boot-leg prohibition days with the "revenooers" out for prey.

We returned to San Francisco to research the gay community. I talked to Robert Mc-Queen, the editor of the *Gay Advocate*, who said the gays were using their consumer power as a threat of boycott to get the respect of the community that they deserved. It was the same approach that, back in the fifties, Malcolm X had used to try to crack white prejudice. And it seemed to be working in California: there were innumerable ads featuring sexy young men which were obviously beamed at the homosexual community.

Robert McQueen suggested that I get in touch with the Sisters of Perpetual Indulgence, a group of gay male nuns who described themselves as an activist nonpolitical group. They were concerned with just causes and with people discovering the child quality, the "fairy" quality, within themselves.

I spoke to Reverend Mother Bill Graham, "she" of the booming voice (privately they like to be "she," publicly "he"), and the following week I photographed six of the nuns. When I asked their names so I could identify them for captions they offered their alternate names. Following is a copy of a leaf from my notebook:

Neighbors,
Craig, Nebraska, 1981

231

October 6, 1981

THE SISTERS

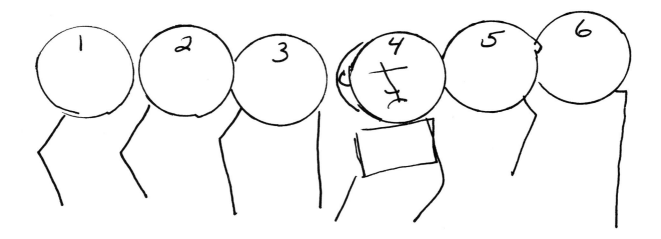

left to right: 1. Homo Fellatio
2. Boom Boom—is Sister Rose of the Bloody Stain aka: Si. Rose
   of the Bloody Stains of the Sacred Robes of Jeesus
3. Marie Ever-Ready
4. Missionary Position
5. Reverend Mother
6. Sleaze du Jour

Member of Sisters of Perpetual Indulgence,
San Francisco, 1981

At some point during the session (perhaps when we were talking about attitudes toward them and their attitudes toward the world) the word "violence" was used. Somebody made a crack that violence would appeal to Sister Rose. "No," he said, with a look of pleasure on his pretty face. "S&M—yes, yes I love it—but violence, that's something else again."

The next week was spent on various subjects. There was a political demonstration when Duarte, the president of El Salvador, came to town. There were two opposing groups, the other said to be composed of Moonies—demanding that Cuba and Russia get out of El Salvador. The pro-American faction pelted the others with raw eggs; the pro-Cuba/Russia group used Coke cans in which a hole had been punched and with which they spattered their opponents. At first the cops were friendly. One stuck his tongue out at me. A female cop stuck her chest out when I photographed her and gave me her card so that I could send her a picture if one "came out." I wanted to say that pictures didn't "come out"—that I made them—but I didn't get a chance because just then I got a riot stick in the small of my back, and instructions to move on.

Then there was a Japanese Autumn Festival with terrific drummers, a hang-gliding contest and a group of "new age rabbis," who conducted Kol Nidre in a Unitarian church and ushered in Yom Kippur, the holiest of holy holidays, there.

But perhaps my most amusing time was spent renewing acquaintance with Margo St. James, the founding head of Coyote, the hookers' union. I had met her years before at a symposium for women's rights. It was in New York before a Democratic National Convention, and the police had tried to clean up the city by locking up all the prostitutes to keep them off the streets. St. James was enraged and called a press conference to de-nounce the police for taking away her colleagues' livelihood.

It was difficult to get a perspective on the America I had left in the early sixties. Two decades had gone by, and there was a different country to portray. It would have been simpler, I thought, to do it in words. Photography is often misleading. It might not lie, but certainly it is unable to tell the whole truth. Its very parameters limit it. The photograph can only encompass a small number of elements; it demands of the viewer a frame of reference, but most people are not visually literate, even though we depend more and more upon pictures for information.

Since people looking at photos often cannot penetrate the visual because they are either visually illiterate or generally uninformed, I feel it is my responsibility to provide words. This is a battle I frequently have with the more art-oriented of my colleagues. From their point of view, the sheer visual experience is sufficiently illuminating. But for me the photo without clarification falls short. It pleases me to see an elegant Cartier-Bresson photograph, but my pleasure is enhanced (after enjoying its symmetry and sheer beauty) by reading that it was photographed in Mexico in the thirties or in France in the nineties. In addition to appreciating this simple information, I get enjoyment from seeing that the master hasn't lost his touch in six decades.

When I first worked for the *Sunday Times* we tried an experiment to see how people viewed visual material, and found that if the photograph was arresting or even reasonably interesting, the person would read the caption; if the caption added information, the viewer would then look at the picture again; and if the picture plus caption captured his imagination he would read the text if there was any—and often return to have another look at the picture. The time spent looking at the photo was longer if words were available.

After a Christmas break with my family I reviewed the progress made on *In America* in the first year of shooting. I had done most of the basic research and photographed three of the nine regions. The six remaining should be easier, because I had worked out methods, organized a plan into which to slot pictures and text. I hoped to finish by the end of the year.

Not yet adjusted to New York time, I flew to Seattle, and next morning, still groggy from the flights and the time differences, I took off in a rainstorm with my new driver-cum-assistant, Kiff Slemmons, for the Quinalt Rain Forest. We drove the highways seeing endless used-car lots, motels, drive-in banks, taco parlors and an efficient cemetery where the gravestones were placed flat and recessed so that the grass would be easier to mow. Kiff commented that the banks and the funeral parlors were flourishing but the economy was sick.

The commercial landscape was replaced by vast gouged-out areas where lumber was cut and nothing done to restore the trees—their corpses haunted us. Usually this blatant devastation is kept away from the road, or at least a curtain of saplings is planted close to the highway to hide the rape of the forest, but here no one had bothered to hide the disgrace.

Back in Seattle, I asked Kiff to check out facts about the plight of the "new poor," a chilling term I kept hearing. Its definition was a person who had been working who was suddenly unemployed, and had used up his savings and his resources. Desperation had set in, and the dangers were drugs and alcohol.

We spent days touring the broken-down waterfront areas that were being razed and replaced by high-rise steel-and-glass structures. The new buildings were displacing the seamen, loggers, railroaders and shipbuilders who could not possibly afford the rentals asked for the new housing. But it wasn't all doom and gloom. Boeing Aircraft was still at work turning out planes. It was a lovely place to photograph and helped lift our spirits. We went on from there to a thriving microchip factory that employed 2,700 people.

Perhaps the most poignant story I did in Seattle was of a literacy class for recent Asian immigrants. They were both men and women, ranging in age from thirty to sixty-five, who had come in the wake of the Vietnam War. There were Chinese who were highly literate and there were pre-literate Laotian tribespeople whose language had never had an alphabet, and who were being taught how to pronounce and write their own names, and how to write a dollar sign.

After the Northwest I embarked on a hegira to the Deep South: Louisiana and Mississippi. Here I wanted to examine the situation for both white and black since the changes in the laws regarding integration. During World War II there had been a large exodus of black people to the North, where they had sought to better their lot by doing war work. There they found prejudice, and work had petered out; they were living in ghettos, and now many were returning to the South. Had they integrated? What was happening?

For possible answers I went to Natchez, Mississippi. Natchez was a port city, which might be less closed-minded than landlocked cities, but Mississippi had a reputation for repression. Natchez had a white mayor, but the electorate was three black to one white, so whites paid attention. The consensus was that things were better for black people in Natchez, but that the rest of the state was still unreconstructed.

White women talked about the change in their lives when the black people who had been their servants left to go north or got jobs in local factories and they were forced to do their own housework. They showed still-visible scars—burns on hands and arms from cooking, for which they had not been educated. There was another group of ladies whose lives had also changed—the ones who during the depression had been faced with losing their grand antebellum houses and had ingeniously placed them on the tourist circuit. People paid good money to traipse through the houses, look at the furniture, paintings and table settings on the "pilgrimage."

I commented on the numbers of genteel old ladies about in Natchez. One wag replied, "Can't cremate our little old ladies. They've had so much bourbon they wouldn't stop burning, they would go on like the eternal flame." This gag was told me in a country home for the aged where there was a mixed group of clients—blacks and whites who got along well together. The prime example was the upper-class white lady in her seventies drinking her afternoon cocoa beside her black "yard boy"—a situation that would have been unthinkable twenty-five years before.

We continued our searches through the black chamber of commerce and the white chamber of commerce, the schools and the courts, and then drove to Lafayette, Louisiana, for the Acadian Mardi Gras—a wonderful respite—but we had an important appointment in Baton Rouge at a Chemical Dependency Unit. Now was the time to use the information Tony Gilbert had given me in his crash course on drugs in New York. I hoped to find a story where people were being helped to kick their addiction; where there was hope.

The Baton Rouge unit was a good choice. The problem was faced squarely. The patients were in hospital garb to forcibly remind them that they were ill, and some of them wore signs that said "I am an Alcoholic" or "I am a Junkie." But these measures were pointed toward a successful end of the treatment.

The young group, ranging in age from twelve to nineteen, looked so vulnerable, so exposed, with their burgeoning few hairs on their chins and their pubescent pimples! We could hear some of them screaming in their agony, cursing and demanding their drugs or drink. There were doctors and nurses in constant attendance, as well as other addicts who had been through their own hell and come out the other side.

During this trip, Clare Cosner, a young researcher, who was a friend from New York, worked with me. She had grown up in the South, and was knowledgeable about it, and suggested a story on guns. We investigated a survivalist group who, according to a local New Orleans sheriff, "outgun and out-equipment" the city itself. They had automatic guns, hand grenades, two helicopters and jeeps. It seemed to me that under the guise of survival there was a paranoia brought on by a personal need to defy the law.

We also photographed in a gun school where women came to learn how to shoot. One woman said she didn't feel secure even going to the supermarket, so she was learning to use a gun. Another, who was pregnant, said she wanted to protect her unborn child. Some interesting statistics were presented: if attacked you had two and a half seconds in which to shoot before being overpowered and killed; the chances were one in ten thousand that a policeman would be available to come to your aid.

On the flight path,
Daly City, California, 1981

The next trip was through the South Atlantic states. I drove south and east with Jodi Buren. Our plan was to stay fairly close to the coast and when it suited us to veer inland to explore. When we reviewed our itinerary upon our return we had photographed in Washington, D.C., Virginia, Tennessee, Kentucky, North Carolina, Georgia and Florida.

We drove through the Bible belt. There was a renewal of fundamental religious belief in the country, as evidenced by an explosion of preachers on radio and television. The electronic church had arrived. The Reverend Jerry Falwell, head of the Moral Majority, had perhaps the largest following of all. When I photographed him in Washington he invited me to Lynchburg, Virginia, to his ministry.

Falwell was a sharp operator and a thundering preacher—a good subject to photograph because of his aura of pompous self-confidence. He had welcomed me warmly and said he would leave me to set up my lights. I surprised myself by saying that I used God's light and needed no extra time. He loved that and became even more expansive. I was embarrassed.

His church, the Thomas Road Baptist in Lynchburg, was remarkably well organized. There were huge parking lots to accommodate the vast number of cars that brought his parishioners and their families. There were nurseries where hundreds of parents left their infants while they attended services. There were Children's Ministries: the Beginners, for two-to-five-year-olds. "In Beginners we capitalize on their character-forming years to train the child up for God." There were Primary Groups for children from six on, where the child was "challenged with scripture memorization." Reverend Falwell said, "We want our children to feel that coming to church is the *most fun* they will have all week." There were endless services. As soon as one ended, more parishioners arrived. There were three thousand at each of three services, all of them spotless: shoes carefully shined, hair shorn and neat. At the altar there were masses of sickly-colored plastic flowers and a translator for the deaf. Four television cameras were stationed throughout the church, ready to roll. What was shocking was the number of security guards inside and outside the church, who were carrying guns. Apparently Falwell's life had been threatened.

The Reverend introduced me jovially to the congregation as "the pretty little lady from London you see on the aisle, who will take your picture, maybe sit in your lap"—which only made everybody around me self-conscious and made it more difficult for me to photograph. Before I left, an aide asked me to sign a release saying that

HRH Oba Oseiijeman Adefunmi,
Beaufort, South Carolina, 1982

none of the photos I had taken would be sold to pornographic magazines.

There followed a chain of people and situations to photograph which started with a letter from Michael McCabe, a man I didn't know. He had been on a trip around the United States and offered me a list of names and addresses that proved invaluable. I thought of them as "begats"—Michael begat Guy Carawan, whom I had photographed during the civil rights crisis in the sixties when he went around America with his guitar singing "We Shall Overcome." He introduced me to Highlander Center in Tennessee, which had an interesting workers' adult education center. This begat Nimrod Workman, who claimed to be the oldest coal man in the United States. He had known Mother Jones, and talked of the early struggles, the strikes and the gunning-down of miners. This begat the Richardsons in Whitesburg, Kentucky, who begat Appalshop, a community-based organization in the coalfields of rural eastern Kentucky. Its purpose was to document the history and culture of the miners and to reveal the lives of the mountain poor to audiences through film, video, theatre, recordings, print and still photography.

So we went zigzagging from community to community, state to state, each session suggesting the next, until we came by accident to the most unexpected story of them all. During my researches in New York I kept hearing that there was a Black Kingdom in the South, ruled by an absolute monarch. Nobody could come up with any more information as to who or where he was. By sheer accident one day in South Carolina, while trying to escape the highways, we took a country road and there nailed to a tree was a primitive sign: African Village. It was a replica in adobe of an idealized Nigerian village, complete with imposing huge-breasted statues of god-

desses, garishly painted. I had photographed the king in 1960 in a boutique in Harlem, where he was introducing the Afro and the dashiki. Now he asked to be photographed on his throne in his state robes. He was His Royal Highness Oba Oseiijeman Adefunmi the First. Behind him on the throne was a rampant golden leopard clasping an ankh in one claw and a sword in the other. (Leopards are a traditional emblem of African royalty.) He now spoke Yoruba, as did his seven genuflecting wives, his twenty children and the rest of his congregation. The movement was based on the Orisha-Vodu religion. The adults were all ordained priests and priestesses and practiced their own African brand of psychiatry.

We photographed two of the wives, who were quite beautiful. One had been a receptionist in New York at Random House, the publishing house that distributed my books, and the other had been an exotic dancer in nightspots in New York.

It was good to see the mounting pile of edited transparencies and captions as each segment of the book was finished. They helped me ignore the mounting fatigue that almost engulfed me by the end of each foray. You always fear that fatigue will cut down on your freshness and ability to see; there's a danger of being a beat too late or too soon, thus missing the photo *juste*. To counter this I took time off to get in trim and then left with my grandniece Claudia Raab for New England and American Independence Day.

New England was a Norman Rockwell *déjà vu*. The Fourth of July was a country jamboree, but there were surprises: a lapsed Catholic nun who was a Jungian proselyte, a state trooper who was bitter about Vietnam, and a horde of people who were fearful of what the Reagan regime would bring.

Wherever we turned, there were people

searching for meaning to their lives as well as searching for a means of livelihood. Many spoke of looking for both human and spiritual values, but they also spoke of restlessness and of America being in transition and in turmoil. There was a group at the Inner Life Institute at Maine who believed that a quantum leap in human consciousness was taking place.

As the trip unfolded, I was aware that it was leaving me with a sense of diminishing returns. It was hard to keep the enthusiasm high, and it became harder to keep the pictures fresh. I had left London in the beginning of 1979 to do the China book, and here I was in mid-1982, three-quarters through shooting the American book. I was weary, and in danger of losing focus on the work in hand. I needed to get a fresh perspective, a new wind.

When I returned to New York, I went to see Bob Gottlieb, intending to talk to him about my problem. Before I could raise the question, he suggested spending a day with me while I was photographing, and he and his colleague Martha Kaplan drove with me out to Queens and then to Asbury Park, where I did the equivalent of shooting on public streets. I don't know exactly what Bob did—to me it seemed like adjusting a spring on a watch that was running down—but whatever it was it worked without words. When I took off for Chicago and the Midwest, vitality was restored.

I was happy to be in Chicago again; I knew the city from the time in World War II when I set up a processing plant there for Stanbi Photos. My assistant for this part of the job was a young man I shall call Mark. He was a photographer who had carefully compartmentalized the photography that earned him his living into two areas: one was precise architectural work, exterior and interior, large tripod, well-lit, etc., and the other was his "art"—3200 ASA, forced development, grain as

big as bullets, out of focus. He kept the two techniques completely separate. I was curious, because I too was placing my work in separate categories: the editorial and the commercial. It was wonderful throughout the two years of shooting in America to be in contact with young picture-takers whose photographic arteries had not yet hardened. Mark and I had ongoing conversations during which I asked a lot of questions. For instance: did setting up "my photography" as opposed to "what pays the rent" create a schizoid world? From others I had heard both a beseeching voice for the need for self-expression to explain the first, and an apology for the need to keep alive to excuse the second.

It was not only in photography that I kept hearing a refusal to compromise and capitulate to the materialist world. Many people clearly felt the need to reject commercialism. I tried gently with Mark to examine the premise that even the personal pictures that are sold need a marketplace; galleries and collectors, publishers of books and magazines, all depend on sales. I had often been told that the photographer would be his own entrepreneur—would set up his own shows and publish his own books. I hadn't the heart to press to the logical conclusion—that dollars still had to be paid for the pictures. Mark insisted early on that he (and others) refused to regard "business" as part of "art." That was his way of dealing with the problem. After our initial discussion we tried to stay away from this subject, but it was like an infected tooth that the tongue keeps going back to.

The art-vs.-commercialism discussion wasn't new to me. It had become a divisive force within Magnum after Capa's death. While he was alive he took the pragmatic view that a little commercialism didn't hurt anyone. It was he who introduced us to working as stills photographers for films when he worked on the John Huston *Moby*

Dick. Cartier-Bresson had always been a proponent of *art in photography* (with a small a) as opposed to the *art photograph*.

It was always more a subject for discussion than a real problem until the late sixties, when a number of the Magnum photographers started to work in advertising. Then it almost wrecked the organization, as lines were sharply drawn between the purists who felt we should continue with only photojournalism and the others who felt that if a photograph was well and honestly made, it didn't matter whether it was used as editorial matter or advertising matter.

The problem was finally resolved with the decision to let those photographers who wanted to work in advertising have their own agents outside our offices. However, commercial jobs like advertising and work for corporate clients have come back into our various offices because many of our members earn very handsome fees doing them. And although the members are grateful to those who do the commercial work, because the percentage they pay into the organization annually helps enormously to keep us afloat, still the pride we take in Magnum is reserved for what we initially came together to do—photojournalism which in some cases can be classified as art.

When Mark and I weren't arguing, we were out on the job. We drove around the Chicago black ghetto. Everywhere were barred windows, shops selling cut-rate liquor and cigarettes, dealing in food stamps and credit clothing. There was a South Side law clinic, a funeral parlor, an amusement parlor with computer games: Atari, Odyssey, Bully. There was also a large crowd lined up at a check-cashing shop, where welfare checks were being cashed. This meant that down the street there would soon be huge lines at the lottery and betting shops.

We went to the Reverend Jesse Jackson's Saturday-morning meeting, held in a huge pillared Greek Revival–style deconsecrated synagogue. The movement was called Operation Push. The consensus of what people had to say was: "When integration came, the spirit was real high. Now we seem to be forgetting what really happened. We've relaxed too much and things are getting too loose. Employment's been cut in half. We'll have to get out and Push, get more black candidates coming up and keeping coming up. To live is to struggle, but what comes out of the struggle is what counts."

In contrast that evening we went to a party on elegant Lake Shore Drive that was given by a black psychiatrist and his wife, who held an administrative post in the public school system—Dr. and Mrs. Ellis Johnson. The affair was to honor Adlai Stevenson III, who was running for governor. The guests were a mixture of bourgeois whites and movers and shakers from the black community. It was all very Saturday-night cocktail dressup. There followed a series of cocktail parties, dinners, a Polish picnic, a Shriners' parade, a trip to the top of the Hancock building to see the city in its glory at dusk, and a visit three hundred feet beneath the city to see a tunnel being dug into the rock. This—Joanne H. Alter, the commissioner of the Metropolitan Sanitary District of Greater Chicago, told us—would be efficient in handling "a million people's poop."

I felt like a gadfly—I touch down here, I touch down there. It all seemed pure chance, and transitory. I wanted something more substantial, and started planning ahead to find a farm family, a farm situation. Meanwhile there was more to do in the city: a runners' marathon, the Chicago Art Institute, an interview with Studs Terkel in his baseball cap, sitting in front of a piled-high desk. I was reminded of W. C. Fields in *The Bank Dick*. Studs talked about the faceless buildings going up all over America, where windows are sealed and air conditioning takes over—tech-

Chess Pavilion,
Chicago, 1981

nology taking over from man. He marvelled that people have just accepted the little dehumanizing humiliations which daily affront our dignity. He spoke of asking directions recently in another city and being told to "go to that megastructure" (talking about a seventy-story building). Megastructure! Even the language is becoming inhuman.

We go to the unemployment lines and the welfare lines, where since Reagan's administration things are bad because federal budgets are being slashed and staff to handle the unemployed are being fired.

Although the problems I discuss in the cities of Chicago and New York are almost identical in terms of human need, visually they are sufficiently different for me to want to keep shooting, to have choices. This is perhaps part of the "just one more" syndrome of the reportage photographer—part, perhaps, of the chancy essence of the work itself: the photographer is uneasy because of the uncertainty factor of the work, feels reassured by sheer quantity of images, and so is impelled to go back and back to the same subject in search of perfection.

After weeks of photographing in Chicago—the beaches, the chess pavilion, the commodities market with its bedlam of young men in ties and colored jackets—I went out into the countryside searching for happy farmers, even though I kept hearing phrases like "resigned despair," "high interest rates" and "mortgage foreclosures." We did find a happy farmer, though—and incidentally the cover of *In America*—in the person of Edward Klessy, a man whose interests were focussed on the environment and the conservation of energy. And luckily for me, his farm in Cleveland, Wisconsin, was pure visual Americana.

Milwaukee and environs had been a pleasant interlude. I felt easy in mind when I met my next driver-cum-assistant, Jason Lovett, in Detroit.

He was a photographer I found through Richard Reeves, the *New Yorker* writer who had retraced de Tocqueville's steps in America. Jason was thirty-nine, black, highly intelligent, informed and articulate. Over a beer in the lobby of the Book Cadillac, with drunken American Legionnaires in a frenzy all around us, he systematically presented the city and its problems in graphic form: it was seventy percent black, it was a one-industry town—cars—and when industry shut down people suffered. He felt that the country was going through some kind of revolution—industrial and technological. There was no leadership, no galvanizing voice. There was no way that this government, with its entrenched position and basic philosophy, could change. It could only hold off disaster.

Jason talked of the drug problem, the riots of 1967, the black mayor. He said things were bad economically in the town, and that black men would always be fired first. Now they were running out of black men to fire, so they were beginning to fire white men.

We discussed which stories would fit into my already bulging inventory of work on the book, and decided on a plasma center where people out of work came to give their blood for eating money.

The other story he suggested was a group of black bike riders called Satan's Sidekicks, a self-styled group of outlaws who bragged: "We got irons. Do you want to see the bazookas? The Thompsons, the Magnums? You're hanging around with the most notorious, most motherfucking members of any club in this town."

I had gone to the Sidekicks on my own after a phone introduction from Jason. They were zonked—whether on drink or drugs I couldn't tell. But all afternoon they kept referring to their dead. Before they drank a beer they would spill a bit on the ground for dead comrades, then reminisce about them. Many had died from head injuries because they didn't wear a bike helmet.

The Sidekicks were fighting the authorities for their right to ride without headgear. Their leader said, "I shouldn't have to wear a helmet. I ride my baby down to the corner on the bike, if she falls off then the Lord wants her. If it's her time to go, it's her time to go. That's between her and J.C. Jesus Christ was an outlaw. He is the spirit, and the real ones are tested tough."

Jason also arranged for me to ride around with the police. It was early in the day. We drove through southwest Detroit. Blue-collar poverty is what you got there: Chicanos, blacks, Puerto Ricans, Asians and Chaldeans (the term used in Detroit for Arabs). There seemed to be a prostitute on every street corner that early wet morning. "Ten to fifteen dollars for some head, twenty for a straight lay, and then up depending on how exotic you want to be. Some police think running whores is not really police work and just move the girls right along. They feel it's a service people demand—and where there's a demand there'll be a supply. The one thing that you have to watch out for is the transvestite males who pass themselves off as straight women. The police tend to be tough on them because they think it's a dirty trick."

We went on driving through Detroit. It felt strange to be in a predominantly black city. I had a sense of being within a photographic negative reversal, a term for when the black values and the white values have changed places. It is the exact opposite of being in most European or even American cities, where the population is predominantly white. I was reminded of a prior experience that I couldn't quite pinpoint. It troubled me until suddenly my mind was flooded with images: South Africa—Soweto, Zululand.

When I saw racial hatred and bigotry in South Africa I had been grateful that we in America had taken the road to integration. Now what I was seeing in my own country was just as horrible, even though it was not condoned by the government and not written into law. Yes, it was on a small scale, it was localized, and most people in the country loathed it, but the seeds were there—and given what I had seen of the strong move to fundamentalism as I had travelled around, I found it very worrying.

Detroit was depressing. I longed to get away from problems and back to New York, but felt time pressing to finish the book and decided to continue my researches and wanderings. With Jason's parting words—"Detroiters are gonna survive. They don't give in to depression, either kind—emotional or economic; there's a lot of vitality around here"—still buzzing around my head, I flew back to Milwaukee, where I was picked up by Pat Wolf, a twenty-one-year-old flute and harp student. She had commandeered her father's super-comfortable Lincoln Town Car, and we rode in air-conditioned splendor through Wisconsin, Missouri, the Dakotas, Nebraska, Kansas, Iowa and parts of Illinois.

This part of the United States was the closest to what I had grown up with, still the God-fearing small-town America in which people saw no need to lock their doors. Although I wasn't seeking Apple Pie America, there it was off every highway. We drove through a never-ending cornscape. The sun shone, the car radio poured forth Mozart and hillbilly music. If we turned off country roads and drove on thruways we would be reminded that these old-fashioned, seemingly forgotten areas we were enjoying were part of the greater whole of America. Suddenly there was an advertisement for a motel featuring water beds; on a strip of highway, like one in Omaha where we counted eight different taco restaurants within one mile: Taco Bell, Taco Grande, Taco Villa, Taco Gringo—what were the others? Or a radio broadcast that for me bound everything together, with all the contradictions and incongruity—a tribute to Marilyn Monroe. It was the twentieth anniversary of her death. A feminist proclaimed that it was a pity she had died, she would have been such a great feminist, she knew so much about being an object and being exploited. Yes, she repeated, she would have been a great feminist. A man sang a song he had written about her, banal beyond belief, also about her being treated as a love object and how awful it was that Hollywood had created this object. It angered me. They had it all wrong. Marilyn, not Hollywood, had had the imagination to create that object. She created herself out of whole cloth, and she exulted in being the sex symbol. She loved turning people on, and it's a shame she never got credit for this, never got the acceptance when alive that death brought her. Alas, she was a dead legend, not a living one, and as misunderstood in death as she had been in life. Even so, she would have loved being wafted over the airwaves of the Nebraska cornfields.

On and on we went through traditional American villages and towns like those I had known in the fifties on Long Island: community picnics, church suppers, rodeos; the niceness, the neighborliness, the kindness had not yet disappeared. It felt good to be recording it even though I had been thirty-eight days on the road and slept in thirty-seven different beds.

I returned to New York, but I didn't linger there. Within two weeks I was in Houston, Texas, tackling the last of the regional areas. My China show was on exhibit at the Fine Arts Museum, so there was press and TV to handle, executives at Exxon, the sponsor, to see for lunch. There was also a strange dinner given me at a gourmet health food restaurant (no salt, no cream, no butter, etc.) which was in a hospital. The hospital building also housed a bank. Only in Texas.

Greg Gomez, my friend from the Navajo reservation days, came up from Dallas in his recently acquired pickup truck. We went out for a few days to explore and to photograph. It wasn't exactly a low-profile recipe for how to be unobtrusive while photographing—a red pickup truck, a grey-haired female photographer and a full-blooded Indian brave in leather, feathers, braids and beads—but it was fun.

April Rapier, a young art photographer (her term), came highly recommended by Anne Tucker of the Fine Arts Museum. She was to be driver-cum-assistant for the Texas trip. She was clever, informed and fearless—there was nothing I asked that she wouldn't tackle. April had managed to get permission for us to call on the Imperial Wizard of the Knights of the Ku Klux Klan of the Realm of Texas at Channelview. The Klan had been in the news recently because it had harassed and then burned the boats of Vietnamese fishermen who had settled in Galveston.

Over the years the Klan would go underground when the political climate demanded, only to reappear when it deemed the time right. In the 1920s the State of Texas was so embarrassed by the Klan's atrocities that a law was passed making it illegal for anyone to wear a hood, and the organization dropped from sight. It was now reactivated and spitting hate.

James Stansfield, the Imperial Wizard, saw us at the enclave where he lived with his family and other Klan families. In all my life I had never heard such terrifying talk. He fulminated against blacks (he pointed out that the Klan was moving with the times; "they" were no longer called "niggers"), the Vietnamese, the Jews, the Catholics, homosexuals and Communists, whom he accused of having hatched a plot of birth control to make the superior white American stop breeding. He inveighed against women, too. "Woman," he told us, "is only second to a man, something to do with her genes or her hormones." According to him, women were put on earth for men, there should be no question of equal rights, there should be (for whites) no abortion, and blacks should be sterilized. He raved: "I am a white radical racist Christian for God, Race and Country. I don't think you ever seen a black angel, only a white one. Think about it."

We sat unmoving for two hours while he carried on his tirade. My fingers were numb from taking notes and my brain seemed to stop functioning when he started to talk about how the children of the Klan were armed and taught to shoot. When we were leaving I asked permission to come back to photograph. He invited me back for the ritual Saturday-night cross-burning. When I told him that I was planning to leave on Thursday, he said there was no problem; they would just move the ceremony to Wednesday night. But meanwhile I should meet his colleagues who had burned the Vietnamese boats, and also go to the Klan library where their (hate) literature was.

I remember the time spent on the Klan story as the most terrible (next to the McCarthy period of terror) days of my professional life. Three nights running, April and I returned to her pretty house numb and chilled by the blast of evil we had seen and heard. We were unable to speak, and unable to break out of the circle of horror in which we were caught. When I could think again, I decided that our reaction of silence was the result of neither of us having opened our mouths to challenge the unspeakable awfulness.

When we returned to Klan Island the afternoon of the picture taking, the whole Klan community was engaged in preparing a crude wooden cross. At dusk, a burning taper was put to the kerosene-soaked cross. As the fire caught, the group of hooded figures danced around the burning cross and chanted a pagan prayer:

"God bless the white Christian race; we appreciate the glorious thing given us. Lord, the lighting of the cross is dedicated to the sun. Thank you for all you have given us. Watch over us and protect us, the white Christian race. Amen."

Another difficult photo session April Rapier arranged (through Mary Sue Koontz) was at a state prison where the inmates, mostly black first offenders, aged between eighteen and twenty-six, worked under the gun. A law called "the good time law" arranged for an exchange whereby each day's work was credited to each man's record to help reduce his sentence.

Effectively I was finished with the photography for *In America*, but I couldn't bear to stop. I had envisioned a valentine to my homeland but had found so many disturbing situations that I felt it would be insulting to avoid showing the serious problems our country was suffering. Also, to end the travels with the Klan was unthinkable. What was needed was beautiful landscapes, and some light relief. I flew to Utah for the first and to Los Angeles for the second, where I hoped to find a film comedy being made. But Hollywood was in the doldrums; there were a few dreary TV movies being made but little else.

Someone suggested a story on the old age home for actors. There were fifty-four cottages, a lodge, a fully accredited eighty-bed hospital on the premises, a skilled nursing staff, seven resident doctors as well as access to various consultants and specialists. It was all very impressive, but seeing so many old people gathered all in one place, even though they were marvellously looked after, was hardly a barrel of laughs. I spent the better part of the day in the recreation rooms taking pictures and talking to people.

overleaf: Prisoners,
Sugarland, Texas, 1982

There was a sad, aged woman in a wheelchair who broke my heart. There were remnants of beauty, but she was palsied and seemed trapped within herself. I tried to reach her, to talk to her, but there was no response. It would have been cruel to photograph her, so I passed her by. When we were leaving, the head of the home thanked me for my consideration to the woman. Who was she? I asked. Norma Shearer.

It had been a difficult assignment. It was so painful to see the country I loved going through such a troubled time. I tried to keep both a photographic balance for the book and an emotional balance for myself, but the question kept intruding—what are we doing to ourselves?

When *In America* was published, Knopf sent me on a publicity tour. What stays in the mind is the early-morning talk shows: *Good Morning Philadelphia*, *New York*, *Chicago*, *San Francisco*, *Los Angeles*, *Dallas*, etc. The most memorable of these was *Good Morning Boston*. There was the usual magazine format. My five minutes were spent wedged between a woman who was preparing a vegetarian tofu stuffing for a turkey and a woman promoting a book on kazoo music. She had distributed kazoos and the audience was blowing "Yankee Doodle Dandy." I was laughing so much I could hardly get through my stint. Only in America.

Motion Picture Home for the Aged,
Los Angeles, 1982

n America had exhausted me. I wanted to get away from the total responsibility a book demands. I was tired of dreaming up ideas, then following through to picture, to interview, to layout, to production, to printing, to publication, to promotion—to finally feeling completely drained. The perfect answer was to work on a film in an exotic country. John Huston offered a couple of weeks on Malcolm Lowry's *Under the Volcano*, which he was directing on location in the shadow of Popocatepetl. All the action took place in agonizing flashbacks into the life of a British consul in Mexico during an epic drunken binge on the Day of the Dead in 1938.

When I looked at the complicated call sheet for the first day's work I was happy to be the one recording the scenes and not assembling them. It read:

Location: Cuernavaca Plaza Zócalo, Fiesta in Progress.

Cast Working: Consul, Yvonne, Hugh, Dr. Virgil: 50 revelers, 100 costumed peasants, 30 International Set Men and Women in evening clothes.

Bits: Girl with armadillo.

Extras: 8 street urchins, 13 dancers, Pariah Dog.

Requirements: Carousel Ferris wheel, centrifugal Ferris wheel, concession stands, band stands, mariachi band, sugar skeletons, cakes shaped like skulls, calliope music, black coffin, 3 armadillos, passport, '30s vintage coins, wallet, cigarettes, dark glasses, cane and of course bottles of whiskey.

Between takes, John Huston talked about the problems of making *Bajo el Volcán*. Over the years he had received telephone calls from film companies that wanted him to direct the film, and then either they would send him unreadable scripts or he would never hear from them again. It was indeed the problem of turning the massive, almost autobiographical novel into a working film script that defeated such fine directors as Buñuel and Losey. Even the novelist Gabriel García Márquez wrote a script (it didn't work). Interestingly, the final screen version was written by Guy Gallo, a Yale Drama School student who was only twenty-eight years old.

For me the film was a visual treat. The location, the sun, the color, the celebration of the Day of the Dead, with local people eating their picnics at their family graveside, the photogenic bone structure of Indian and mestizo extras—all were a treat to see and a treat to photograph. But perhaps the most memorable scenes were the ones in which the Consul meets his death at the bar, the Faralito, in which Lowry used to drink.

A Mexican prostitute who plays
a whore in *Under the Volcano*,
Mexico, 1983

253

Rock breaking
in the clay pits,
Delhi, India, 1984

For this scene the script called for eighteen whores, a dwarf and a transvestite. They were all authentic, recruited from the best brothels in Mexico City by the producer, who spent days checking, interviewing and taking Polaroid pictures for Mr. Huston's approval.

Usually the stills photographer recreates rather than creates the photograph on a film location. The director sets the scene, the photographer will then record it. On the day of the brothel scene I was due to leave for New York and then on to London, which meant that I would miss the shoot with the whores. They were a jolly group and I was sorry to miss them. (I had met them the day before, when they had been bussed in to Cuernavaca to try on their costumes.) When I drove out to the location to say goodbye to John, he was put out when I explained that I had to miss the brothel scene, and asked when my flight took off. We figured I had an hour in which I could do the scene, but there was a snag: the actors were not in place, the *mise-en-scène* was yet to be organized by the director. "Go ahead, Eve," he urged me. "You do it." So with the entire crew standing about awaiting my instructions, and the cast and director watching, I deployed the "ladies," the transvestite and the dwarf. It was a heady experience to play director on the location of one of the world's great film directors.

On the plane I worried about the hour's cost I had added to the director's budget. I remembered his saying that when he was a day behind on a shooting schedule, the film company would estimate it was forty thousand dollars behind; if he was a day ahead they would estimate four thousand dollars ahead. Was he ahead, was he behind—and what was the arithmetic for an hour either way?

Back in London after five nomadic years, I found it hard to adjust to an earthbound existence, and to deaccelerate I took an assignment in India that ended up a nightmare of stolen equipment and a saga of chicanery, threats and demands for bribery from customs in Bombay when the new equipment finally arrived. I refused to be used thus, and offered a counterthreat: I said I would tell Mrs. Gandhi. When the official was not impressed, I dialled her number. He backed down and gave me the gear. But imagine the difficulties of trying to work with borrowed, untested equipment. None of the meters matched, so I had to assume they were all inaccurate. The only way to ensure workable pictures was to bracket (expose the same image at different stops). It was hell, and although the story fulfilled the brief we started with, the *Sunday Times* didn't run it. There was some question about the text. The entire exercise had been ill-starred from the beginning.

Again in London there was the usual combination of advertising, editorial and film work: eight color ads of nine-month-old babies being athletic: on bouncers, doing push-ups, crawling, using their fingers on an abacus, etc.; a portrait of Angela Carter for a magazine; stills on *White Nights*, a movie with Mikhail Baryshnikov, Gregory Hines and Isabella Rossellini.

Baby photography is one of the more difficult commercial tasks. It is hard for the photographer to get away from the banal—impersonal, adorable—baby look. Everything moves so rapidly, especially with the very young ones who tire easily, that there isn't time to do anything but follow the infant's lead. No matter the plans, the preparation, it is always a shambles. The most tractable child will suddenly dissolve in tears, fall asleep, yell for food, want to have his diaper changed, or for no obvious reason (except the bright lights, the black box, the strange people, the unusual activity) be off-schedule. Mothers are endlessly muttering, "He never did that before, that's not like him, today is an off day, I don't

Isabella Rossellini,
Finland, 1985

know what got into him. . . ." But, even so, there are wonderful quiet still moments when the child takes over. One can only hope that one's reflexes and skill are up to the situation.

For a gambler like me, a baby session was always a crap game to enjoy. After every campaign I would swear never to do another baby picture, then would be seduced by the sheer improbability of the work and accept the assignment.

There was a baby in the Angela Carter picture for the *Sunday Times* too. I loved her writing and what it spoke to me about her. She had, when over forty, given birth to a son, and I thought she might like having a photo of herself with him. Then I added the father of the boy. The best picture of the take was one of the three of them touching each other and looking happy together. When the picture ran full-page in the *Sunday Times* she sent me a charming note and asked for a print. I intended to send one but never got around to it. At her death, I was dismayed by my negligence. The best I could do was to make sure that the picture she liked was used with her obituary notices.

Since I began this account, other people I've photographed have died: Yves Montand, Francis Bacon, Marlene Dietrich. In each case there was a call from our French editor, Jimmy Fox: the office was being besieged with calls for pictures. Each time I was wakened with the news of the death, and questions like "Where are the negs?" and "Can you write a text block and captions?" And each time I felt like a ghoul, hating the thought of charging money for these pictures. The only thing I can do is make sure that the best ones are used and that the copy is accurate.

White Nights was perhaps the most enjoyable movie I ever worked on, simply because I made so many friends during the filming. Usually my inclination is not to presume on the relationship between the actors and the photographer, but to look on it as a working friendship. If the other person makes the first gesture to turn the situation into a real friendship, then I'm game, but I don't make the first overture—perhaps because I fear rejection, perhaps because I don't want anyone to think I'm interested because the person is famous. None of that applied on *White Nights*. The four of us—Isabella, Misha, Greg and I— were an instant mix. We liked one another, we worked well together, we enjoyed the same bad jokes, we saw each other away from the location and we have remained friends. Although the same ingredients had obtained on other films with other actors, this was different. There was an immediacy and an almost chemical reaction I hadn't experienced before.

We worked on the film in England, Finland and Portugal, and then Isabella and I went to France (where she was modelling for Lancôme) to continue a personal story on her for *Life* magazine. We were to continue the story in America. Meanwhile, Francis took Michael and me on a week's holiday to Brighton. It was delicious. We stayed on Marine Parade facing the Channel and an amusement park complete with Ferris wheel, swings, dodgems, slides and other delights dear to the heart of a six-year-old. Grandma found that Tibet, Afghanistan, India and the Caucasus paled by comparison. None of the others had Michael in them.

My concern after finishing the books was not only to fill my days but to fulfill myself. I had been badly bitten by the book bug, and had become accustomed to knowing in advance what work I was going to be doing. Even with its difficulties I had come to love the long-term security of book-making as compared with the short-term assignments. This was a corrupting frame of mind for a freelance.

The books were the best way to work I had

Mikhail Baryshnikov
in rehearsal,
New York, 1987

I *n America* had exhausted me. I wanted to get away from the total responsibility a book demands. I was tired of dreaming up ideas, then following through to picture, to interview, to layout, to production, to printing, to publication, to promotion—to finally feeling completely drained. The perfect answer was to work on a film in an exotic country. John Huston offered a couple of weeks on Malcolm Lowry's *Under the Volcano*, which he was directing on location in the shadow of Popocatepetl. All the action took place in agonizing flashbacks into the life of a British consul in Mexico during an epic drunken binge on the Day of the Dead in 1938.

When I looked at the complicated call sheet for the first day's work I was happy to be the one recording the scenes and not assembling them. It read:

Location: Cuernavaca Plaza Zócalo, Fiesta in Progress.
Cast Working: Consul, Yvonne, Hugh, Dr. Virgil: 50 revelers, 100 costumed peasants, 30 International Set Men and Women in evening clothes.
Bits: Girl with armadillo.
Extras: 8 street urchins, 13 dancers, Pariah Dog.
Requirements: Carousel Ferris wheel, centrifugal Ferris wheel, concession stands, band stands, mariachi band, sugar skeletons, cakes shaped like skulls, calliope music, black coffin, 3 armadillos, passport, '30s vintage coins, wallet, cigarettes, dark glasses, cane and of course bottles of whiskey.

Between takes, John Huston talked about the problems of making *Bajo el Volcán*. Over the years he had received telephone calls from film companies that wanted him to direct the film, and then either they would send him unreadable scripts or he would never hear from them again. It was indeed the problem of turning the massive, almost autobiographical novel into a working film script that defeated such fine directors as Buñuel and Losey. Even the novelist Gabriel García Márquez wrote a script (it didn't work). Interestingly, the final screen version was written by Guy Gallo, a Yale Drama School student who was only twenty-eight years old.

For me the film was a visual treat. The location, the sun, the color, the celebration of the Day of the Dead, with local people eating their picnics at their family graveside, the photogenic bone structure of Indian and mestizo extras—all were a treat to see and a treat to photograph. But perhaps the most memorable scenes were the ones in which the Consul meets his death at the bar, the Faralito, in which Lowry used to drink.

A Mexican prostitute who plays
a whore in *Under the Volcano*,
Mexico, 1983

253

Rock breaking
in the clay pits,
Delhi, India, 1984

ever known: travel, adventure, responsibility, shooting and writing on subjects of my own choosing all added up to a terrific way to spend my days. After a short time of commissioned assignments, I began to miss the discipline and the sense of achievement, so when Stephen Rubin of Bantam Books asked me if I would do photographs for a book on Baryshnikov I jumped at it. It was only when the work was already in progress that I discovered that both Misha and John Fraser, the writer, had suggested me. Neither knew that the other knew me. I had met John on a train from Shanghai to Beijing, and had run into him again by chance in Chicago, where we were both promoting our books on China. The book, John's idea, was about Baryshnikov and the American Ballet Theatre. The thought of spending months watching Misha dance was an answer to the sudden drop in energy which followed my nightmare time in India.

Dance photography, of course, is a highly specialized field. What I wanted for the book was not the great dance moments—I wasn't really equipped to catch those—but the sweat, intense hard work, concentration, pulled tendons and pain that go on behind the scenes.

When I started work on the Misha book I was apprehensive. My fear was that it might impair our friendship. It was one thing to see him briefly when I would come to New York; it was another to photograph him at work on a daily basis and to do a book on which he had complete picture approval.

It was a ticklish situation, because he was so delightful that it would have been easy to make just flattering pictures, but I wanted substance and I wasn't sure how to go about getting it. A superstar (which he is) even in an ordinary situation with good friends seems to use up all the oxygen and you find the atmosphere unnatural. Fortunately, this didn't happen with Misha. He was wonderful to work with, and considerate with the choice of pictures; the whole enterprise made us even better friends.

Dancer
Lisa Reinhart,
New York, 1987

erhaps it was the year spent with Misha that started me thinking about returning to the USSR, or perhaps it was the great changes taking place: glasnost and perestroika between them seemed to sweep away the Russia I had known and photographed in the three trips I had made in the sixties and seventies. Now it was the end of the eighties and time for another journey. I came up with the idea of going back to the places I had photographed to update my material in the light of present change and, I hoped, to track the differences in attitudes and situations.

For the book projected I wanted a perceptive writer, someone stimulating who understood photography. The obvious choice was Bruce Chatwin, since we had worked seamlessly and happily in India. We each respected the other's thoughts and space and made a good team.

Bruce was delighted with the idea. He too had come up with a plan for a book on the USSR and was currently studying Russian in France with a sect of Jesuits. He was bubbling with ideas, and kept saying "Great," and "It will work." The reason he thought it right for both of us, he said, was that I seemed to break down barriers with people; people would talk to me. He cited the case of Mrs. Gandhi accepting me and confiding in me.

We had a rollicking lunch in my kitchen. I teased him about a story a mutual friend had told me about him. This is the tale:

Bruce and a friend had spent months in Australia, where Bruce was writing *Songlines*. One day when they were ready to leave Australia, Bruce wrapped up his manuscript and, when he was packing their Land Rover, put the parcel on the hood of the car. They then drove off without checking and must have gone thirty miles before they missed the manuscript. Bruce's friend, in telling the story, said, "You know, Bruce—we never found a single page."

Bruce told an entirely different story. He said he had put the parcel on the hood of the car and turned his back to adjust a suitcase, when suddenly out of the forest came a tribe of monkeys, picked up the bundle and raced back into the forest.

They both gave chase but were not able to retrieve a single page. Which version to believe—the novelist's or the layman's?

During the period I was trying to make arrangements for the Russian trip, Bruce became ill, and in six months he died. Besides my deep personal sorrow for his death, I lost heart for the project. It would just be too desperately sad (after our grandiose plans) to go alone. In addition, the wait for visas lost us the immediacy of the ferment that was overturning seventy years of Com-

American tourists, amateur
theatricals, Rostov on Don,
Russia, 1988

munist rule. Things were moving at such speed that by the time we could publish we would have been overtaken by events. So the Russian project was shelved and Knopf agreed to replace the Russian book with a book on Britain that I had been gathering together since the early sixties.

While the Russian negotiations were sputtering along I was assigned by the *Condé Nast Traveler* to go to Russia with Jessica Mitford on tour by ship up what she called the Mighty Vodka.

Over the years I had seen the USSR from different points of view depending upon the visa arranged: in 1965 it was a deluxe visa at thirty-five dollars a day, in 1966 it was a businessman's visa at seven dollars a day (the very best way to go, because the Russians were desperately anxious for trade), and now I was about to take a trip on a tourist's visa which amounted to hundreds of dollars a day. It was to be the most confining.

We were to document a cruise of 150 American tourists on a trip on the River Volga. We embarked at Rostov on Don and disembarked at Kazan. The tour was a Rotary Club afloat on vodka. The tourists were affluent, mainly retired couples. They said they "did" a new country every year. They had been to India and China, and since Reagan had just been in the USSR, this year was Russia's turn.

They came complete with friendliness, generosity and naive prejudice. It was an education to watch them listen to the two lecturers, a defected Russian from a small Pennsylvania college and a Russian Communist from Moscow, debate politics for the benefit of the Americans.

Imagine the shipload of tourists endlessly at meals or at drink complaining and waiting to be entertained. As comic relief there were amateur theatricals handled by the Russian tour guide. The compelling image that stays in my mind, and on film, is of two bare-chested, bare-bellied and hairy-bare-legged men (over sixty) in city short

socks and shoes and in white gauze tutus, dancing *Swan Lake*.

It was great to be able to get to know Jessica. She is a *grande dame* (ex-Communist). It was fascinating to watch her at mealtime demolish fools or at lectures about the USSR talk about World War II as a class war and hear her describe the British aristocracy and her own family. One sister was married to Oswald Mosely, the head of the British Fascist Party, and another sister had been Hitler's friend.

I was still deeply distressed at Bruce's death and toweringly frustrated at the failure of the Russian book to materialize. Also I had hoped on the book trips to the USSR to find time to learn more about my forebears and their lives in the Ukraine. Before leaving London I had a letter from my oldest brother, Michael. He wrote that his children and grandchildren had heard him talk about our mother a lot, but what about Father? What did I remember, and could I do a bit of research about him when I was in the USSR that he, Michael, could use at a family reunion?

The last day on the good ship *Maxim Gorki* I found myself deep in thought about my father. I sat down to write my brother what little I knew. Perhaps I could plan a return trip to check out the villages from which our parents came. Sadly, we had over the years not talked to them about themselves and their early lives. What a treasure trove it would have been for our descendants. I started to piece together what little I knew.

Here is the letter written to my brother:

Dearest Mike:

You asked me for memories of our father, of Volka. It seems fitting that I turn to thoughts of him here in the USSR where he was born and grew to manhood. I am on a trip up the Volga on assignment for a travel magazine.

264

As I listen to spoken Russian—sounds I do not understand, but which persist (like a race memory) in bringing back our childhood in Philadelphia; images of poverty, laughter, irritation, bare feet (shoes were at a premium) and love crowd each other: evanescent and kaleidoscopic.

I hear Volka's voice, quick to anger—a man whose partial deafness had him miss essential words, and thus meaning. He was a proud man and he would dissemble to try to have us believe he had heard properly. Many times it was comical and we would laugh—cruelly as children do—when he got things wrong. But he had a great sense of humor—and would see the joke and, ruefully, laugh along.

He was a literate man, a born teacher—and he was irreverent. Even when he became a rabbi he would say to our mother, Bessie, who was a fundamentalist in her beliefs and would insist upon carrying out the letter of Jewish dietary law—one must be "froom" (orthodox) but not "meshugah" (crazy).

He was an educated man in his native language—Russian—and a scholar in ancient Hebrew, Aramaic, Yiddish, Torah and English. He would talk to me, the agnostic, about comparative religion in a worldly inquiring way, and when I was sixteen we read the Song of Songs in the original—he drawing me on with his fluent Hebrew, I following haltingly but with mounting excitement at the imagery.

He was a handsome man—medium height—Bessie was tall for a woman—when they stood together they were of equal stature. He had light eyes—grey—that changed intensity with his moods. His hair was light brown, and in his middle years he had a jaunty beard that was streaked with grey. George was the only one of his children who inherited his good looks. Now Michael Arnold, my grandson, looks like him—fair,

attractive and with the same kind of humor.

Pictures appear on the screen of my mind: either a real memory or one often repeated so that I think I remember. I am three years old. I have had a serious ear infection and for weeks have been listless and silent, a change from a noisy boisterous child to a sick one. Volka is bringing me back from the free hospital ward where the abscess has been lanced. We are waiting on the street corner for a trolley car, he is holding me in his arms. Suddenly the abject child starts to sing: "Shoemaker, shoemaker, mend my shoe—I won't be back till half past two." The tears pour down his face.

Another incident: I am eight years old and long-blond-curled, but envious of all the other kids in the neighborhood who have Buster Brown bobs. I badger Bessie until she manages the fifteen cents for the barber. When I return home shorn, father is furious, spits out at mother, "You have spoiled the child's looks." He is angry with her until the Saturday, when, according to the Torah, it is a mitzvah to bed your wife.

Then there were the stories he told of his early days in America. When he was thirteen his father brought him to America, but they didn't stay. Our grandfather found the U.S. a godless country, so they returned to Russia. Good thing too, or he would not have met our mother.

His meeting with Bessie: he came to her shtetl as a tutor for her brothers. When he saw her first she was kneading dough for bread. She moved her hand to push away a strand of dark hair from her lovely brown eyes. He looked into them and was lost forever. It was a love match.

He was a courageous man, but never thought of himself as such. He talked matter-of-factly of their early struggles. When he set off to return to America he was already married and had an infant son. He was held up for six months in London. I don't know why. Daily he kept himself sane by going to the British Museum to teach himself English.

His arrival in America: these are bitter times. He sends for his wife and their firstborn, Louis, who is to die of spinal meningitis at thirteen. An aside: at the boy's funeral Tante Rezel (or was it Tante Perel?) says in Bessie's hearing, "Why does she keen so? She still has all those other paupers." Bessie hears and screams at her, "You have ten fingers, you lose one, it hurts as though you have lost the whole hand."

They go through years of soul-destroying poverty. At one time she takes in other people's clothes to wash. He tells a story of peddling rags. His horse is always ill or dying. He makes jokes about just as he had taught the horse to eat less and less food, until he could manage without eating at all, the ingrate goes and dies on him!

Another story: On the day before Passover, when he is destitute, not a penny with which to bring in the holiday, he is riding on his wagon, calling out, "Any old rags, paper, bones." He is in an elegant neighborhood. A lady calls to him. She wants her basement cleared out and gives him a treasure trove of old books, magazines and miscellany which he sells for ten dollars—a fortune. He tells the tale, his eyes moist: "I had money for matzos, chicken, sacramental wine and even nuts for the children."

Enough. My own eyes are moist. My heart is with you in this family get-together. I am sad not to be able to join you—but I hope this letter reaches you in time for the reunion. Enjoy—celebrate Bessie, celebrate Volka—a splendid pair— I am proud to be of their seed.

All my love, Eve

When the Russian book finally dropped out because things were moving too rapidly in the USSR, Sonny Mehta, who had taken over at Knopf when Bob Gottlieb went to *The New Yorker*, agreed to my working on the British book with Bob as my editor.

So now in 1989 I had the British book to prepare along with an exhibition to accompany the book for the National Portrait Gallery in London. The book was called *In Britain* in Britain and *The Great British* in America. There was also an exhibition at Castelli in New York of the Baryshnikov material and the editing and preparation for publication of a picture book for Bantam Books called *All in a Day's Work*.

All in a Day's Work was a collection of pictures of people at work, from Zululand to Afghanistan, that I had made over a period of thirty-five years specifically for a book which had never been published. The photos were a particular pleasure to compile because they had been taken for my own interest; they were not assigned, so there were no strictures to shoot to layout, and no worries about whether they were vertical or horizontal. Also they were single images, which meant simple captions. So although there was still the problem of how the photos related to each other on facing pages or as after-images as one turned the page, the book looked entirely different from any of my other books, which were inevitably made up of picture stories and related text. To add a bit of spice to the single images I found quotes from various sources which seemed either amusing or simply apposite.

When working on *All in a Day's Work* I became increasingly interested in the way photographs are viewed. I had read Barthes on how the juxtaposition of facing images and text affects response, but it was in the handling of these pictures for pagination that the obvious truth came home to me strongly that unless one can hold the single image in the hand or see it isolated on a wall, the meaning of the photograph will inevitably be affected by the surrounding material. I hadn't thought of this before because I was thinking mainly in single images, not in terms of layout of pictures.

I had flown to New York to work with the art director on the proofs rather than to Japan, where the printing was being done, because I wanted to be closer to home as we awaited the birth of Sarah Jane, my granddaughter. It was at once a privilege to be able to imagine the new person, because her sex was known before birth, and a bit of a letdown, because part of the mystery surrounding the birth was gone.

On Sarah's birthday, as I rode the train to

Manchester to meet her and make her first photograph (as I had with Michael and was to do later with David), I remembered an Italian proverb that seemed apt: May she have her share of laughter and tears.

The British book began to take shape. The more I worked on the pictures, the more evident it became that there should be words—lots of them, because Britain was close to my heart. It had been my home except for the five years I was away to do the China book and the America book, from 1979 to 1984. The more I examined the visuals, the more memories they called up, and the more I wrote, the more pictures my mind conjured.

Usually before embarking on a new book or even a new assignment there would be dithering and nerves, fear of the unknown journey into myself and my work—a recurring phenomenon that would leave me, no matter how often it occurred, surprised by its onslaught and its persistence. But the British book did not produce these symptoms. Perhaps it was because I was too busy mourning the death of my beloved friend Marcia Panama. Nothing in the months following her death seemed to penetrate the shell of concentration I pulled about me.

We had shared a great deal of our lives over the quarter of a century we knew each other. We were both Americans abroad, worked in the arts: she a sculptor, I a photographer. Most of the time we were single ladies who enjoyed the theatre, our friends, antiquing, short trips around Britain and to Europe. Our children—her daughter, Kathy, and my son, Francis—were both medics and friends. We loved to exchange ideas, recipes, dinner parties and gossip. It was the kind of rewarding friendship that is usually best with another woman.

Marcia was my unofficial family in Britain and I hers. When she married again in the early eighties our friendship continued. Then she developed leukemia. She was heroic in the way she faced her death. During the last year, when she was able, she would climb my stairs on Mondays (the day she would go to the hospital for a blood transfusion) and I would cook lunch for her and we would talk. Somehow, to be writing the British book and slowly preparing the National Portrait Gallery exhibition (it wasn't due for another year and a half) brought me close to the London years I had known with Marcia. As ghosts from another time inextricably linked in my mind with her, the project became a celebration of her and helped ease the pain of loss.

Work was interrupted to make time for the Magnum fortieth anniversary celebration. I was on the book committee, which involved trips to America and Paris, and was involved in the BBC three-hour television miniseries on Magnum. There were exhibitions to attend in connection with the celebration: a gala in New York following the show at the International Center of Photography and a luncheon for 150 in Paris followed by the vernissage at the Palais de Tokyo which *tout Paris* seemed to have come to enjoy. The whole thing was capped by a disco party (that smelled of pot) for just Magnum families where we laughed and reminisced and danced the night away. The celebration ended sweetly for me next day when Francis and Michael took me to lunch in Paris and Michael ordered for us in French. We were celebrating Michael's twelfth birthday. He had left Manchester on a child's two-thirds-price ticket and returned on a full adult's fare. He loved that rite of passage.

There was yet one more birthday that I remember from that summer. Isabella Rossellini and Misha Baryshnikov and I met for lunch in New York at an Italian restaurant somewhere in

A scribe and his client,
Afghanistan, 1969

Greenwich Village. I was the first to arrive. I looked up from the first sip of a long cool drink. There was my Russian friend in a flowered visored baseball cap, a wild red shirt and a pair of oversize sunglasses. The garb was to render him incognito. He was thrilled and excited, having just come from the maternity hospital, where he had first seen his son, Peter.

When Isabella arrived we alternated drinks all afternoon between the champagne Misha ordered and the bottle of special vodka that Howard Gilman had ordered for us when Misha called him to spread the news. I think my memory may be faulty, but I seem to recall that at some point Misha scooped me up and we danced among the tables.

When I either got stuck for words or couldn't decide about a picture for the British book, I would immerse myself in editing my archives. It was essential that they be in order for the preparation of the next book, the big book, the retrospective. There were diaries, documents, text and captions, and letters to cull from my files as research.

I went through thousands of contact sheets and ordered one thousand black-and-white work prints. The color was more difficult to handle because it was divided into single small (1 by 1½ inches) transparencies. These I would project enlarged (in the dark) onto a white wall so that by day's end my poor head was spinning images and my retinas complaining from the abuse of invasion by successive light and darkness.

It was an extraordinary feeling to be researching my own life and to try to be objective about it. I would stand back and attempt to observe the personality and motivation of stages of my development as though in search of information on which to base an assessment of someone I didn't know very well. Sometimes digging around in the recesses of my mind delighted me, but often I would be puzzled and uncertain of why I had behaved in a certain way or why I had taken an unexpected direction. It was both enlightening and frightening.

It also reinforced my belief that through picture journalism I had come closer to people than would have been possible in practically any other field of work. The medium itself demands an intimacy, no matter how brief, in order to observe and understand the person in front of the camera so that what is seen can be translated into images. The experience between subject and photographer is both physical and emotional. So whether it was the first five minutes of a baby's life or two and a half months recording Marilyn Monroe acting in *The Misfits*, I was an essential part of the process. Clark Gable used to joke about phoning a shot in if he didn't want to be photographed a certain way. Well, obviously there is no way to get the image without the vital participation in the process by the picture taker as well as the subject.

I had always been aware of the sheer magnitude of images that forty years of intensive work had produced, but facing it on a daily basis was unsettling. It seemed unfair that there were so many decisions to make in choosing what to present of my life's work at so late a time in my life, when my faculties were not as acute as they were when the pictures were made. Would my judgment be unclouded? Could I depend on it? The only thing to do was select the undeniable "best" and then, as I had done with Bob Gottlieb on other books, make final decisions with him.

Being desk-bound, projector-bound and house-bound began to bore me. I needed something fresh to stimulate me, so I accepted an advertising campaign for British Rail that Saatchi & Saatchi offered. It was dead of winter, and, of course, true to the contrariness to be expected in advertising, the pictures were to be jolly warm-

Sculptor
Marcia Panama,
London, 1975

271

weather enticements for people to ride the rails. The idea behind the series was that women would leave their cares at home for a day, take the train with a woman friend or friends and go off for an adventure: to view the gardens of a great house, a picnic on the Lakes, a day at the beach, a day at the races, etc. There were to be six advertisements. The money paid for the series was obscenely high as compared to books or editorial work. It seemed a grotesque exercise in symmetry that the day rate offered me was precisely what I had earned as a semiannual payment when I came to work for the *Sunday Times* in the sixties.

The whole campaign was photographed in the most appalling weather conditions: rain, sleet, hailstones the size of marbles hitting our legs. Two strong assistants held me while I photographed, to keep me from being blown off the Blackpool Pier into the Irish Sea. Afterwards there were enough rainbows and lightning and thunder to satisfy a Wagnerian production.

In the Lake District where we were to photograph, the picnic trees were being uprooted by a tremendous storm. The entire train system in Britain was at a standstill, so that our models got as far as Oxford and were then returned to London. Since we couldn't work outdoors, we decided to look for indoor locations. The roads were icy and a forty-ton truck plowed into the back of our BMW. Luckily, the four of us in the car escaped serious injuries. We wound up with headaches and muscle bruises. The backs of my calves were so battered that they looked like intensified Kodachromes shot on a sunny day.

When we finally were able to photograph the picnic, we found that the storm had blown some swans our way. They added immeasurably to the picturesque quality of the scene, but when I started to click away, the male swan was bothered by the sound—perhaps he felt it was a rival bird trying to steal his mate with a new love call. He started furiously nipping at my ankles while I was trying between squalls to photograph three pretty women having a jolly picnic on a summer's day. My assistant had to keep that bird with its terrible wingspan off the backs of my bruised legs.

The next shoot was at a stately home with magnificent gardens in Perth in Scotland. It was delightful to be working on a clear-blue-skied day after one of the wildest British hurricanes this century, but my troubles were not yet over. As I lifted my camera to my trusty right eye I suddenly realized that it was blind. I could not see a thing. For the blink of that darkened eye I did nothing. Before me was a huge van filled with people and housing a complete dressing room. I looked around at the three models, copywriter, creative head, and art director, location-finder, makeup artist, stylist and my assistant, and announced that we would shoot the new pictures differently—like a motion picture. I would give the camera to my assistant to operate, and would then set up the shots and direct the models and him; I would make bad jokes and perhaps make everyone laugh. All through that benighted day I never let on to anyone that I couldn't see. My assistant was pleased. He still doesn't know that it was not only my trust in him to play photographer to me as director that prompted me to hand over my precious camera to him.

In the evening, still playing court jester to keep my little band smiling, I dropped off in Manchester to spend the weekend with my son and his family. When I arrived, he was busy making a béarnaise sauce. I could no longer keep my dread news to myself and blurted it out. The look on his face gave nothing away, but he dropped the spoon he was using to stir the sauce. Then he went immediately for his ophthalmoscope, checked my eye, said a few reassuring things, and added that he was a general surgeon, not an eye man, but that he knew a good one. My problem turned out to be a cataract. They usually come on gradually; atypically, this one came on almost full-blown. We agreed to an operation in the summer to give the cataract a chance to ripen fully. I then returned to Scotland on Monday to finish the ads with my assistant as cameraman and no one in the *équipe* being told why.

In August I went to Manchester for the operation, which was routine and uneventful. I returned to London happy to have it over, but I had a funky, wobbly feeling—not quite a mild amnesia, but a sort of mental miasma. My mind seemed to have gone off on a holiday of its own, and I found that the new eye was not focusing properly and that I couldn't work with the left eye. It is hell for a right-eyed person to try to switch over. I had to wait five weeks to find out the final results of the operation. Would I have to wear glasses, and how would they affect my pictures? It felt like living in a soap opera. Gradually my wobbliness cleared and my mind returned in good form when the doctor found he had made the stitches too tight and so rendered me astigmatic. He zapped the stitches with a laser. I waited another three weeks for the final verdict: glasses necessary for reading but only to magnify the type. Jubilant, I picked a moving target to test my post-op pictures: Sarah Jane, then two years old. No problem, no glasses necessary for camera work. Hallelujah!

There were two happy events to look forward to that year. David Robert Arnold, my youngest grandson, was born in September, and my British book was published. As I had with Michael and Sarah Jane, I went to Manchester to be introduced to David and to photograph him. Then I flew to America for the printing and publication of *The Great British*.

The book was launched with a party given by my friend Howard Gilman—a party full of playfulness and intelligence masterminded by Howard and his staff. The theme, of course, was British, so there was everything from the Union Jack to British music to garden roses flown from England to British food that tasted un-English, prepared by Howard's chef: toad in the hole, Scotch eggs on a quail's-egg base and lots of other unfamiliar but delicious morsels. Even the weather was in keeping—it rained.

The vernissage of the British book, *In Britain*, was still to come—in conjunction with the National Portrait Gallery exhibition. Printing for an exhibition is different from printing for a book or a magazine. One has to decide beforehand the overall look one hopes to achieve; try to visualize juxtaposition of pictures and how images impinge upon each other when placed next to each other; decide scale and size, and whether black-and-white and color should be displayed side by side or kept separate, all the while trying to keep a grid in mind of what the rooms will look like when the show is hung. I decided that the pictures should be in various sizes to encourage the viewer to move in close or step back from each picture. To have them all of a size lessens the interest. Even so, no matter how careful the planning there are always worrying adjustments when the exhibition is hung.

There was also a great deal of promotion and publicity to handle. After all, this was about Britain. When my friend Rosemary Bowen-Jones of the BBC came to interview me as a preliminary to making a twenty-minute film about the book and show, she asked after my grandson Michael. I told her that he had asked for a camera and a few lessons for his fourteenth birthday. She suggested he be given it on camera so her crew could film it.

Michael and I both got carried away by the occasion, so we just played on camera. When I asked him why he wanted a camera, he said it was silly to have me for a grandmother and not know how to take a picture. We went on to the obvious silly but essential advice, from "Don't forget to remove the lens cap" (I've lost more pictures that way) to "Don't stick your fingers in front of the lens." By the time we were finished with our banter I had dreamed up a whole more sophisticated program about photography that I'm currently developing for television.

The National Portrait Gallery exhibition was a success. There were a thousand guests at the viewing the night of the opening, which was followed by a dinner for forty held in the Victorian Room upstairs. Friends had come from New York and Paris. We drank our champagne under the watchful eyes of a young Prince Edward (later King Edward VII) in full pinks and a portrait that Bramwell Brontë had painted of his sisters. Not bad for little Evie from Philadelphia.

I had been so rushed preparing books and exhibitions that it came as a shock to realize that except for using the camera to test my eyesight and the occasional snap of the grandchildren I had not photographed professionally for two years. It was a great cause for concern, but before it became a real problem, Michael Rand, my longtime editor-cum-art-director friend at the *Sunday Times Colour Magazine* called with an assignment and what an assignment: to photograph the British prime minister.

It was too important a job to refuse, so of course the answer was yes, but it turned out to be one of those jobs that require more diplomacy than photography. First, the editor, Robin Morgan, went to Number 10 Downing Street to see the PM's press secretary, Gus O'Donnell. Next, Michael Rand took some of my books over to Number 10 for a meeting with other officials who handled press, then he and I went together so I could be vetted. We were taken on a guided tour of the house. Except for the three or four grand reception rooms, it was small, crowded and disappointing. It was hard to remember that a great empire had been run from there.

The prime minister was just coming into the reception hall as we were leaving. It was surprising to see how different he looked off-camera. He is taller, more animated and decidedly more impressive, and he appeared relaxed and unflappable when he stopped to chat.

He touched my shoulder, a spontaneous gesture, and said that it would be different when we met in the cabinet room—"It would be mixed." I assumed he meant that there would be the two women ministers mixed in with the twenty male ministers.

The arrangements with Number 10 were to go through many changes. At first, it was to be a day in the life of Number 10, along with a quick few shots of the PM. Then it turned into a day in the life of the PM. And finally it escalated into a profile on the PM in and out of Number 10. I wound up working on the story over a period of six weeks, which included an overnight trip with Mr. Major on the Queen's Flight (Her Majesty's plane) to Rome and Athens.

There was an amusing situation in Rome when the prime minister met with the Italian prime minister, Giuliano Amato. They were to talk over lunch. I was promised a chance to photograph them then, but was first whipped off to an elegant meal in another part of the palace. When I asked again about pictures, I was told it would be at the end of the luncheon. As time got shorter I asked again. This time I was told it was not appropriate because there would be dirty coffee cups on the table. When I said that would just

overleaf: Prime Minister John Major of Britain with Prime Minister Giuliano Amato of Italy, press conference, Rome, 1992

add an intimate touch, the answer was a definite no. My next request was to be allowed to photograph the two men when they passed through a salon on their way to a press conference when Mr. Major was leaving. This was grudgingly agreed to, and I was taken to a grand chamber that I had noticed when we arrived in which historic pictures of all Italian prime ministers were on display. I had staked out just the spot I needed, and posed the two politicos for a moment leaning against a massive ormolu table and against the background of a serious Benito Mussolini.

Access seemed to expand from situation to situation. For instance, I didn't ask to photograph Mrs. Major; suddenly she was offered. But despite the seemingly easy approachability, my actual shooting time with the prime minister was strictly limited. I had three minutes in the study with him, five minutes in the cabinet room with his ministers, perhaps twenty minutes on the plane, etc. So if I added up my entire time with him over the intermittent days that made up the entire take, I had perhaps an hour in all shooting time. When Mrs. Major asked me how I was managing, I mentioned the little bits of time allotted. She shook her head and said, "You've had more time with my husband in the past two weeks than I have."

The only thing that made it possible to get the story was that I worked without lights, tripods, motor drives or any of the other modern devices most pros use. My only luxury was my assistant, who carried the bag. When we went to Europe and it wasn't feasible to have an assistant, Ian Beaumont, the press officer, carried my bag. If I had had to set up lights and other equipment, I couldn't have worked in the allotted time; it was my lifelong experience of working with available light, no matter how dim, that made the whole thing possible.

My other tool was patience—just being available for days at a time so I could be slotted into the PM's hectically busy days. It was a matter of endless cups of tea and boredom. To keep sane, I kept busy documenting the functioning of government at Number 10, beginning with the milkmen at seven a.m. and continuing long past dusk. One story I documented and was disappointed the *Sunday Times* didn't use was the way the government handled the news. Twenty-four hours a day, a staff of nine watches television, reads the newspapers and listens to the radio. Daily, they prepare a précis for the press secretary. He briefs the prime minister and then he briefs the media. Twice daily, morning and afternoon reporters, both TV and flat press, come for what the British call "the lobby"—what we might view as a press briefing. When I asked someone at the press office what "the lobby" was in aid of, she said it was to give reporters information about which they could say, "A source close to 10 Downing Street told me . . ."

I was particularly interested in watching the way the PM was prepared for Question Time. Every Tuesday and Thursday he takes questions in Parliament. The day I photographed the PM's briefing by his press secretary and his meeting with his ministers was a particularly fraught one, because the chancellor of the exchequer was to present his autumn budget. I enjoyed watching the various ministers in the antechamber to the cabinet room clutching their papers and cooling their heels until exactly ten-thirty, when they in turn would brief the PM. As I observed the day's activities leading up to the chancellor's speech and the prime minister's appearance in the House, it seemed to me that the entire apparatus was geared to react to both the press and the opposition, not to act. The PM was prepared with answers for all probable and improbable questions that might be tossed at him. That fifteen minutes in the House must be the most taxing, adrenaline-producing quarter of an hour any citizen in the kingdom is expected to undergo.

John Major was a difficult man to photograph. Whereas in person he projected charm and personality, when being filmed he seemed deliberately to hold back. It was as though he had decided to keep a core of himself to himself, and thus keep the public guessing as to whether there *was* a core. The viewer expects authority from a prime minister, the sense of power high office bestows, and when confronted with this low-key "nice" man, doesn't know what to make of him. Where is the ambition, the fire, the drive that must have brought him to this eminence? Either Major had decided to go low-key as a prudent antidote to Mrs. Thatcher's flamboyant style or he is badly served by the camera. Photographers say the camera doesn't lie, but this may be a case where the camera does lie—or at least tells only partial truth.

It was a difficult job. I was expected to run in shooting at rat-tat-tat speed and emerge with instant masterpieces. After years of photographing the great and the near-great, where usually every gesture is carefully choreographed by the subject, it was a relief to find a man who didn't play the expected image game. Even so, I was conditioned to try to reveal more than the usual grey image and kept longing to put a red scarf around his neck and to be working in color.

John Major was the fourth British prime minister I had photographed. Alec Douglas-Home carried my camera bag when he ushered me into the Hersil, his ancestral home in Scotland. Edward Heath raced ahead of me so that I had to run (clutching my camera bag) to keep up when I went electioneering with him. Margaret Hilda Thatcher hijacked every situation by telling me

where to stand, thus controlling the pictures. But John Major just gave me a hug. . . .

Because I had not photographed for two years, for days before the shoot I hadn't dared to question whether what I had learned over decades by instinct and habit was still part of my arsenal of photographic skill. It was safer to concentrate on the ideas behind the story, on the kind of black-and-white film to be used. Would the really fast film TMX 3200 ASA be too grainy, or would TMX 400 ASA rated and pushed to 1600 ASA give better results? Also there were decisions on whom to take as assistant; the assistant is part of the package and has to fit in seamlessly. All this cogitation kept worry at bay. Only after the work was finished and I had seen the results and found them good did I get a nervous reaction and indulge in considering how I would have handled the situation had I lost my touch and been unable to meet the professional standards required of me.

As it was, Michael Rand was pleased. We did eight pages and a cover. The cover made me uneasy. It wasn't even my work. One evening when the PM was in a playful mood at a cocktail party before the opera he announced that he wanted to be photographed with me and he put his arms about me. I made sure that he looked right and arranged a camera in my hand, and my assistant David Hindley snapped the picture.

It was this photo that Michael Rand ran on the cover. I thought it questionable journalism, but Michael felt it said something fresh about Mr. Major, and he sweet-talked me into submission by saying it was an affectionate tribute to me.

When the article had gone off to press, my son asked me how it felt to get back on the horse. How had it felt to be photographing after a two-year hiatus? It felt natural.

Ever since my return from my last trip to Russia I had been thinking of my parents. I started to find out about possibly going to the villages in Kiev where they had grown up, and I started to dream about my mother.

We were very much alike—strong, often opinionated, purposeful women each determined to have her own way in spite of obstacles. From my childhood on we were adversaries—loving adversaries, but adversaries nonetheless. Our lives together were seldom easy. My mother practically never edited what she thought, and could say wounding things. She, who came out of a Russian ghetto and had suffered poverty as a young and also middle-aged woman in America, aspired to an easy bourgeois life for her three daughters, Dora, Charlotte and me. She felt we should be supported in style by our husbands and was outraged by my wanting a professional life of my own. She felt it was a *shande*—something between an embarrassment and a scandal—for me to go out to work.

I remember her outburst when I proudly told her about an assignment to photograph Mamie Eisenhower. She looked at me pityingly, and in Yiddish baited me with "*Koptsen vu krichts du?*"—literally, "Pauper, where are you crawling?" Furious, I tried to explain that the assignment was an honor. She refused to understand. It was fruitless to argue with her, so I left her until my anger cooled. When next we met she was hurt and kept repeating, "*Vos hab ich den gezackt?*"—"What have I said (that so angers you)?" She really had no way to bridge the difference in our views of the situation.

My earliest memory of her was being waked in the night by her bitter keening over the deaths of her eldest brother, David, his wife and eight of his children in a pogrom in the late 1920s in the shtetl in the Ukraine where he had owned a sugar beet factory. One son, Ben, two years old, was shoved under a bed and slept through the murders. Later, his married sister Dina came from Kiev to claim him. He had been hidden meanwhile by Christian neighbors.

That year a nephew of my mother's, Frank Levin, was dispatched to the Ukraine to bring out the rest of the family: two aunts, their spouses, a widowed sister and assorted siblings, including Ben and Dina. I remember vaguely their being billeted with us, the poor relations, and Bessie's cooking endless pots of borsch and baking hundreds of knishes.

She was a good cook but an expansive one. If she peeled a beetroot, the kitchen looked as though an ox had been slaughtered in it. In her old age, she would sometimes talk about her

My mother, Bessie,
with my son, Francis,
Long Island, 1950

early years in America and the problems of trying to bring up nine children in poverty.

Her favorite story was of reaching a nadir in which there was literally nothing in the house to eat. She was a proud woman and did not want the neighbors to know—she had a horror of being offered charity. So she put a large pot of water on to boil on the coal stove to raise a bit of steam to keep the nosy neighbors from finding out that indeed the cupboard was bare. She would dramatically relive her anger and her pride in the dressing-down she gave one poor soul who dared to lift the lid off the pot. I still remember her temper. She could go from irritation to fury in a trice and then when the recipient was roundly insulted, she would shrug and say, "*Vos hab ich den gezacht?*"

There was another story about her cooking. When she was seventy-five she came to visit us on Long Island. She found a stepladder and climbed a cherry tree. She picked the fruit, made the dough and cooked cherry varenikas (a sort of Russian tortellini). When she served them to Francis, who was then four years old, she told him that she wanted him to remember that when his grandmother was seventy-five she climbed the cherry tree, made the pasta and cooked him cherry varenikas. Recently I asked him whether he remembered. Alas not, but *I* remember, and have told my grandchildren about it.

It was only when she was in her sixtieth year that in a routine physical a doctor discovered that nature had collapsed one lung. When she was in her early thirties she had been diagnosed as having tuberculosis. She had refused to accept the diagnosis and had gone on to bear two more children and rear all nine of us under circumstances that were daunting beyond belief.

She was funny about her age. She was the only woman I ever knew who added years to her age. Initially, she didn't know her birthdate. She knew it was in the summer, she thought July, so we settled on July 15. She was uncertain of the year and then found that if she said she was older than she thought she was there were compliments. Bessie, you don't look seventy, eighty, ninety or whatever. She lived to be ninety-four by her count.

When she was widowed at fifty-four, Charlotte, her youngest daughter, was twelve and Jack, her youngest son, was fifteen. She was devastated by the death of my father. He had been husband, lover, friend, through adversity, and finally, when they could have lived comfortably and with their nine children almost all grown, he died a terrible death of cancer. She was desolate but strong, and she was clear about her life. She said, "When I was a girl I was my father's daughter, when I was married I was my husband's wife, when my children came I was my children's mother, now that I am widowed I am at last my own person." She also finally came to accept my being a professional woman. She teased me and bragged to neighbors about her daughter who in spite of growing up barefoot and having no sense of direction had been travelling around the world and had become a successful photographer.

Sometime in her eighties she moved to York House, a housing complex in Philadelphia where the aged each had separate living quarters and had the choice of eating in a communal dining room or doing their own housekeeping. There were all sorts of activities arranged. Bessie took on the responsibility of a knitting circle, and she prided herself on the fact that annually they raised five hundred dollars for charity for their efforts. She drove the knitters hard to meet her rigid standards.

She kept things lively at York House. Her brother Labe and her sister Sonia had their own apartments there, and there were endless family contretemps to enliven their days. Sonia was a year and a half younger than Bessie. Their mother had died giving birth to Sonia, and Bessie never forgave Sonia. All their lives they had fought. Bessie would recount their quarrels with great glee. One day I took her to task. I said it was a *shande* for two old ladies to be endlessly at each other's throat, and went on to say that my sisters and I never argued. Bessie looked crafty. "You don't know what you are missing," she said. "It keeps us alive."

When she became ill sometime in her early nineties she went to live with Charlotte, her youngest daughter. George, Charlotte's husband, was wonderful to her, and she deeply appreciated him. He was a Catholic, and although she had opposed the match, they became close friends. One morning she told him that she had had a dream. In her dream, she learned that there was only one mother-in-law seat in heaven and because of George she would occupy that seat.

During her final illness I came to the States to see her and to finish *Behind the Veil*, the film I had made in Arabia. When I was in the dubbing the-atre, my sister Dora called. Mother was in hospital in Philadelphia. Somehow I managed to excuse myself and get on the next train. When I reached there, mercifully the blood clot that threatened her life had cleared. I stayed a few days and then had to return to England. We talked and talked and suddenly all our differences dissolved and we were very close. She said she didn't want me to return again to see her. She said, "Do not grieve for me. I have lived a good life. I have used myself." On the plane thirty thousand feet in the air I wrote to her and was able to tell her all that was in my heart, to thank her and to tell her how much I admired and loved her. I felt in a state of grace.

Six months later she was hospitalized. One day she decided she had had enough. She had the nurse braid ribbons into her hair, had a session with the rabbi, called the entire *meshpocheh* to her bedside, bade them farewell, and next day she died. I hope that when my time comes I have the gallantry and style she had. I hope to be able to say, "I too have used myself."

Diary Entry, 1994

Today Michael came for lunch and a photography lesson. I looked at my grandson's lovely sixteen-year-old face across the table and seemed to see there that poignant moment between childhood and the threshold of manhood. I wanted to capture that moment on film. I also wanted to impart to Michael some of what I had learned about portraiture.

The lesson would of necessity be both subjective and objective. He would sit for his photograph and thus have a sense of what the person in front of the camera feels and experiences so he could begin to understand that part of the process. By watching me and listening to what I had to say while I worked he might begin to understand the objective sense of what the photographer feels and does. I would also explain more fully when we had finished, and he would, I hoped, get a chance to ask questions. Then we would trade places—he behind the lens and I in front of the camera.

We worked by daylight from a skylight in my apartment. As I began to assess the way the daylight brought out the bone structure and the planes of his face (he looked almost incandescent), I talked to him about time and light, the two quintessential ingredients of the photograph.

The picture was about this precious moment in his life—and, I couldn't help thinking, in my life as well. It was about relationships: ours to each other, our love and affection for each other, and our trust in each other. It was also about our relationship to the camera.

I wanted to call upon the intimacy built up between us as grandmother and grandson—and I knew exactly what I wanted the portrait to be. This hasn't happened to me very often. Usually I have an idea before the session—but more often I treat the project as an organic entity that I let unfold. In this case I wanted the simplest of photographs: no artificial light, no special angles, no posing, no darkroom embellishments—just Michael. Although I visualized the final image, it was the work in the laboratory that completed the cycle, evoking days and nights spent in the darkroom forty years before. Now, holding the picture in my hand, I realized that I had come full circle and began to ask myself questions.

What drove me and kept me going over the decades? What was the motive force? If I had to use a single word, it would be "curiosity." Curiosity was a constant challenge. The very unpredictability of photography enthralled me. The possibilities were endless. The decisions of what to include and what to exclude, the

My grandson
Michael Arnold, age sixteen,
London, 1994

framing, the business of trying to define the moment, of watching the light move across a face, the kaleidoscope of emotions to choose from—all so varied and interchangeable. The photographic questions to find answers for were inevitably intertwined with the lives of people.

I was hungry for answers, and the hunger to know led me to learn the profession that permitted me to travel the world, to see many lands and many cultures, to assess what I saw and to try to understand what I saw and photographed in terms of my background and experience. A friend once commented on my life as a one-woman cultural exchange.

Now I was looking backward and I was looking forward. The line stretched from my parents to my grandchildren. I was in the middle looking both ways, trying to assess my past, trying to figure out where I wanted to go from here, but it seemed to me that in order to see my photographic way forward I had to look at the *now* in terms of the *then*.

I had tried to define for Michael what I had learned when I started photography lessons with him. It was something I could not teach and something he could not learn. It was something he would have to bring forth from within himself. Sadly I remembered a phrase from my youth. A photographer in Philadelphia I had wanted to apprentice myself to told me: "I can teach you the steps, but you will have to feel the music."

In other words, technique can be learned, the rest is up to you. Still, there was a process by which I had worked. Perhaps it could now help me to see my way back to photography. There had been forty intensive deeply committed years—and suddenly nothing: no compelling ideas falling over each other, no itch to pick up the camera, curiosity nil, challenge nil.

Even so, I still continued my search for picture ideas, I still read voraciously everything from the classics to daily newspapers and current periodicals (I am a news junkie), watched television, listened to radio, went to films and theatre and discussed all sorts of ideas, no matter how seemingly unsuitable, with all kinds of people in my effort to pinpoint the kind of human drama needed to make my kind of photos.

The crucial questions were always is the subject visual and will the words enhance the pictures. If the subject interested me, then I was arrogant enough to think that I could make it interesting to others. I also had to bear in mind the marketplace. It was then essential to be able to prepare a compelling outline (either written or oral) for the editor or art director so he could feel comfortable with the idea he was expected to assign. I had done this all my professional life and had garnered major assignments of everything from a single portrait to large essays to books on various countries.

That was then. Now where were the editors that the sixties, seventies and eighties had spawned? These people who had money to spend, had the authority to assign large space for feature essays, were receptive to fresh ideas.

There is now a shift in photography from material of substance to glitz and packaging. Personality and celebrity endorsed by the media are now in demand. This reinforces the thought that we do not remember people as they are, but as their photographs show them to us. Gimmicks and special effects abound. I am not trying to make out a case that we were that pure in my day. I am simply trying to figure out what is happening now.

My generation had a clearer path in many ways. The structure was looser; no one issued provisos prior to the shooting. It was left to the photographer to find the pictures that best told the story. Assignments were open-ended. There was sufficient time allotted for thinking. There was a chance to find and develop ideas that could only be handled on location and not by edict from someone sitting behind a desk. This way of working permitted unlimited opportunities to find the fresh and the unexpected.

I could spend two years without editorial interference on a *Life* assignment on Malcolm X. There are still a very few dedicated photographers, like Eugene Richards (who has done brilliant reportage on the American drug scene) or Abbas (who has spent years photographing the Muslim world), but they are struggling on their own to try to express their time and also to express themselves, to make the kind of pic-tures that could transcend their initial use beyond the magazine or newspaper assignment that engendered them. Some of the most memorable photographs ever made have entered the public consciousness as art even though they may have originated as journalism: Bob Capa's dying soldier, George Rodger's Nuba wrestlers and practically the entire Cartier-Bresson oeuvre.

Public information is now influenced by the quickie TV sound bite, and the "photo opportunity" is now manipulated so the photographer seems less a witness and more part of the construction of the news.

A case in point was the American landing in Mogadishu for a "humanitarian exercise." They had come to "break the famine, get the gunmen off the streets and return law and order to the Somalis." When the Marines landed in full gear, expecting resistance, they were met instead with TV lights, camera crews and hundreds of stills photographers. The expedition had been organized as a media event. The photos I saw looked like film stills intended for entertainment.

One photographer told me it was impossible to work. Wherever he pointed his camera there was another photographer in his sights. In my day there might have been perhaps Bob Capa and a few men attached to the military unit going in to record the event rather than as part of a welcoming party that were there to make the news.

The public is not hoodwinked—it is now becoming more aware of tricks being played. Whereas the photograph had been accepted as objective truth, now that truth is coming into question. It is no longer automatically accepted that the camera doesn't lie or that the lens confers truth.

The fuss that was made in America when the *National Geographic* moved the pyramid in a cover layout to improve the composition and provide space for logo, credits and the price of the magazine is an example of technical tinkering made possible by the new technology that people are beginning to question. In 1990, Fred Ritchin reported that when readers commented, the editors' answer was that the new photo was one the photographer *might* have taken if he had been standing in a slightly different spot. Formerly the most an intruder could do was to crop the outer edges, airbrush areas within the picture or retouch wrinkles. These were stationary areas, but with computer technology it is now possible to move entire elements within the picture.

A system called "imaging" enables the practitioner to stretch, bend or twist an image to subtract or add elements, to change hue or color and to gerrymander the whole so one can take the head of one person and superimpose it on another person's body or construct an entirely new image by taking figures from different photographs (or other sources) and composing an entirely new picture—as Richard Avedon did for the Oscar ceremonies. The resultant picture was presented as a photograph, as though the subjects had been standing together, when actually they were cobbled together from different sources. Many of my colleagues feel that this is trickery and that one shouldn't play around with or distort reality. I feel that if one chooses to do so, then the result must be clearly labeled and not passed off as reality.

There are obviously, too, legal as well as moral and ethical questions arising from the new technology that allows elements within pictures to be so easily lifted to accommodate this kind of manipulation. These problems will become even more murky as electronic interactive systems come into their own in the home.

Photographers have always grappled with the application of the mechanical as it applies to the creative. Since they are completely dependent upon the technologies which are the tools of their trade, the problem is always to try not to overbalance so the human aspects of the photograph are not in danger of being lost. This has always been a threat; now it has become even more complex and calls for greater vigilance to make sure that the human eye is not suborned by the electronic one.

When photography was born the cry went up "From today, painting is dead." Photography did not replace painting, and I do not think that imaging will replace photography. Art found other channels of expression without becoming corrupted. It is devoutly to be wished that photography will likewise not be defiled.

As I think of the day approaching when the celluloid that contains my life's work will be translated into pixels and stored in a single disc that I can hold in my hand, I realize that I had the best of serious picture journalism. There was an innocence in our approach, especially in the fifties and sixties when we naively believed that by holding a mirror up to the world we could help—no matter how little—to make people aware of the human condition. Now I question whether we were a combination of voyeur and exhibitionist as well as witness and crusader.

All the above is engendered by my questioning whether I have reached a way station or whether I want to continue photographing. There is still the plan to return to Russia to find the villages where my parents grew up—but this I cannot do until I publish the current book. Meanwhile I feel perhaps I should keep in practice.

I know I do not want to stop. The old forms are no longer either interesting or possible for me. Perhaps I should experiment with the new technologies to see for myself if there are more humane and responsible ways to use them. I ask myself whether I can change enough to be able to work with the emphasis on technology, to redirect my concern more to how an idea is expressed and away from what is being said.

Also, am I physically and emotionally up to it? I question the personal equipment I shall need to bring to making a fresh start (or is it a coda I'm talking about?) in professional photography. Paradoxically, I think the photographer should be an amateur at heart—someone who loves the craft. Then she must have a healthy constitution, a strong stomach, a distinct will, quick reflexes and a sense of adventure, and be willing to take risks.

Can I still call on these attributes and how will I fare in light of the radical technical changes taking place in photography? The imagery may not change, but the means to create the images will demand new skills and personal adjustments. It is futile to ask—the proof is in the doing.

I try to put aside fears of inadequacy, of diminished physical ability (I suffer from the photographer's occupational disease—a chronic bad back from schlepping cameras around the planet), and as I write I feel myself getting excited. Ideas begin to trickle in, then come faster and faster. Where shall I start? There are whole areas of photography I haven't explored or have only touched on. What shall it be? Landscape? Nudes? Still life? Color for color's sake? New areas of printing with the computer? The choices are endless. . . .

A Note on the Type

This book was set in a modern adaptation of a type
designed by the first William Caslon (1692–1766).
The Caslon face, an artistic, easily read type, has
enjoyed more than two centuries of popularity in the
United States. It is of interest to note that the first
copies of the Declaration of Independence and the
first paper currency distributed to the citizens of the
newborn nation were printed in this typeface.

Separations and printing by Coral Graphics,
Hicksville, New York
Bound by Horowitz/Rae Book Manufacturers,
Fairfield, New Jersey